spark ✶

THE AUTISTIC CHILD'S GUIDE

Presenting spark*: *Self-regulation Program of Awareness and Resilience in Kids*

Dr. Heather MacKenzie

Wired Fox Publications

Second edition published in 2019
by Wired Fox Publications
wiredfoxpublications@gmail.com

Cover design by Joneric Amundson

Library and Archives of Canada Cataloguing in Publication
The Autistic Child's Guide – Presenting **spark***: *Self-regulation Program of Awareness and Resilience in Kids*
Heather MacKenzie
Includes bibliographical references and access to resource files
ISBN **978-0-9684466-6-9**

TABLE OF CONTENTS

ACKNOWLEDGEMENTS

Special thanks are extended to my friend Chris Barson, of Positive About Autism™, who provides ongoing support for my work and for **spark*** in particular. Chris has generously given me guidance and encouragement in making **spark*** and my ideas come alive in workshops and presentations.

I want to thank Susan Deike for her ongoing support and help with 'friendlifying' my ideas and message. Because of Suzy, the text in this book 'matches' my approach and attitudes more closely.

Joselynne Jaques, a wonderful speech-language pathologist in the U.S., has provided me such good feedback from her implementation of **spark***. Her insights are invaluable.

I want to thank reviewers of the first edition of this book who provided thoughtful reviews and helpful feedback as well as encouragement. They gave their time, knowledge and expertise so generously. I am greatly indebted to Susan Deike, Karen Duff, Joanne Ginter, Susan Greaves, Carmen Hengeveld, Janine Montgomery, Laureen Schellenberg, Teeya Scholten and Allison Waks.

Thanks goes to the wonderfully creative Moshe (aka Joneric) for making the concepts come alive in the cover.

A large thank you must go out to Janine Montgomery for her tremendous support of **spark***. She has been instrumental in developing the research component to **spark***. I must thank also Asperger Manitoba Inc. for its support of the **spark*** groups at the University of Manitoba, the students who implemented the program and Brenda Stoesz who masterfully led the data analysis.

I want thank Troy Janzen from the University of Alberta for suggesting the inclusion of "the Language of **spark****".

Heartfelt thanks go to my husband, Bill, for his unconditional support and editorial comments throughout this process.

PREFACE

My goal in writing *The Autistic Child's Guide* is to inspire others to improve the lives and futures of children with autism spectrum condition[1] (ASC) by building foundational self-regulation skills. That is, we help our children achieve greater independence through learning important behavioral, cognitive and emotional skills and strategies. With well-planned and well-executed teaching, we can help children with ASC to grow, develop and, at the same time, become more independent and happier.

In the past, people believed the brain was fixed and unchangeable. That meant that a child with a developmental disorder was seen as unable to make substantial gains in development. If a child failed to make progress, it was thought the child was too "low functioning." This suggested there was a limit on how much the child could be expected to learn. Parents are often told that their child would never attend a regular school, graduate from high school, or be able to live on their own. The experienced clinician in me, and my inner optimist, finds this situation both sad and frustrating. We know so little about the brain and neurological system of children diagnosed with developmental disabilities. How can we say a child can't do something until we pursue all possibilities first? Children with ASC do have neurological differences compared with so-called "normal" children but their development and overall functioning *can* be significantly improved. We need to use different approaches and goals. Most of all, we need to raise our expectations for these children. Reuven Feuerstein, a visionary educator from Israel, has found that every child can learn - we need to find the strategies that work best for them.

> *A lack of learning ... should first be interpreted as a result of the inappropriate or insufficient use of teaching strategy rather than an inability on the part of the learner.*
>
> Gold, M. (1980)

I know from personal experience with many children with ASC they can learn and, perhaps more importantly, they want to learn. Like any child, they're born wanting to discover more about the world and make sense of it. Some of their learning strengths may be considered 'unconventional' but these can be used to create more positive futures for them. We need to help each child in ways that make sense to them.

I remember listening to Antonio Damasio, a brilliant American neurologist, talk about how injuries sustained by some patients suggested that they shouldn't be able to do certain things. Over time, however, he found that other areas and networks in their brains took over the functions. Brains are quite 'plastic': that is, if one part isn't functioning well, other areas and circuits can compensate or take over. This neuroplasticity, or cognitive modifiability as Feuerstein called it, is critical to how we view children with ASC. Their brains and neural networks can change and become more efficient with appropriate intervention and assistance.

Writers like Oliver Sacks[2] and Norman Doidge[3] have intrigued and inspired us with wondrous accounts of people who have overcome brain injuries and neurological differences. Both men allude to the old adage 'use it or lose it'. The neural networks of the brain need to be 'exercised' so we don't forget how to do things. If we don't use certain pathways, they may be taken over by other more highly-practiced functions. Our brains don't necessarily become 'set' over time, but certain functions and habits do come to dominate. It's difficult to break a thinking 'habit' but it can be done. Our brains continue to change and adapt throughout our lives, not just when we're young. Change is just a little easier then because we've practiced them less.

Plasticity is the essence of early intervention: we start therapy early because we believe brains can change. It's just recently, however, that the brain itself has become the focus of this intervention. We know that the brain can be re-organized. Gone are the days when we think a child either learns or doesn't. Brains can change with experience and new neural connections can be developed. With practice, these connections grow more solid and things get easier.

We can't pretend we can change which neurons fire at what time or in what sequence. Neuroscience may find specific connections or areas of difficulty, but our understanding of the brain is still quite limited. The fact that the structure and function of everyone's brains can change doesn't mean that we can 'cure' differences. It should, however, make us all rethink how we view and approach children with exceptional learning needs.

The central thesis of this book is that children with ASC can learn and want to learn. Without our help from the early stages, though, they experience difficulty moving forward and their development may not reach their true potential. We need to give our children with ASC the very best chance possible to lead a happy and productive life.

Autism in everyday life

When you meet a young child with ASC, their difficulties with regulating and adjusting behavior, thinking, and emotions become apparent. You may notice fleeting or a complete lack of eye contact. Children with ASC often walk right past you as though you weren't even there. The child may be in their own world – possibly enjoying a toy or a game but not sharing the experience with you. Interacting with the child can be challenging. You can call their name, offer them their favorite treat, and they won't react. Carrying on a conversation take a lot of work. Staying engaged with them is just as challenging. The child may become over-wrought if even a minor change is made to their environment or daily routine. Striking out, hitting themselves, crying, tantrums and even biting can be their way of expressing their frustration. It's hard to calm a child down in the middle of a meltdown.

Some children with ASC may be unable to communicate at all, or perhaps will use a few words or phrases. Others will go on at length about select topics. Although children with ASC may enjoy their toys, they're often not typical toys. Electric fans, pieces of string, a branch from a tree can be mesmerizing, as can kites, flags, clocks, or anything that spins.

Of the hundreds of children I've worked with over the years, one young boy with ASC prompted me to think specifically about teaching self-regulation. When I first met him, he displayed all the characteristics of ASC. He made little to no eye contact and sometimes appeared to be unaware of other people. He was in constant motion and almost seemed to buzz. His parents were told, when he was a preschooler, that he had oral apraxia and not to expect him to talk. When I first met him, he did talk but it was almost unintelligible. He said the same things over and over and over, perseverating on significant recent events ("go Chicago", "go Chicago", "go airplane", "go Chicago"). His body was tense, and he seemed to be in a constant state of high anxiety.

When I visited this child's classroom, I noticed he frequently asked the same question over and over: "Go gym today?", "Go gym today?" The teacher would reply, "Yes, we're going to the gym today". He was then told to sit down and do his work. After a minute or two, he was back at it, asking the same question over and over. It was relentless!

While in my office awaiting a ride home, the child would pace, squeezing their hands together, contorting their face, and, sometimes, squealing. Excitement about an upcoming event seemed to result in this behavior. Forewarning him of events wasn't wise because he'd become almost overwrought. His mother and I reminded him to stop the hand-wringing and pacing because other people would think they were "weird" (mom's words, not mine!). He'd stop briefly but then the behavior would start again.

I wondered what was going on in his brain and body. He laughed when someone fell or hurt themselves. I really believed he didn't find it funny. This boy was a highly anxious and tightly-wound person. He laughed out of excitement, agitation, and tension. I knew he was a kind and tender person who cared about other people, so this 'reframing' of his behavior made perfect sense. Laughing was still not socially-appropriate, but it no longer seemed so inappropriate and callous.

This little fellow was hugely dysregulated and driven by anxiety. He couldn't possibly learn and cope in their day-to-day life in such a state of imbalance. He was in a fight-or-flight mode a great deal of the time. A fight-or-flight mode is like the hyper-alert state you'd be in while walking down a dark alley alone at night. You almost prickle with awareness and are ready to run off or do battle at any second. No one can learn in such a state and no one should have to live like that.

His family and I figured out how to structure his life so it was less anxiety-provoking. I knew I had to find ways for him to assume more control. We set up some clearer routines and schedules but, if anything changed, he'd fall apart and, once again, become dysregulated. I taught him some forms of self-regulation. I coached him to use what I referred to as their "GQ" stance, adopting the pose of male models in the up-market magazine Gentlemen's Quarterly. By having him place their fingertips in each front pocket of their jeans, he was no longer squeezing his hands together when anxious. I also taught him some cognitive self-regulation in the form of listening skills. He learned to look at one thing at a time, say directions over to himself, and repeat "think in my brain" and "don't get distracted". The success with this boy led to further successes with other children. They too learned it was possible to regulate their own thoughts and actions.

Since that time, I've expanded my ideas about the forms and extent of self-regulation that can be taught. The successes continue to buoy me. Even my preschool-aged clients have quickly learned to modulate their own behavior. I remember a little five-year-old who said, "I'm going to ignore that." when the phone rang in my office. I was tickled and amused by her resourcefulness. Those were words I had taught her to keep herself from becoming distracted. She was showing that she was in command of her behavior, her thinking, and her emotions.

Whenever we work with children, we have to keep in mind where we're heading. I don't mean just looking ahead to the next year or years. Envision the child as an adult. Ask: How will they be able to function? Can we give them a chance at living independently, being gainfully employed, and enjoying meaningful relationships? Those things all require the ability to assume control over your behavior, thinking, and emotions. They need to take responsibility for their actions, following rules, and being safe even without adult supervision. They can make decision for themselves. It means they can self-regulate their emotions so they remain calm and adapt to different situations, people, and events.

Overview of this book

In the chapters ahead, we'll examine these issues and see how they relate to ASC. Then, the ***Self-regulation Program for Awareness and Resilience in Kids*** (spark*) is presented. spark* is a systematic, incremental approach to teaching self-awareness and self-regulation of behavior, thinking, and emotions.

spark* is a unique evidence-based model for teaching self-regulation. I've developed this program over many years of clinical work. It's been tried and tested on individual children and with groups of children. It works progressively from imitation of easy actions through to self-direction and control of behavior, thinking, and emotions. The model takes into account and addresses the major executive functions underlying each self-regulation activity and the importance of attention to learning.

Children are taught to be become more resilient and to advocate for themselves so they can cope and learn more readily in everyday settings. They're helped to identify where and when to use these skills and strategies and how to use them even in the presence of distractions, temptations, and disruptions.

The skills and strategies presented in **spark*** aren't exhaustive but represent a solid foundation on which more advanced skills can be built.

Unique features of **spark*** include:

- ✓ Focus on three areas of self-regulation: behavioral, cognitive, and emotional

- ✓ Based on current neurology

- ✓ Emphasis on attention and five major executive functions

- ✓ Suitable for children from two years of age to about 9 years of age

- ✓ Careful progression from awareness of simple motor acts to more complex cognitive and emotional self-regulation – the skills and strategies learned to deal with Behavioral Self-regulation serve as a base for Cognitive and Emotional Self-regulation

- ✓ Early and consistent inclusion of self-calming strategies

- ✓ Systematic withdrawal of adult direction while promoting self-direction for each child

- ✓ Inclusion of Resilience and Self-advocacy in the application of each form of self-regulation

✓ Explicit teaching of generalization of self-regulation skills and strategies

✓ Concentration on improving self-awareness and self-monitoring

✓ Practicing skills and strategies in enjoyable, fun activities

Chapter 1 is a review of self-regulation and its most important features. We then discuss why self-regulation is important to children with ASC and how dysregulation can impact daily life. Key findings from research in self-regulation and their effect on learning and development are then highlighted.

Chapter 2 reviews the five major executive functions which underpin self-regulation in the **spark*** model. The main features of each executive function are presented along with their associated neurology. This chapter is concluded with an overview of typical development of self-regulation from birth through early adolescence.

Chapter 3 presents information on dysregulation in children with ASC and current research into their executive function deficits. Although the research has limitations (such as, most results arise from studies with adults only), the main trends can provide us with insight. The chapter is concluded with a discussion of how lack of self-regulation skills may affect children with ASC over their life spans, including quality of life, ongoing support needs, attention, and problem behaviors.

Chapter 4 looks at available information about different types of intervention for improving executive functions and self-regulation. The **spark*** model is then described along with its main components and the areas of focus for Behavioral, Cognitive, and Emotional Self-regulation.

Chapter 5 discusses important reminders when preparing to implement **spark***. Vital factors for implementing **spark*** are highlighted, with particular emphasis on the Language of **spark****.

Chapters 6, 7 and 8 present the Behavioral, Cognitive, and Emotional Self-regulation units, respectively. Each chapter includes the main areas of focus and skill development, including Awareness of Ability, Awareness of Need, Resilience and Self-advocacy. Each lesson contains information on executive functions, task variations, objectives, task structuring, materials, Language of **spark*** used in each lesson, introductory script, practice methods, as well as suggestions for prompting the child, promoting self-monitoring and for solidifying and highlighting skills in everyday settings. Each chapter also presents observational assessments and progress monitoring procedures.

Chapter 9 summarizes the main trends and progressions in the **spark*** program and the long-term implications for learning and for everyday life for children with ASC. Results from research into the impact of **spark*** are presented. Suggestions are made for promoting self-regulation skills in day-to-day situations.

The appendix contains references and endnotes.

NOTE TO READER: If you really detest science and discussions of executive functions and self-regulation, why punish yourself? There's helpful information in the first four chapters, but you might want to skip ahead to Chapter 5. That'll get you started with spark*.

In the 77 Resource files accessible through the Self-Regulation Central website (www.selfregcentral.com), you'll find stimulus materials, songs, games and suggested storybooks and other resources. Eighteen newsletters are also included that introduce families and others involved in the child's life to important concepts and engage them in providing information and support to the child's learning. Three certificates of completion for each **spark*** are included to celebrate achievements. Forms for planning and evaluating intervention are also included. A complete list of the contents of the Resource files is below.

Contents of the spark* **Resource files**

EXAMPLES
Awareness of Need chart for controlling hands
Awareness of Need chart for systematic approach
Audio directions with pieces of information obscured
Foot or body movements
Listening with pieces of information obscured
Stories for visualizing information
Verbal direction worksheet for determining the most important information
Visual matching worksheet for determining most important and relevant information
Worksheets for using systematic approach

FORMS
Achievement of Lesson Objectives – Behavioral Self-Regulation
Achievement of lesson objectives - Cognitive self-regulation
Achievement of lesson objectives - Emotional self-regulation
Child background information
Observational Assessment – Behavioral Self-Regulation
Observational assessment - Cognitive Self-regulation
Observational assessment - Emotional self-regulation

ILLUSTRATIONS
Action intensity variations 1 and 2
Action manner variations

CHAPTER 1 - SELF-REGULATION

What is self-regulation?

Self-regulation is the ability to control and direct your body, thinking, and emotions in healthy and situationally-appropriate[4] ways.

Self-regulation is conscious, deliberate efforts to plan, control, or direct their behavior, thinking, and emotions in healthy and appropriate ways. This means that children look at a task or situation, figure out what they want and what's needed. Then they decide what steps and strategies they should use and try them out. They monitor their progress and make adjustments as needed. This means they stay focused on the task, even if they become distracted or have difficulties.

In developing self-regulation, children shift from living moment-by-moment. They begin to build mental images and frameworks for guiding, planning, directing, and evaluating their actions, thoughts, and feelings. They also get better at delaying rewards and take greater pleasure in their achievements. Self-regulated children are more likely to be intrinsically motivated and less dependent on receiving rewards.

What does it take to become self-regulated?

When thinking about developing self-regulation, consider the process a person has to go through to get a driver's license.

They need to learn the basic rules of the road, what different street signs and signals mean, and how to adjust to them.

They must learn how the accelerator, brake, gear shift, seat belts, mirrors, and various gauges work and what they do. Then comes practice driving, accompanied by a licensed driver or instructor. There may be restrictions to reduce distractions, such as disallowing passengers, because learning is still fragile.

The student driver discovers how different speeds feel and how freeway driving can be more challenging.

Over time, the driver builds Resilience so they can tolerate more traffic, higher speeds, and driving with a car full of people. Knowledge and skills become more solid. Distractions are less likely to interfere.

They also learn where and when different rules and behaviors are appropriate and when they're not. If rushing to the hospital, they can speed. If driving near a children's playground, it's wise to slow down. When the weather's bad, they need to drive more cautiously because the roads may be slippery.

Throughout these phases, the student becomes more independent but still needs guidance from a mature driver. Increasingly, driving becomes more skillful, automatic and enjoyable. Soon, they can head out on their own.

Just like the beginning driver, a child learning self-regulation need help through stages of increasing independence. They have to learn, first, that they're capable of controlling their body, thinking and emotions; just like the young driver learns to control the accelerator and brakes. They learn to control their impulses. The child must be taught how to plan, coordinate and organize themselves. They need to keep in mind what they're doing, what their goal is, what the rules and standards are, and what they should be doing. They monitor what's going on around them.

When learning self-regulation, ['pthe child comes to understand how to take responsibility for their own body, thinking, and emotions. They learn the extent of their control and things they can't control. They become more independent, making better choices.

Self-regulation needs to be personalized to each child's cultural, religious and individual family contexts as well as other important settings, including school. Standards for behavioral, cognitive, and emotional self-regulation need to 'fit' within situations important to them and their family. Our goal isn't to make the child conform or comply. We want to help them be more comfortable and not stick out as odd or frightening.

Self-regulation is central to a child's becoming an independent, self-motivated learner and adult. They learn to make appropriate choices and to learn from their experiences. It's through self-regulation that they can realize their true potential.

What self-regulation isn't

Self-regulation isn't the same thing as 'individualism', where the child's free to do whatever they want without any constraints. We don't want them to become either a law unto themselves or a robot. Our focus is on helping them act and think in ways that are in line with family and cultural values, as well as their own best interests. Children learn about limits. They figure out how to make reasonable decisions that keep them safe.

Self-regulation isn't simply impulse control or the ability to delay gratification. We're not just teaching the child to stop and think before making a choice. We're not merely training the child to wait to get something they want. Self-regulation involves considerably more than learned self-control. Each child learns to plan and evaluate their responses and reactions to the world around them.

Self-regulation isn't just teaching the child to calm or alert themselves. We want them to learn about how to maintain calm alertness and focused attention for learning. That's not enough. It's important for them to regulate not just their bodies, but also their thinking and emotions.

Finally, self-regulation isn't a way to stop behavior, thoughts, and emotions. If that were the case, all excitement, adventure, and joy would be taken out of learning and from life. Children learn to adjust their behavior, thinking, and emotions to different contexts. They learn there are times when they can just let loose and be themselves without any constraints. Of course, they have to be safe, but they need chances to feel free. If they like to bounce, flap their hands or twirl string, they need help to find appropriate times and places to do them.

Impact of dysregulation in everyday life

A child with weak self-regulation will likely act in the moment and not focus on the impact of their behavior. They may dive into a task without making sure they have the directions and materials they need. They might not consider what could happen; for example, they may pick up scissors and start cutting, not realizing they're chopping up the couch.

A child may look stubborn or lazy because they don't start an activity right away. A dysregulated child often doesn't know where and how to start.

They can seem disruptive. They may interrupt others. They might interact with others in odd ways, such as by crashing into them. These may be due to difficulties with memory, organization, and self-awareness rather than 'bad' behavior or attention-getting.

When doing a task, they may get caught up in non-essential parts. They might become absorbed in sharpening all of their pencils or picking at a spot on the page. They may skip steps or become over-focused on a small feature of the task. They only occasionally check their work for errors.

Children with poor self-regulation lose things frequently. They forget mittens, shoes, or their homework. They might get lost in the middle of following a request. You might ask them to go to their room, tidy up, put their dirty clothes in the laundry, and then join you for a snack. Sometime later, they'll come back with their dirty clothes in hand and their room still untidy. For the child with dysregulation, this isn't mis-behaving. Their problem is due to difficulty with organization, remembering, and becoming distracted by other things.

They'll likely have a poor internal sense of time. That means they don't 'feel' the difference between three minutes and 30 minutes. Asking them to do something for three minutes may seem like an eternity. On the other hand, 30 minutes playing with a favorite toy or computer game may feel like a brief blip in time.

Unforeseen events and changes in plans may cause them to become extremely upset. Lack of flexibility is part of having weak self-regulation. Their reactions often seem inappropriate or out of proportion. They likely will have difficulty stopping one activity to move on to another. Interrupting their computer or TV time to go to bed or eat supper will be met with emotional outbursts. Children with cognitive flexibility problems are more likely to perseverate, doing the same thing again and again, and have difficulty moving on.

What can improved self-regulation do?

Research shows positive results in all areas of life for people with stronger self-regulation. Some of the key research findings show:

- Better mental health and greater happiness[5], greater psychological wellbeing[6] and increased positive emotions, with reduced anxiety and tension[7,8]
- More successful interpersonal relationships[9]
- Greater intrinsic motivation[10]
- Higher feelings of competence[11]
- Increased interest and enjoyment in learning[12] and better engagement in learning[13,14]
- Higher creativity[15]
- Higher effort in learning[16,17] with more determination and will to succeed[18]
- Greater persistence[19,20], perseverance[21] and less procrastination[22]

- Improved learning performance and outcomes[23]

- Greater use of adaptive strategies, such as planning and time management[24]

Self-regulation skills learned during the preschool years provide the foundation for positive classroom behavior[25,26]. Children with stronger early self-regulation skills can regulate their engagement in learning[27] better. They also have a greater sense of autonomy[28]. Self-regulated learners have stronger belief in their abilities which makes a difference to the goals they set for themselves as well as their achievement[29,30].

Over the long term, preschoolers with stronger self-regulation skills show greater social-cognitive competence, goal-setting, planning and impulse control as adults[31]. A group of 1,000 New Zealand children were followed from birth to 32 years of age. They looked at their self-control and its impact on their lives[32]. Self-regulation was found to have "its own association with outcomes, apart from childhood social class and IQ"[33]. It predicted the status of each individual's health, wealth, and crime involvement three decades later. The researchers concluded that, if early intervention can achieve even small improvements in self-regulation, there could be an important shift in health, wealth, and crime rates in society.

Here are some examples of what can happen in everyday life when a child has stronger self-regulation skills.

- **Improved planning and goal-setting with less impulsive responding.** John thinks ahead to what they want to do with their Lego. They decide they want to build a rocket ship and takes out the pieces they need so they're all close at hand when they need them. That way, they can concentrate on building and doesn't have to keep going back to the box to get pieces.

- **Stronger development and use of strategies that can optimize abilities.** Neha tells herself to ignore the noise the other children are making so they can concentrate and get her work done. She tells herself the noises aren't important, and they picture a shield in her head that makes the noises bounce off.

- **Better self-monitoring in order to detect and correct errors.** Lucas is printing their name and they see that **they're** running out of space on one line. They decide to erase their name and start again a little farther over on the page rather than attempt to squish the letters into a smaller space.

- **Improved time-management.** Sarah checks the clock and sees they have just 10 minutes to finish her story. She speeds up so they can get it done in time.

- **Stronger belief in themselves as a learner.** Kai is struggling with a book they were assigned to read. They're feeling increasingly frustrated. They stop, take a breath and quietly say to themselves, "I can do it. Keep going."

- **Greater intrinsic motivation which comes from a sense of pleasure, curiosity or challenge rather than a reward or external praise.** Heather enjoys solving and completing crossword puzzles because they're challenging and stimulating. She also likes to exercise and stretch her vocabulary skills.

- **Better determination, persistence and clearer understanding of how much effort needs to go into learning and mastery.** Becky has a vision of the perfect pebble for her collection. She goes to the beach and is confronted by miles of pebbles. She realizes this isn't going to be easy but decides on a place to start and how they'll proceed to give herself the best chances. That way they aren't overwhelmed.

Key points in this chapter

Self-regulation is the ability to control and direct your body, perceptions and thinking in healthy and situationally-appropriate ways.

Children need help learning self-regulation, taking them through stages of increasing independence, resilience and coping in everyday settings.

Developing self-regulation includes learning you have a set of brakes as well as an accelerator. Self-regulation is about learning when and where you need to use these tools.

Learning self-regulation means much more than learning impulse control, stifling a child's ideas or letting them take over control of their life.

Children with weak self-regulation skills are less able to use their abilities effectively and efficiently and don't develop a strong sense of competence.

Children with stronger self-regulation skills show better adaptation to and achievement in life.

CHAPTER 2 - SELF-REGULATION & EXECUTIVE FUNCTIONS

Self-regulating the executive functions

In our daily lives we have many thoughts, ideas, and options. Our brains receive a tremendous amount of information. We sort through them, figure out what's most important, and what can be ignored. We decide what we want to accomplish and how to go about it. We often have to divide out attention and do a number of things at one time.

The main organizing and coordinating center in our brains that lets us do these things is the executive function system. Executive functions are the "brain circuits that prioritize, integrate, and regulate other cognitive functions"[34]. Our executive functions are a collection of processes that allow us to put our thoughts and intentions into action.

The processes of the executive function system are similar to what a good business executive would do; thus, the term 'executive'. The business executive is responsible for putting the company's resources into action by:

- Setting goals
- Determining what's important to the business
- Committing necessary or available resources to tasks
- Planning and overseeing procedures
- Monitoring progress
- Changing procedures and goals as need be

These duties parallel those of the brain's executive functions. There are lots of different, inter-related processes that come together to form a working goal-directed system.

Figure 1 on the next page shows executive functions at the center and self-regulation as the buffer between the brain and context. Self-regulation skills help children consciously modulate their executive functions. This allows them to put their knowledge into action.

spark* focuses on helping children gain more control over their executive functions by developing self-regulation skills. Children learn to regulate their executive functions and then use to cope and learn. They're helped to align their behavior, thinking, and emotions with the demands of each situation. If a child is at the library, mosque, temple, or church, they learn the clues that tell them to speak quietly and not run around. Other situations give clues about how to behave. For example, when you enter a fast-food restaurant, the entire script of actions and words downloads from your memory and guides your behavior for ordering the food:

> You know to line up at a till where an employee is. You wait your turn, standing a reasonable distance from the person in front of you. While you stand in line, you read the menu and make decisions about what you'll order. Once you're at the counter, you wait for the employee to look at you. Then you tell them what your want. You listen for the amount of money you owe and then you pay. You move to the pick-up line.

Figure 1. Schematic diagram of the relationship among executive functions, self-regulation and context.

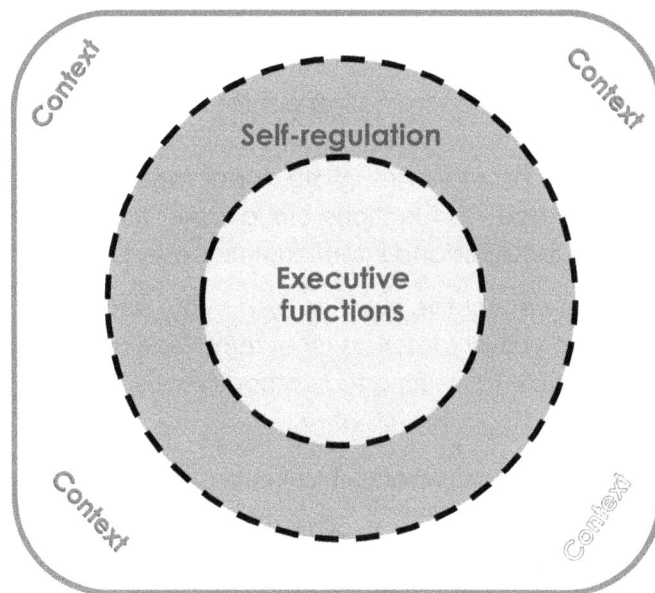

These behaviors are thanks to self-regulation of your executive functions. When you start counting the steps and decisions you have to make just to order fast food, you begin to realize all of the executive functions involved and the self-regulation needed. Day-to-day life is remarkably complex when you consider how to put your thoughts and intentions into actions.

A few words about the brain, learning, and 'neuromyths'

Human behavior and learning ultimately start in the brain. Neural circuits in our brains develop through active, dynamic interactions with people, objects, and events. These experiences help organize and enhance how our brains work. These complexly-interwoven circuits become stronger or weaker, dependent on how much they're used.

Not that long ago, it was thought that different cognitive functions occurred in specific locations in the brain in an almost one-to-one fashion. We now know that learning promotes the development of connections between different areas of the brain. These networks spread across many regions. This means that different brain functions involve whole networks instead of just one particular area of the brain.

Myths about the brain and how it functions continue to be popular. These 'neuromyths' often come from "a misunderstanding, a misreading and, in some cases, a deliberate warping of the scientifically established facts to make a relevant case for education or for other purposes"[35]. They're often presented as 'fact' and can sound plausible.

One common belief is that people are either left-brained or right-brained. This is untrue: our whole brains and both hemispheres contribute to nearly all activities, not just half or just specific areas.

A second 'neuromyth' is the concept of 'critical periods'; that is, there are critical periods in early life when the brain's ability to learn is considerably greater than in adulthood. There are important 'sensitive' periods when learning certain things is easier and changes ('neuroplasticity) can be greater. However, the ability to develop new neural connections isn't limited to the preschool years. Learning and resulting neural changes occur throughout our lives.

Another myth is that you can take information directly from neurology and brain scans to develop plans for teaching children. There's a lot of buzz about 'brain-based education' but, unfortunately, most of it "rests on very shaky ground"[36]. Sadly, it's not that straightforward. It involves a lot of speculation and isn't necessarily founded on accurate neuro-anatomical and/or neuro-functional information. The structures and functions of the brain are very complex, making it almost impossible to say, "If you do this, it'll make the brain work in this way." There simply is no linear, one-to-one relationship with behavior[37].

New technologies are helping us to understand more about our brains and how they function. This knowledge is advancing at a remarkable pace. Functional Magnetic Resonance Imaging (fMRI) provides information about blood flow, a measure of neural activity. If an fMRI shows greater activity in an area of the brain, that area is considered to be part of the act or thought that's occurring at that time. Differences in tasks, instructions, age of subjects, and statistical analyses often make it difficult to compare results among the different research studies. It complicates our ability to draw any solid conclusions. Because of this, there continues to be a lag between new technology for viewing brain activity and the ability to interpret the findings. This means that fMRI data need to be interpreted with caution.

We're just beginning to understand the connection between the brain and behavior. There's a long way to go before we can look at altering, solidifying, and refining specific neural connections to improve learning. However, neuroscience is inspiring us to think differently about children, disabilities, and development. It's challenging us to develop better interventions and practices.

At this stage, we can't conclude that differences in brains or brain function of children with ASC mean they directly cause learning deficits or strengths. Nor can we conclude that differences in their brains necessarily lead to deficits or problems. We know that experience changes the brain and its organization so some differences found in brain scans may reflect the diversity of events and experiences that person has had rather 'brain impairments'.

Executive functions

The executive functions are so intertwined and interdependent it's not easy to separate each one. There's no gold standard for measuring executive functions so the separation of distinct processes is open to some debate. However, the following five executive functions hare key to the lives of children with ASC:

1. Planning and organization
2. Inhibitory control
3. Working memory
4. Self-monitoring
5. Cognitive flexibility

Planning and organization

Planning and organization are involved from the instant you decide to do something. You need to look at what you intend to do and form a plan of action. Your perceptions, thoughts, intentions, and actions must be organized and integrated into a coherent plan to accomplish your goal. The planning and organization system must also deal with unanticipated events so other approaches can be used as needed.

Planning and organization processes are primarily associated with the dorsolateral section of the prefrontal cortex[38]. See Figure 2 on the next page for a schematic diagram; the prefrontal cortex is highlighted within dotted lines. This area is involved in activities that require setting goals, anticipating future events, and sequencing.

Inhibitory control

Inhibitory control allows you to direct your attention and actions even when there are temptations and distractions. This executive function helps you override interruptions, your emotions, and usual ways of doing things. Inhibitory control allows you to suppress irrelevant thoughts and actions that may interfere with your goals, such as eating chocolate cake when you're on a diet. Inhibitory control also helps you stop a behavior if it's not helpful or it's inappropriate. Good inhibitory control also keeps you working on a task even if it's difficult.

Inhibitory control takes in a wide range of brain areas, including frontal and prefrontal areas, the parietal lobe, cingulate cortex, basal ganglia, thalamus and the cerebellum[39]. Figure 2 below shows (clockwise from the left) the prefrontal cortex, parietal lobe, anterior cingulate cortex, thalamus, cerebellum and basal ganglia. Neuro-imaging studies indicate that deficits in inhibitory control are associated with disruptions in the circuitry of the frontal and parietal lobes[40].

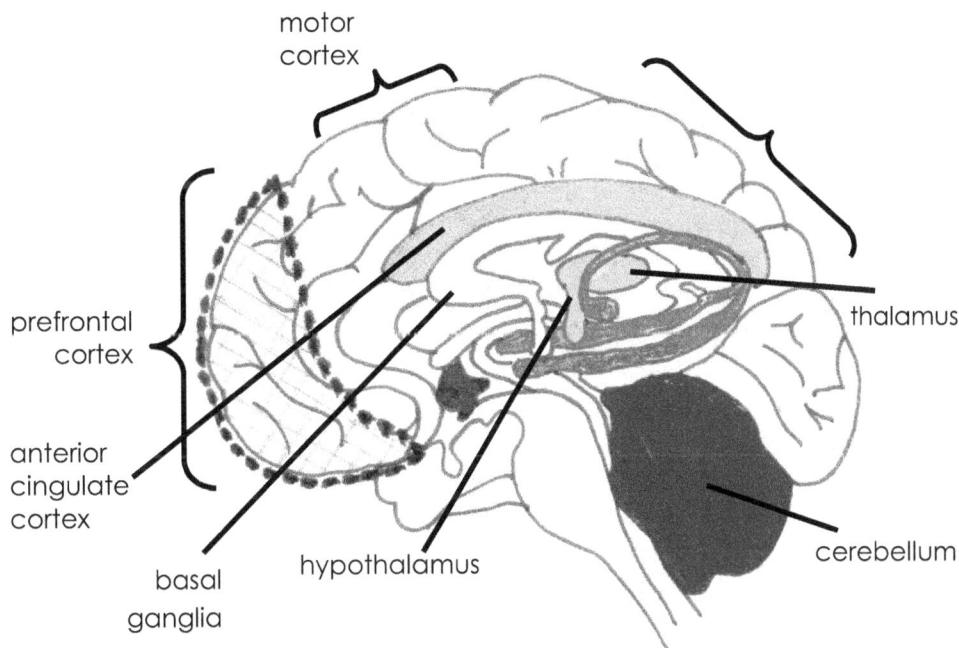

Figure 2. Diagram showing approximate location of the prefrontal cortex, thalamus, basal ganglia and cerebellum

Working memory

Working memory is the capacity to hold information in your mind long enough to generate goals, plans and steps needed to achieve what you wish. The information loaded into working memory can be newly-learned or retrieved from long-term storage. Working memory makes it possible to remember instructions, consider alternatives, multi-task, and connect the present to future possibilities and/or past experiences. It's critical to learning that we can see connections between concepts and ideas and re-assemble parts into new creations. You use your working memory when doing mental arithmetic, remembering a phone number until you dial it or remembering the rules and objectives of a task while completing it. Working memory is also central to our ability to connect new information with things we already know and to create new concepts.

The prefrontal and parietal lobes of the brain are important for working memory. Working memory is strongly linked with reasoning and response inhibition as it shares some of the same areas of the brain[41]. Figure 2 on the previous page shows the prefrontal and parietal lobes.

Self-monitoring

Self-monitoring is the ability to supervise your actions and thoughts to make sure they're heading toward your goal. By monitoring your performance, you can compare what you're doing to a standard or to expectations. This lets you recognize the need to correct your work and to change how you're doing it. This supervisory function ensures the quality and accuracy of your work. Self-monitoring is considered essential for the development of self-regulated behaviors and emotions[42].

Self-monitoring is primarily associated with the prefrontal cortex and the anterior cingulate cortex (ACC)[43]. The ACC provides an interface between action selection processes in the frontal cortex, emotion or motivation processes and regulation of the motor cortex[44]. See Figure 2 to locate the prefrontal lobe, ACC, and motor cortex. The interconnections between these areas suggest that there's a relationship between self-monitoring, attention, and inhibitory control.

Cognitive flexibility

Cognitive flexibility (sometimes referred to as attentional or mental flexibility) is the ability to switch what you're thinking and doing in response to changes. It's the ability to move from one situation or activity to another and adjust to change. Cognitive flexibility lets you shift to a different thought, a different action, or perspective. It's important to your ability to think of alternative solutions to a problem or novel uses of an object (like, thinking of different uses of a box or plastic bottle). It draws significantly on inhibitory control and working memory[45] in order to stop, compare, and adjust to changes.

Cognitive flexibility is associated with the basal ganglia, anterior cingulate cortex, prefrontal cortex, and posterior parietal cortex[46]. Figure 2 shows (clockwise from the left) the basal ganglia, prefrontal cortex, parietal lobe, and anterior cingulate cortex.

These five executive functions are complexly intertwined with each other. There's a lot of inter-dependence among them so, if one process is receiving a heavier load, other functions may be impacted. For example, if working memory is overloaded, your ability to inhibit your behavior might be reduced. If a situation calls for a lot of cognitive flexibility, your ability to plan your steps may be compromised.

Attention, self-regulation and executive functions

Controlling the focus and duration of your attention is important to ensuring your executive functions work harmoniously in functional ways. This means that the amount of effort required to self-regulate is impacted by available attentional resources.

There are at least three types of attention that are crucial to successful learning. They include:

- Selective attention. This is where you pay attention only to the most important and relevant information. Selective attention is important when you need to focus only on the most important information while tuning out distractions. When you're trying to study or memorize a song, you need selective attention that will let you concentrate your efforts only on those things.

- Sustained attention. This type of attention focuses on the length of time you maintain your focus. You keep your attention on a task as long as it takes to finish it.

- Shifting attention. Shifting attention is needed to multi-task and deal with multiple pieces of information. You need to shift from one thought or feature to another in smooth, easy ways and not lose track.

In Table 1 below, it becomes clear that attention plays an important role in all the executive functions and, consequently, in self-regulation. Selective attention is important to planning and organization, inhibitory

Self-Regulation		Selective attention	Sustained attention	Shifting attention
	Planning and organization	✔	✔	✔
	Inhibitory control	✔	✔	✔
	Working memory	✔	✔	✔
	Self-monitoring	✔	✔	✔
	Cognitive flexibility	✔	✔	✔

Table 1. Relationship between self-regulation, executive functions and attentional resources.

control, working memory, self-monitoring, and cognitive flexibility. You need to focus only on the most important and relevant information and to ignore distractions.

Sustaining your attention is critical to planning so you can organize your approach, ignore irrelevant information, and monitor your performance.

The ability to shift attention is crucial to planning and organization, inhibitory control, working memory, self-monitoring and cognitive flexibility so plans can be changed if needed during an activity or event.

An important point in this discussion is that, while you work on conscious control of executive functions, you are focusing on attention. That means attention need not be a separate goal area. When you teach self-regulation, an implicit part of it is improving attention.

Typical development of self-regulation, executive functions, and attention

Self-regulation, executive functions and attention typically develop and mature over at least the first two decades of life - from the preschool years, into adolescence. Figure 3 on the next page shows the normal development of executive functions from birth to the early teen years. Notice that darkening of lines represents progressive refinement of skills, blunt-ended lines indicate attainment of an adult-like level and arrows at the end of a line signify ongoing development.

This developmental progression reflects overall neurological development, changes in the connections among different areas of the brain as well as learning[47]. The emergence, maturation, and refinement of executive functions also parallel development of attentional controls[48].

Between birth and two years of age, the ability to self-regulate behavior and emotions shows significant improvement. For example, children begin to self-sooth (such as, by sucking on their fingers) and can seek help or comfort from others when needed.

Between six months and one year, children show increasing evidence of emotional self-regulation. They can tolerate some delays in events and in gratification[49]; one-year-old children can typically cope with delays up to 10 seconds[50,51]. They exhibit increasing control of their bodies and body parts, including their voices[52]. The emergence of object permanence between eight and 12 months of age (that's when objects are no longer 'out of sight out of mind') indicates that children are developing stronger memory.

Between one and two years of age, children show increasing ability to correct errors and plan new actions. Error correction strategies are observable in the play of children as early as 18 months of age[53]. They begin to respond to commands and warnings from caregivers[54]. Toddlers are capable of complying with simple requests ("Say bye-bye") and prohibitions ("Don't touch").

Around two years of age, they begin to use a rule held in memory to inhibit alluring or habitual responses[55], such as "Don't touch Grandma's Dresden figures." Their ability to inhibit responses suggests that their intentional behavior, planning, and inhibitory control are maturing. Self-regulation of attention begins to emerge and mature toward the end of the first year and continues throughout the preschool and school years[56].

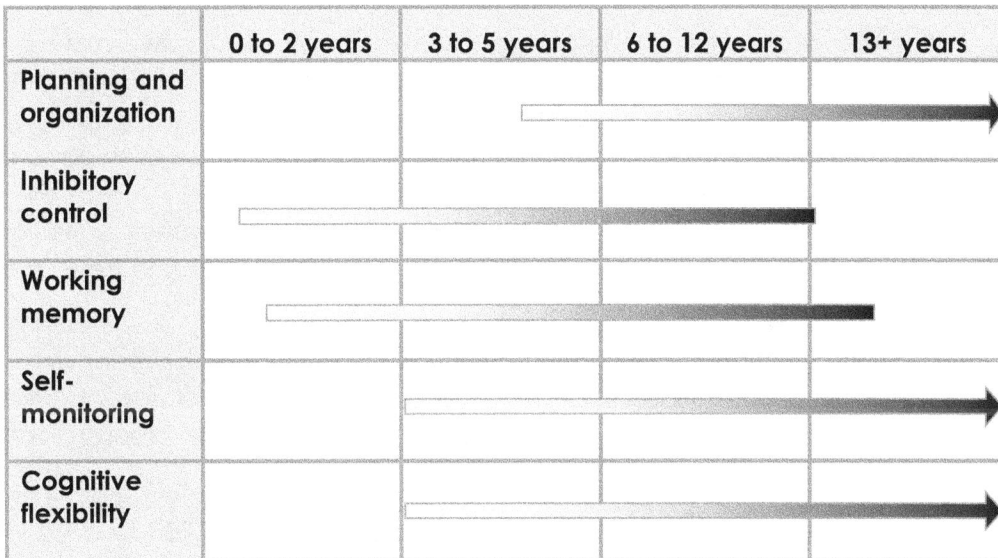

	0 to 2 years	3 to 5 years	6 to 12 years	13+ years
Planning and organization				
Inhibitory control				
Working memory				
Self-monitoring				
Cognitive flexibility				

Figure 3. Developmental progression of executive functions from birth through adolescence

From three to five years of age, children start to develop voluntary control of their attention. Significant improvements are discernible, especially in selective attention and vigilance[57]. They're also increasingly able to control their bodies. They're less driven by impulses, like the temptation to eat or pocket things at the grocery store.

They learn to adapt their behavior in response to different situations (for example, speaking differently to younger children versus adults) and the standards associated with each one.

Working memory and cognitive flexibility show noticeable improvement. They can generate concepts by grouping objects along one dimension, color, size, number or shape, and by two dimensions, color and shape together[58]. Greater flexibility is also seen in the child's ability to switch between tasks more readily and fluidly[59]. Through this period, children can figure out similarities among increasingly dissimilar objects[60], like how a dog and a chair are the same (they both have legs).

Planning and sequencing of tasks and activities improve but they continue to develop through to adulthood[61].

Inhibitory control improves as well with children being able to suppress a dominant, frequently-used but incorrect response in favor of a less prominent and infrequently-used but correct response[62].

As young as five, children show metacognitive awareness, an appreciation of their thinking processes: they understand the purpose of remembering and some awareness of what forgetting is. They also begin to use simple metacognitive strategies, like repeating things over to themselves so they won't forget.

Between four and five years of age, children become more aware of their emotions and increasingly use culturally-determined rules to exercise control. They understand that they must speak quietly in church, mosque, temple or synagogue but can yell in the playground. They develop more strategies for coping and dealing with frustration[63]. They monitor their own performance more frequently[64] and use self-talk to guide their behavior and thinking[65] (for example, "Okay, now I need to put this one here and then take this one ...").

From six to 12 years of age, there's continued development of behavioral, cognitive, and emotional self-regulation. By about six years of age, children develop basic control and regulation of their actions, arousal, and emotions[66,67].

Considerable progress is seen in cognitive flexibility up through 10 years of age, but development continues through adolescence and beyond[68]. Children use feedback more effectively to improve their performance. They can also shift more easily from one dimension to another when grouping or sorting information[69]. It's during this time period that children can more successfully play games, such as *20 Questions,* that require shifting from category to category and remembering and accumulating information[70]. Working memory is believed to reach adult level by the end of this period[71]. Planning develops rapidly during the elementary school years but continues beyond adolescence[72].

The most notable trends in typical development of self-regulation are the child's increasing ability to be future-oriented and imaginative. Children rely less on the physical presence of objects[73]. In infancy, children are primarily driven by in-born reflexes and biological needs, like hunger. As they reach toddlerhood, behaviors and thoughts are increasingly under voluntary control. In the later preschool years, there's significant movement toward active control of behavior, thinking, and emotions. That means, self-regulation shifts from being primarily biological and reflexive to more cognitively- and socially-oriented.

What happens after that? You can see in Figure 4 on the next page that self-regulation continues to develop through to the mid-twenties. There's a small dip in the teen years, followed by continued growth. After the twenties, however, self-regulation declines through old age.

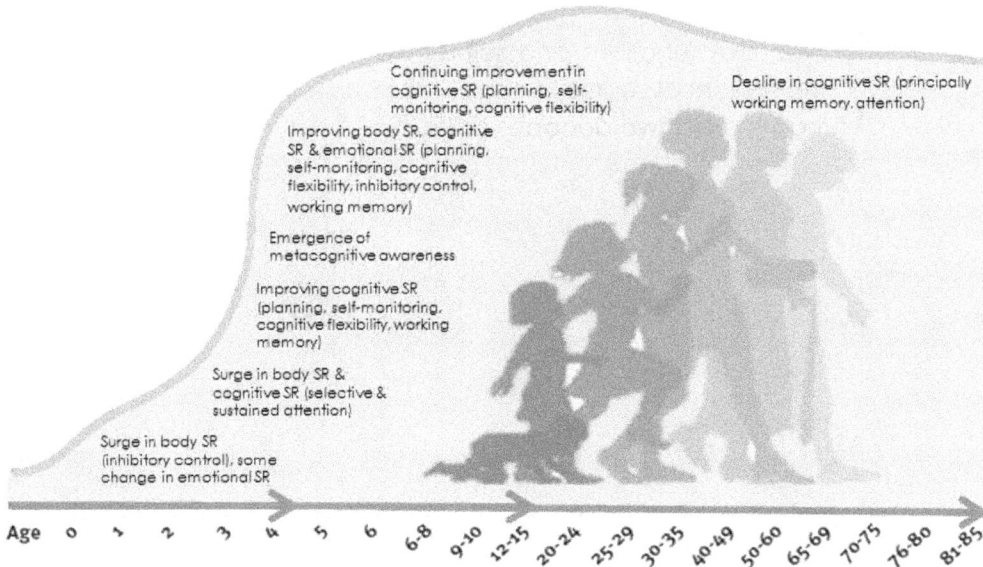

Figure 4
Development of self-regulation from infancy to old age

Key points in this chapter

Executive functions are the main processes we use to plan, organize, integrate, and regulate our behavior, thinking, and emotions. They're what we use to turn thoughts and intentions into actions.

Self-regulation is the conscious control of executive functions, adapting their use to the differing demands and needs of varying situations and contexts.

Being cautious about 'neuromyths' and other misunderstandings or deliberate warping of science is important when choosing programs for children.

A major premise of **spark*** is that children can learn to consciously take control of their executive functions and improve their behavior, thinking, and emotional expression.

The five main executive functions included in **spark*** are planning and organization, inhibitory control, working memory, self-monitoring, and cognitive flexibility.

Sustained attention, shifting attention, and selective attention are important to harmonious interplay of the executive functions. When you teach self-regulation, an implicit part of it is improving attention.

Executive functions and self-regulation start developing during the preschool years but continue to refine and strengthen over at least the first two decades of life.

CHAPTER 3 - DYSREGULATION IN AUTISM

Dysregulation and executive dysfunction in autism

Autism spectrum conditions (ASC) are traditionally[74] defined as having features in three main areas:

1. Social

    a. Significant problems using nonverbal behaviors, such as eye contact, to organize social interactions

    b. Lack of appropriate relationships with peers

    c. Few attempts to share enjoyment, interests or achievements with other people

    d. Lack of social or emotional interactions with others

2. Communication

    a. Delay in language development

    b. Significant difficulty starting or sustaining conversation with others

    c. Stereotyped and repetitive use of words and phrases

    d. Little spontaneous make-believe play

3. Behavior

    a. Preoccupation with just a few interests, often things like trains, dinosaurs, cars or computers

    b. Inflexible adherence to specific routines or rituals

    c. Stereotyped and repetitive mannerisms, like hand flapping or finger flicking

    d. Preoccupation with objects or parts of objects, such as fans, flags or wheels

This describes ASC as including delays as well as significant dysregulation of behavior, thinking, and emotions. Social behavior and communication skills require self-regulation to ensure flexibility and finesse. Relationships with others are developed through finely-choreographed interactions that must be tuned to the person, time, and place – all needing self-regulation. These are all areas of significant difficulty for children with ASC. They don't easily adjust to different people and situations. They become over-focused or stuck on some words, phrases, movements, routines, objects, or topics and can't readily move on. They have difficulty stopping themselves from doing and thinking about some things. Planning and organizing different ways of dealing with the world and people around them are challenging. They can't easily inhibit some thoughts or actions, monitor changes, and then adjust according to those changes.

Difficulties with self-regulation may not explain all of the characteristics and behaviors of people with ASC. But viewing ASC as difficulty with self-regulation is compelling. Repetitive behaviors, like hand flapping or talking about the same topic, and preoccupations can be productively viewed as self-regulation problems. Perseveration and over-focus show that the child is unable to inhibit behaviors or thoughts and shift focus.

Weak self-regulation of attention, planning and organization, inhibitory control, working memory, self-monitoring and cognitive flexibility may all be associated with the poor imitation skills often observed in children with ASC.

Impairments in joint attention, which are often the first characteristics seen in young children with ASC[75], can also be viewed as problems in self-regulation. The child's inability to consistently and accurately self-monitor ongoing behaviors as well as poor working memory, inhibitory control and cognitive flexibility are possibly involved.

Other behaviors, such as unusual eating habits and sleep patterns, self-injurious behaviors and extreme temper tantrums are also likely related to difficulties with self-regulation.

Impaired executive functions and consequent weak self-regulation, or dysregulation, are found in children with attention deficit disorder, Tourette's syndrome, schizophrenia, obsessive-compulsive disorder (OCD), phenylketonuria and ASC[76]. Executive dysfunction is "one of the most consistently replicated cognitive deficits in individuals with ASC"[77]. Interestingly, the authors of the *Autism Spectrum Rating Scales*[78] discovered the prominence of self-regulation in identifying people with ASC. When they looked at their data, they identified three main features: (1) unusual behavior (e.g. insistence on routines, lining up objects, insistence on doing things the same way each time), (2) social communication (e.g. infrequent starting of conversations, rarely sharing enjoyment with others, failing to play with others), and (3) self-regulation (e.g. failure to complete tasks, leaving chores unfinished, becoming distracted). Self-regulation stood out as such a strong factor that they concluded that it represents a core feature and should be included in the diagnosis of ASC.

Dysregulation and adult outcome in autism

Generalization of skills and strategies is an important issue that has far-reaching impacts on the lives of people with autism. The outcome data for adults with autism distressing. They simply don't represent the outcomes I know are possible for people with ASC. A large proportion should be able to lead productive lives and achieve independence. Currently, this appears to be the exception for adults with ASC rather than the rule.

Overall, research into outcomes for adults with autism[79,80,81,82] paint a distressing picture. Figure 5 below summarizes the findings, comparing them with expectations for non-autistic adults.

Some improvements have occurred over the past decade[83] but still only a minority of adults with ASC lives independently or semi-independently. Regardless of intellectual abilities, rates of university or college completion are less than half that for the general population[84]. Unemployment rates of 57% to 78% are considerably higher than the 5% to 7% typically found in Sweden, France and England[85] where the major studies were conducted. Marriage rates between one and 16% are significantly lower than the 95% found in their home countries[86].

A significant percentage of all adults with ASC continued to exhibit core behaviors of ASC, such as resistance to change and ritualistic behaviors, in addition to about 84% having one or more mental health issues, such as OCD, depression and anxiety.

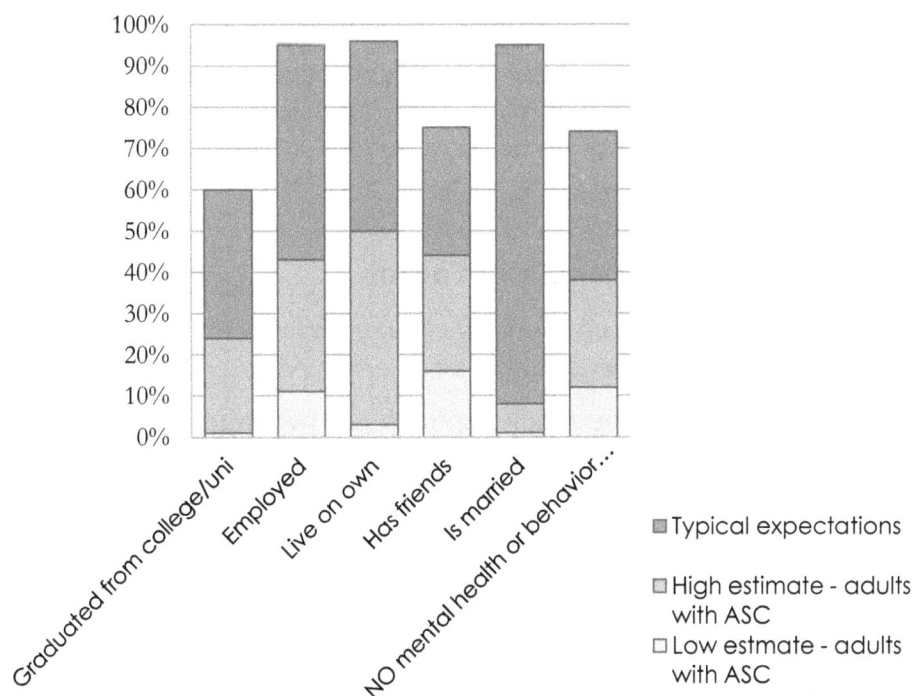

Figure 5. Summary of research on six key adult outcomes showing reported range for adults with ASC (low through high estimates), compared to typical expectations.

Three main reasons for the failure of people with ASC to achieve higher levels of education, employment, and independence have been suggested[87]. One issue relates to difficulty regulating, modulating, and coping with the demands of community settings. Because of their tendency to be overwhelmed by the many social and sensory demands of educational, vocational, and employment settings, adults with ASC may opt for less challenging situations. This leads to failure to achieve at a level consistent with their abilities, to unemployment or underemployment, as well as reduced social contact. Lack of social contact can, in turn, lead to increased difficulty dealing with all social situations and a greater likelihood of isolation and mental health problems.

A second factor concerned problems planning, organizing and executing goal-directed activities. Adults with ASC often have difficulties deciding on a goal and then figuring out how to reach it. This means that, even if the person has aspirations, they're unable to organize their life to achieve them.

The final reason was a lack of self-advocacy skills. Adults with ASC often don't understand what they need in order to function in challenging settings and don't appreciate that they can advocate for themselves. Families and carers of people with ASC often jump in to 'rescue' them when they see their child becoming overwhelmed and floundering in demanding situations[88].

These three areas all point to problems with self-regulation. Adults with ASC seem to lack awareness of their ability to manage and direct their bodies, thinking, and emotions. They also appear to have little understanding of how to advocate for themselves so their lives can be more satisfying. The apparent failure to meet some of life's challenges indicates that they continue to be fragile and tentative in their approach. They haven't had the opportunity to learn how to be more resilient and resourceful in coping with day-to-day life.

Executive functions in people with autism

The next section presents an overview of current information on the five key executive functions as they relate to people with ASC.

When discussing executive functions, there are two issues that come up. One is that it's artificial to separate each executive function. The do act together and are interrelated but we have to try to make sense of them somehow. A second issue is that most studies of executive functions use isolated, highly-structured tasks. These tasks don't necessarily relate to real life. That means a person may respond to a test in a laboratory differently than how they might in day to day life.

At this time, conclusions about the relationship between specific executive functions and behavior in ASC are somewhat speculative. In general terms, however, development of executive functions has been found to predict how well children with ASC will respond to treatment[89] as well as their long-term outcome[90].

> **A note of caution before proceeding**: It's often difficult to compare study results due to differences in age of the subjects (many studies include adults only), in functioning levels and co-morbid conditions (like ADHD) as well as diversity in the types of tasks and responses required. Making generalizations from adult subjects to children is usually a problem because learning over time changes how our brains function. Adults' responses can't be used to represent how children might act. In addition, studies tend to include only small numbers of subjects, so the results don't represent the full range of people on the autism spectrum. Therefore, when reviewing the findings of research into executive functioning in ASC, caution is needed.

Planning and Organizing

Research into planning and organization in people with autism[91,92,93,94] give somewhat mixed support for impairment in this executive function. It seems that, when information load is increased, they experience more obvious deficits in planning and organization. This will likely be compounded if the child also has ADHD, a frequent co-morbid condition in children with ASC.

Inhibitory control

Results of studies to date[95,96,97,98,99,100,101,102,103,104] appear mixed in relation to the existence and/or severity of deficits in inhibitory control in people with ASC. The perseveration and stereotypical behavior seen in children with ASC provide compelling support for impairments in inhibitory control. Because almost half of children with ASC have comorbid hyperactivity, impulsivity and inattention[105], inhibitory control problems may be more prevalent than some studies suggest. Inhibitory control is believed by some researchers to be the major executive dysfunction in those with ASC"[106].

Working memory

Overall, research studies[107,108,109,110111,112] suggest that certain types of working memory may be impaired[113] in people with ASC. For example, spatial working memory, memory for things you see, appears to be an area of deficit. However, verbal working memory needs to be examined more fully before conclusions can be made in that area.

Self-monitoring

Some theories and research suggest that deficits in self-monitoring may contribute to social-emotional and social-cognitive impairments in children with ASC[114]. Deficiencies in self-monitoring can be seen in inconsistent focus on social cues, social information processing and social learning[115]. That is, children with ASC aren't consistently checking on their performance and on changes that are occurring in social situations.

Cognitive flexibility

Impaired cognitive flexibility is often considered to be a hallmark of ASC[116,117]. We often see resistance to change, difficulty with transitions between activities, perseverative, stereotyped behavior, and difficulties in the regulation and modulation of actions[118,119,120]. Cognitive flexibility problems may also be at the core of children with ASC's pragmatic (social communication) difficulties[121]. A child's ability to interpret words with multiple meanings or speak about a variety of topics may be restricted by their problems with cognitive flexibility rather than lack of words or social skills.

These results support the idea that many key features of autism arise from impaired self-regulation. Not all individuals with ASC have difficulties with all of the executive functions but, all have problems with some. Studies are needed that look at executive functioning and self-regulation in people across the range of ASC, over the longer term, at different age levels, within the laboratory and in day-to-day life.

Dysregulation, family quality of life and ongoing support needs

Families report difficulties caring for their children with ASC. These families are less likely to attend religious services. They also participate less frequently in community activities and events than families of typically-developing children[122]. These difficulties largely result from the behavioral challenges their children experience.

One behavioral challenge a lot of families deal with is running away (also referred to as "elopement"). This is where children run away without supervision. A recent study[123] found that almost half of the 1200 autistic children surveyed had tried to run off from their families. Over one-quarter of the children were missing long enough to cause serious concerns,. Sixty-five per cent were in danger of traffic injury and 24% in danger of drowning. Many parents indicated that risks of the child's running away prevented the family from attending or enjoying activities outside the home.

These issues, in addition to adult outcome research, point clearly to significant amounts of ongoing support needed by people with autism. They can learn many of the skills needed to function more optimally but there's a significant problem with generalization of that knowledge. For years, we've heard about how children with autism can learn a skill or strategy in one situation but don't use it in different settings and/or with different people[124]. When it comes time to use the skills in everyday life, they usually don't unless an adult prompts and guides them[125,126]. There may even be regression and loss of skills if close supervision and adults' prompts are removed[127].

There appears to be some sort of 'disconnect' between learning the skills and putting them into use. There's a breakdown when it comes to using them in everyday life. I've found this on many occasions with children I've worked with. We practiced a strategy or skill but, when it was needed outside the therapy room, they failed to use it. I recall one boy who was a very kind-hearted and gentle child but, when another child said they were a girl, he bit her. We talked about the incident: yes, he knew what to do if someone teased them or used mean words but, no, that practiced skill didn't come into consciousness during the name-calling.

I found some important similarities between people with ASC and those with known deficits in executive functioning[128] due to injuries to their frontal lobes, the 'home' of executive functions. I came across the work of Hans-Lukas Teuber who did some of the important early research into the functions of the frontal lobes. Teuber observed that individuals with frontal lobe damage exhibited "a curious dissociation between knowing and doing"[129] – they knew how to do something but didn't apply that knowledge. This was strikingly similar to what we see in people on the autism spectrum – that breakdown at the stage of generalization. Could working on self-regulation help them with generalizing skills and strategies into everyday life? Executive functions and self-regulation skills may be important keys to extension of learning into daily life.

Other features of autism and dysregulation

Attention

Children with autism have difficulties with attention[130]. Failure to look where other people are looking may be one of the earliest signs of autism in children, being observable as early as eight months of age[131]. They rarely look to see where a noise or voice came from. These differences appear to persist into adulthood[132].

Sustained attention isn't necessarily a problem in children with autism; they can fixate on things for long periods of time. Unfortunately, this tends to be overly-selective where they ignore most other things.

Shifting attention is typically a problem in children with autism[133]. They have difficulty switching their attention from one thing to another and then back to something or someone else[134]. If they're occupied with a favorite object, it's even harder to shift attention[135].

Attention problems affect social-emotional development in children with autism. Children with ASC have well-documented difficulty understanding emotions in others[136]. They have problems recognizing emotions from facial expressions, tone of voice, and body language which may persist into adulthood[137]. Young adults with ASC often have trouble telling a fearful expression from an angry one and over-rate trustworthiness of unfriendly faces[138].

Current research suggests that impaired executive functioning may contribute to social-emotional difficulties in children with ASC[139]. Their differences in recognizing and appreciating emotions may be due, at least in part, to reduced attention to faces and facial expressions[140,141]. Children with ASC are more likely to look at the mouth than the eyes of someone talking[142] even though the eyes provide more complete information about emotions. When they do look at another person's eyes, it's only briefly[143,144].

Problem behaviors

Problem behaviors in children with ASC haven't been clearly examined relative to executive functions.

Many children with ASC have atypical eating behavior[145,146], with strong preferences and/or restricted ranges of food.

Problems with sleep are also common, with two-thirds or more having difficulties falling asleep or staying asleep[147,148,149].

Self-injurious behavior, such as head banging or hitting or biting, is another area. Approximately one-third of children with ASC injure themselves while a slightly larger proportion acts aggressively toward others[150], mainly parents and siblings.

Tantrums, extreme forms of dysregulation, tend to continue on almost a daily basis in three-quarters of children with ASC[151].

Differences in executive functioning of autistic children are reflected in problems with engagement in school, cooperation, independent functioning, and peer relations[152]. Children with better emotion regulation and inhibitory control develop more helpful, caring relationships with peers. Teachers view children with autism as less cooperative, less engaged in school and learning, less independent, and having more negative social relations – all of which are fundamental to school success in children[153]. The sense of engagement and pleasure in school develops early in children and may stick with them over their entire educational history, impacting their long-term academic performance[154].

The many characteristics and learning difficulties found in ASC may not be explained completely as impairments in self-regulation and executive functions. Most areas of difficulty can, however, be improved with enhanced self-regulation skills. Working directly on self-regulation is well-suited to children with ASC because they value structure and a personal sense of control. Teaching them how to regulate and organize themselves and the world around them can result in reduced stress and anxiety[155]. They can then become more open to learning and to interacting with others.

Impact of improved self-regulation

There are very few studies that look at what happens when children with developmental concerns, like ASC, have stronger self-regulation skills. The research that exists suggests that well-developed self-regulation skills can have a positive impact on academic performance[156] and participation in school[157]. Teaching children to self-regulate their behavior, thinking, and emotions can establish a foundation for learning[158]. Children with disabilities who develop stronger self-regulation also become more independent[159], exhibit more goal-oriented behavior[160] and greater self-confidence[161]. They transition more successfully after graduating from school[162], find and hold onto a job more easily[163] and are more likely to complete post-secondary education[164]..

Key points in this chapter

Many of the key features of autism may arise from impaired executive functions and self-regulation, including emotional dysregulation and weak generalization of skills and strategies.

The currently poor outcomes for people with autism in terms of education, employment and independence may be related to difficulty regulating and coping with community settings, problems planning and organizing and lack of self-advocacy skills.

People with autism appear to have varying degrees of impairment in planning and organization, inhibitory control, working memory, self-monitoring and cognitive flexibility.

Poor self-regulation skills in people with autism impact the quality of life for their entire family and necessitate high levels of ongoing support.

Impaired executive functions may be at the heart of the uneven skill generalization common in people with autism.

Selective, sustained and shifting attention are complexly intertwined with executive functions and impact learning and social-emotional development in people with autism.

Most areas of difficulty in autism, including behavior problems, can be improved by strengthening self-regulation.

CHAPTER 4 - INTRODUCTION TO THE spark* MODEL

In the previous chapters, executive functions, self-regulation, and their interrelationships were reviewed. Typically, development of self-regulation extends over at least the first two decades of life and requires long periods of time to refine and adapt to changing life circumstances. Current research into self-regulation and executive functions in people with ASC showed the challenges they face in translating knowledge into action.

Before going on, we need to look at different approaches for improving self-regulation. Out goal is to find out what works best.

Intervention to improve self-regulation

Interventions for improving self-regulation and executive functioning in children and adults have taken five main forms: (1) computer programs, (2) neurofeedback, (3) physical exercise, (4) mindfulness practices, and (5) curricula and programs. Interestingly, little of the research into these interventions involve people with autism.

Computer programs

Computer programs have been developed to train executive functions. Typically, they focus on just one or two functions at a time.

One area is *working memory*. Both children[165,166] and adults[167] significantly improved their visual working memory after concentrated training with specially-designed computer programs. There was generalization of training effects from visual to verbal information[168]. Interestingly, there were neurological changes[169], involving increased activity in the prefrontal and parietal regions of the brain. A meta-analysis[170] of working memory training with typically developing children found large immediate gains in verbal working memory[171]. The gains were not maintained, however.

Training *inhibitory control* in young children[172] produced a significant improvement. However, there didn't seem to be any generalization. The researchers suggested this may be due to the children developing strategies that were too task-specific.

Cognitive flexibility was studied[173] in three-year-olds. They researchers found that cognitive flexibility was teachable but certain forms of instruction were more effective than others. Simply telling the children the rule for performing a task was significantly less effective than giving them opportunities for practice guided by an adult.

One computer-based study[174] in the field of autism used *Braingame Brian*. It's a computer game that focuses on improving cognitive flexibility and working memory. After 100 hours of training, the 8- to 12-year-old children with high functioning[175] autism showed significant gains in working memory only. Cognitive flexibility seemed more resistant.

Computerized cognitive ('brain') training has become a multi-million-dollar business. One study[176] of over 11,000 participants in online training showed no evidence to support computerized 'brain trainers' beyond those tasks trained. There was no transfer to untrained tasks, 'even when those tasks were cognitively closely related' (p. 775).

Neurofeedback

Neurofeedback helps people focus on and alter their brainwave activity by providing feedback on a computer screen. Use of neurofeedback in adults showed beneficial effects on cognitive flexibility and working memory[177]. Children with high functioning autism who were trained with neurofeedback, showed significant improvements in controlling their attention and their talking as well as cognitive flexibility and planning[178]. In addition, children showed significant improvements in social interaction, communication skills and behavior. Follow-up 12 months after the original intervention showed continued significant improvements in selective auditory attention as well as maintenance of all other executive functions, communication skills and behavioral gains[179]. But, there's not yet enough evidence to support use of neurofeedback with autistic children[180].

Physical exercise

The impact of physical exercise on self-regulation has been examined in two basic forms, exercise programs alone, and combined physical and meditation training.

Exercise programs can improve some areas of executive functioning. Children who participated in regular exercise programs showed significant improvement in inhibitory control[181,182,183]. They also had better selective attention[184], focused attention[185,186], resistance to distraction[187,] and concentration[188].

A review[189] of research using exercise (e.g., jogging, weight training, bike riding) with children with autism found greatest impact on inhibitory control. Children participating in exercise programs exhibited less aggression, self-stimulation, and self-injury and more attention to task. Vigorous exercise had a more pronounced effect. However, the impact of exercise may be temporary: the children's behavior returned to baseline levels within 40 to 90 minutes.

Physical exercise has been combined with meditative practices, like martial arts and yoga. One study[190] into the impact of tae kwon do found significant improvement in physical, cognitive, and affective self-regulation, prosocial behavior, classroom conduct, and mental math. Another study[191] looked at the effect of practicing a traditional Chinese Chan-based mind–body exercise, Nei Yang Gong, as compared to progressive muscle relaxation. They found significant increases in inhibitory control both in the laboratory and at home for children in the Chan-based exercise.

Yoga practiced with children with severe forms of **ASC** found gains in a number of areas[192]. Their imitation of movements, breathing, and vocalizations all improved significantly. Eye contact increased and they modeled their behavior from peers more frequently. Children who practiced yoga for just one month exhibited significantly stronger cognitive flexibility, planning and organization, and behavioral inhibition[193]. Young adults who were involved in yoga showed improvement in inhibitory control and working memory[194].

Mindfulness practices

Mindfulness is a type of meditation based in Buddhism which is typically used in a non-secular manner. It teaches a systematic approach to regulating attention to the breath to promote focus on the present moment. The three main facets of mindfulness[195] consist of (a) awareness and self-monitoring of the present moment, (b) inhibitory control of thoughts (bringing them back to the present moment if they wander), and (c) acceptance of feelings and emotional state.

Adults practicing mindfulness have repeatedly shown improvements in inhibitory control[196]. Positive change has also been found in self-monitoring skills[197], and cognitive flexibility[198].

Children who receive mindfulness training make gains in behavioral regulation[199,200], attentional control[201], metacognition[202], and overall global executive control[203]. A meta-analysis found consistent evidence of inhibitory control improvement but variable effects on working memory and cognitive flexibility[204].

Mindfulness training with autistic children also shows promise. Teens with Asperger syndrome were taught to mindfully shift their attention from negative emotions that triggered aggressive behavior to the neutral soles of their feet[205]. After practicing for up to six months, aggressive behavior was reduced to zero. In a follow-up four years later, no episodes of physical aggression were observed among the three participants[206]. Other researchers have found significant reductions in symptoms of depression, anxiety, and rumination in adults with high functioning autism who practiced mindfulness in the short[207] and long term[208]. However, other research[209] obtained non-significant changes in executive functions after seven weeks of mindfulness training in 6- to 10-year-old children with ASC.

Curricula/programs

There are a few programs that address executive functions and self-regulation more generally.

The Alert program[210], also known as *How Does Your Engine Run?*, is an intervention protocol typically used by occupational therapists with children with ASC. It's designed to help the children learn to recognize their arousal states and teach them sensory-based self-regulation strategies. This program addresses automatic, stimulus-driven, and largely reactive systems so is considered pre-executive[211] (Barkley, 2012) rather than part of the executive function system. The only juried study of this program in its original form[212] didn't find significant change in self-regulation associated with participation in it.

Command & Control Cognitive Training[213] is a group executive function training program for children with autism, from 11 years through adults, and their parents. It teaches children within a tech/gaming context to be aware of their executive function command centers and how to control them. After 12 sessions, participants showed small to large positive effects on general executive functioning as well as social responsiveness.

The ECLIPSE model[214] is described as one that targets self-regulation, executive function, 'attribution retraining', and sensory awareness, aimed at improving social competence. A pilot study[215] with autistic adolescents found improvements in behavior as well as positive change in shifting attention, inhibitory control, and emotional control. These promising results did not, however, reach statistical significance.

Tools of the Mind[216] is a curriculum developed to teach academic skills and behavioral and emotional self-regulation to children. *Tools* emphasizes the development of underlying skills such as paying attention, controlling impulses, ignoring distractions, remembering on purpose, logic, symbolic representation, and cognitive flexibility. Activities are incorporated into daily routines and play. Significant gains in inhibitory control, working memory, and cognitive flexibility have been found in children who attended the *Tools* program versus those who were in a traditional preschool[217]. They also had fewer internalizing and externalizing behaviors compared to controls[218] and greater growth in receptive and expressive language. To date, this program hasn't been used with children with ASC.

Unstuck and On Target[219] (UOT) is a classroom-based executive function intervention approach for promoting cognitive and behavioral flexibility in high-functioning autistic students ages 8–11. UOT uses a cognitive/behavioral approach that emphasizes self-regulatory scripts, guided practice, and visual/verbal cuing. Children participating in UOT showed significant improvement in their cognitive flexibility[220]. No improvement was found in planning and organization[221]. In a third study, participating children showed significant improvement in cognitive flexibility along with significant change in their ability to compromise, follow rules, and switch from one activity to another[222]. The children also displayed significant change in their abilities to compromise, follow rules and change from one activity to another. Further tests showed that the children participating in UOT also had significantly improved flexibility and planning[223]. At a one-year follow-up[224], gains made in cognitive flexibility were maintained in the laboratory and at home. Gains made in planning and organization were observable in the laboratory only.

On Target for Life (OTL) is an upward extension of UOT for adolescents with ASC. Participants in this cognitive–behavioral intervention program made significant gains in general executive functioning[225] in comparison to participants in social skills training. Children in both groups showed similar improvements in social functioning, anxiety reduction, and behavioral regulation.

The *Zones of Regulation* program[226] is designed to teach children to become aware of and control their emotions and impulses, manage their sensory needs, and improve their problem-solving skills. *Zones* is used widely by therapists and teachers but, to date, only one study[227] is reported. It found that, after 11 weeks of intervention, preschoolers made no significant improvements in their cognitive, communication, motor, social–emotional, or adaptive skills.

Important features of intervention to improve self-regulation

The review above shows that, through intervention, executive functions and self-regulation skills can be taught and enhanced in children and adults. Intervention leads not only to behavioral changes, but also to alterations in brain circuitry. A few studies also reported improvement in executive functions and areas of development that weren't specifically focused on.

A number of important features can be gleaned from the review. Transfer and generalization of learning can be limited. This appeared to be more the case with single-focus approaches (that is, those that worked to improve one executive function at a time). Some of the curricula that incorporated multiple executive functions seemed to have a broader and more enduring impact. In addition, those programs used a variety of activities that involved interaction with others. Two important meta-analyses[228,229] highlighted features of programs aimed at improving self-regulated learning[230] and executive functions. They are summarized below (in grey-shaded areas), followed by ways spark* deals with them :

Focus should be directly on two or more executive functions at the same time. It isn't necessary to concentrate on just one executive function at a time and may be better to focus on multiples[231].

Each spark* lesson places primary focus on two or more executive functions, with secondary attention paid to the others. In some lessons, all five of the target executive functions are addressed. Fewer executive functions receive primary focus in the early stages of the first unit, Behavioral Self-regulation. Increasingly through that unit, more executive functions take on primary focus. In the Cognitive and Emotional Self-regulation units, four and five executive functions are focused on within each lesson.

Metacognitive strategies need to be included. Metacognition involves reflecting on your learning, your understanding, memory, knowledge, planning, and self-monitoring. Metacognitive awareness helps the child become conscious of their thought processes and more engaged and in control of their own learning. Metacognitive strategies teach the child to think about their own thinking and behavior. In order to put the 'self' in self-regulation, children must become aware of their own behavior and thinking. Children who use metacognitive strategies are more likely to learn efficiently and deeply and generalize what they learn[232].

Throughout spark*, children are encouraged to reflect on their own actions, thinking, and emotions. The lesson plans outline how to help children think about what they're able to do and what they did so they can note changes and learn to self-monitor. They're prompted to develop vocabulary related to their thinking, attention, understanding, behavior, etc. so they can use self-talk and self-reflection which transforms the way learning occurs[233]. Children come to understand their motivations and goals.

Cognitive strategies help children engage more fully and independently in learning. Mel Levine, an American pediatrician who championed people with learning differences, proposed an *Essential Cognitive Backpack*[234]. This is a set of skills children need in order to become successful adults. The four main cognitive strategies in the Backpack[235] are: (1) learning how to take in clear and complete verbal and nonverbal information and check to make sure they understand it; (2) learning how to organize activities and projects, make plans, and set priorities; (3) collaborating with others and forming productive working relationships with people of different status; and (4) knowing your own strengths, passions, and weaknesses, and setting appropriate personal goals.

To address these issues, **spark*** uses an information processing model to guide lessons in the Cognitive Self-regulation unit. The three main phases of processing in the model include: intake of information, integration and output or expression. At the intake stage, lessons focus on helping the child learn to work systematically and search for the most relevant information while ignoring distractions. They also learn ways to help themselves hang on to information long enough to figure out what to do. At the Integration phase, the child is taught how to bring together multiple pieces of information to make a whole scene or image, visualize information, and check their understanding. At the output stage, the child learns to provide precise descriptions that are clear to other people. These all contribute to the skills needed to be successful learners.

Generalization of skills and strategies must be explicitly taught. Generalization is typically weak in people with ASC and variable in different approaches for improving executive functions. It's critical that attention is paid directly to turning knowledge into action in realistic ways that represent everyday life.

spark* includes clear and explicit ways of helping children (a) understand the usefulness of the skills and strategies to their everyday life, (b) clearly identify times and places where the skills and strategies should be used, and (c) receive support and encouragement in using them in day-to-day situations. Every skill presented in **spark*** is practiced first to help the children understand that they're capable of doing and modulating it (for example, walking slowly as well as fast). Then they help to identify (with input from parents) when and where in their lives the skill would be useful. To aid extension of the skill into everyday life, the children are helped to become more resilient and use the skill even in adverse situations (like, when they get distracted). The final step is to help the children learn how to advocate for themselves. That is, if they're having difficulty using their new skills, they learn many ways to help themselves regain a sense of equilibrium.

Self-calming strategies are important to helping children improve their self-regulation. We know that severe anxiety occurs in 40% of children with ASC[236] but as many as 84% experience at least some symptoms[237]. Anxiety-related concerns are among the most common problems for school-age children and adolescents with ASC[238]. They may be reflected in specific phobias, obsessive compulsive disorder, social anxiety, separation anxiety and generalized anxiety[239,240]. Anxiety can cause acute distress, intensify the symptoms of ASC and trigger behavioral difficulties including tantrums, aggression and self-injury[241]. Anxiety has adverse effects on thinking and learning as well as executive control of attention and inhibitory control[242]. Even mild stress can overwhelm the prefrontal cortex and cause executive dysfunction[243].

Self-calming, in the form of mindful breathing, is an important element of **spark***. It improves self-regulation and reduces destructive anxiety. In the Behavioral Self-regulation unit, beginning mindfulness is introduced as Turtle Breathing. This calming and centering strategy is used throughout the subsequent lessons and activities and is encouraged and supported in everyday life. Turtle Breathing is a way to redirect the child's attention to the sensation of breathing and away from other things that may be distracting or disturbing them. We also combine Turtle Breathing with 'cooling down' strategies like visualizing pleasant things and people.

Increase independence from adult supervision and prompting. As seen in the support needs of children and adults with ASC in Chapter 1, specific work needs to be done in this area if true self-regulation and greater autonomy are to be achieved.

From the beginning of the Behavioral Self-regulation unit, there's specific focus on reducing adult direction. Each activity is practiced through a progression of five stages: (1) direct imitation of the adult, (2) imitation of actions shown in illustrations, (3) following verbal directions alone, (4) imitation of a peer, and finally (5) self-direction.

Throughout **spark***, the child is asked to evaluate their own performance ("How did you do?"). This is done deliberately and often in order to promote independence. They're learning that they can evaluate their own performance and don't have to relay on adult input.

Include physical exercise/movement. Movement and exercise are important to engaging children as well as helping improve their self-regulation. But, exercise alone without focus on executive functions will produce little benefit.

Quite naturally the Behavioral Self-regulation unit incorporates physical activity. An important part (and culmination) of this unit's the inclusion of yoga. It allows combining Turtle Breathing with whole body movement and balance. Children with autism typically have sensory-motor difficulties[244, 245,246]. Simple yoga can help them with self-calming as well as commonly-found problems with sensory systems, balance and finely-controlled movements[247].

Practice must extend over multiple sessions, but activities need to vary in complexity, novelty, and variety. The program needs to continuously challenge children's executive functions. More time devoted to practicing is better. Learning self-regulation isn't a 'one shot' issue; it takes time and practice to become self-regulated. Remember, typical development of self-regulation takes at least two decades of neurological development, learning, and refinement. With many autistic children, there'll also be some un-learning that needs to take place in order to move ahead.

Children need some novelty in their learning. By doing the same thing repeatedly, children will lose interest.

Children also need help to go beyond their current comfort level. This requires support from knowledgeable, caring adults. Social support positively affects prefrontal cortex functioning, attention, and reasoning. Children's feelings of confidence as learners is important to their success.

spark* has three main units and a total of 44 lessons. Although lessons may be combined, the structure of **spark*** requires multiple opportunities for practice and extension into everyday life. Each lesson describes the level of success/accuracy a child needs before moving to the next lesson. This ensures repeated practice. Activities are also set up so there is some novelty as well as inclusion of each child's favorite topics (affinities). Each lesson can be completed quickly if the child meets criterion for moving on. There is no pre-prescribed amount of repetition.

The program needs to address the negative impact of stress, mood, tiredness, physical health on executive functions and self-regulation. When children are calm, happy, rested, and feeling well, their prefrontal cortexes function better. They can work and think more flexibly and creatively.

In spark*, we use the acronym C.A.N. (Calm, Alert, and Nourished) to ensure that children are ready to work on self-regulation skills. We also help children identify those features in themselves so they can make sure their learning is at its best.

The Language of spark* is incorporated into everything we do. The words and phrases of the Language of spark* support children emotionally and cognitively in their learning. The adult is placed in the role of a guide and coach who both encourages and challenges each child. There is a great deal of focus on building self-confidence and having a sense of a shared quest.

Any program, must be mindful of three main things. It must be:

1. **Developmentally-appropriate**. Ask whether what we're planning to teach a child is appropriate to the child's age and stage. For example, children do not begin to use eye contact like adults until they are at least 11 years of age[248]. This, among other things, draws into question teaching eye contact to young children.
2. **culturally grounded.** Skills and strategies we teach children need to be appropriate and acceptable to each child's culture.
3. **autism-sensitive.** People with autism have significant sensory and anxiety issues so we much be careful to respect these and help the children become more resilient.

The spark* model

The *Self-regulation Program for Awareness and Resilience in Kids* (spark*) is an evidence-based approach to teaching self-regulation of behavior, cognitive processes and emotions. It's intended for children from two years of age to about nine. It was developed to be integrated into an overall program of development but can be used successfully as a stand-alone intervention or as part of individual or group therapy programs. spark* will be of interest to regular and special education teachers, education assistants, occupational therapists, psychologists, speech-language pathologists and parents.

spark* is designed to enhance children's self-awareness, awareness of appropriate time and place, resilience and self-advocacy in relation to self-regulation, attention and executive functioning. It's theoretically derived from the latest scientific research in the fields of neuroscience, social learning, positive psychology and ASC. spark* was developed and refined through clinical experience with preschool and school-aged children with special needs.

The main goal of **spark*** is to improve and brighten the future for children with **ASC** and other special needs. Outcomes will vary with different children but, through **spark***, it's hoped that their abilities can be optimized. We want to move children along the road to improved self-regulation to increased success in learning and happier day-to-day life.

Some of those skills integrated into **spark*** will help children:

- Become more willing to tackle new tasks and unfamiliar situations with confidence.

- Be more persistent with task and situations that are challenging.

- Cooperate, negotiate ,and collaborate with others, sharing and taking turns.

- Make reasoned choices and decisions.

- Plan and organize steps toward achieving a goal.

- Find resources and solutions without help from others unless necessary.

- Learn by watching others and from their own past experiences.

- Cope and learn, even in highly stimulating or distracting environments.

- Inhibit impulses when important and ignore distractions.

- Switch from one task or demand to another and from one situation to another and cope with change in general.

spark* works progressively from imitation of easy actions through to self-direction and self-control of behavior, thinking, and emotions. The major executive functions underlying self-regulation as well as selective, sustained, and shifting attention are explicitly and deliberately highlighted and practiced.

In the early stages of development, the adult acts as the child's main regulator by teaching and modeling the skills. With practice, the child learn to recognize usefulness of the skills and strategies and increasingly assume control over them.

Generalization of self-regulation skills is taught through the Awareness of Need, Resilience, and Self-advocacy activities to ensure practice and use in day-to-day settings. Resilience activities help the children increase their tolerance for distraction, disruption, and temptations. Children are also taught to advocate for themselves so they can maintain their sense of equilibrium.

Main structure of spark*

spark*'s three main units are: Behavioral, Cognitive and Emotional Self-regulation, as shown in Figure 6 below.

Each child must start the program with Behavioral Self-regulation, so they have the opportunity to work successfully on consciously control their body and attention and as well as learn to calm and center themselves.

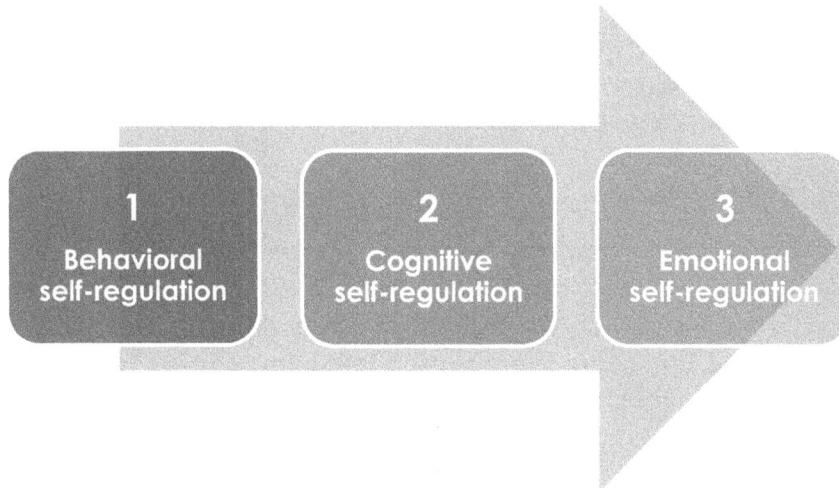

Figure 6. Diagram of the progression across the three main units of spark*.

Within each unit of **spark***, children learn skills and strategies that serve as foundations for those presented in subsequent lessons. The child's newly-acquired ability to consciously control their body, attention, and calmness is integrated into cognitive processing skills within the Cognitive Self-regulation unit. These then combine to facilitate Emotional Self-regulation.

It's **critical that all children start with the Behavioral Self-regulation unit,** complete it, and then proceed to the Cognitive Self-regulation unit. Once the Cognitive Self-regulation unit is completed, the Emotional Self-regulation unit can begin.

Behavioral Self-regulation

Behavioral Self-regulation is the first area addressed. It involves physical activities that can be directly prompted and shaped. In learning to self-regulate their actions, each child develops an understanding that they can vary how, when, and where they use their body and can do so in flexible, situationally-appropriate ways.

Behavioral Self-regulation skills are presented in five different areas of focus: hands, breathing, feet, voice, and whole body. Each of these areas is practiced through a series of four different areas of skill development toward autonomy and self-direction: (1) Awareness of Ability, (2) Awareness of Need, (3) Resilience, and (4) Self-advocacy.

Cognitive Self-regulation

Cognitive Self-regulation is the ability to control and modulate how and when you use your cognitive resources. The child is **helped** to gather important and relevant information, ignore distractions, check their understanding of the information, and form a response.

Cognitive Self-regulation skills are presented in three different areas of focus: (1) complete and accurate intake of information, (2) integration of information and (3) clear and precise expression of knowledge. Each of these areas is practiced through the same areas of skill development used in Behavioral Self-regulation: Awareness of Ability, Awareness of Need, Resilience, and Self-advocacy.

Emotional Self-regulation

Emotional Self-regulation involves detecting, interpreting, and responding to emotions, based on both internal and contextual information. The term 'regulation' may suggest controlling or stifling your emotions, but this isn't the intent. Instead, Emotional Self-regulation is focused on helping the child understand situations and experiences more accurately and then selecting responses that are more appropriate. We want each child to manage their emotions in flexible, situationally-appropriate ways. For example, a child who becomes angry at a sibling but, through self-regulation, can tone their typical response down from hitting or scratching to walking away or telling an adult.

Emotional Self-regulation skills are presented in three different areas of focus: (1) detection of social clues, (2) interpretation of clues, and (3) forming a response. Each of these areas is practiced through three of the same areas of skill development used in the Behavioral and Cognitive Self-regulation units: Awareness of Ability, Awareness of Need, Resilience, and Self-advocacy.

Key points in this chapter

Intervention in the form of specially-designed computer programs, neurofeedback, physical exercise, and mindfulness practices can improve at least some aspects of self-regulation. But comprehensive curricula and intervention programs appear to have broader and more enduring impacts on executive functioning.

spark* incorporates the main features of the most effective programs for improving executive functions and self-regulated learning.

spark* is a comprehensive evidence-based program for improving self-regulation in children with special needs, with specific focus on children with autism.

spark* is comprised of three main units: Behavioral, Cognitive and Emotional Self-regulation.

The three units of **spark*** successively build skills and strategies that form the foundation for each other.

CHAPTER 5 - GETTING READY
TO START spark*

spark* is carefully crafted and structured to increase child autonomy while decreasing adult direction. This path toward self-regulation requires a delicate balance of adult behaviors and language with growing child independence and self-regulation.

Below are important things you need to do before starting spark*. Some may seem obvious, but some may be forgotten,. A little reminding doesn't hurt.

Preparing to implement spark*

Talk to families, preschools and schools about spark*

We encourage **spark*** practitioners to hold an information session for parents, teachers, therapists, and others involved with each child before starting. The session should include information on:

- What self-regulation is and isn't
- Why work on self-regulation can help children with autism spectrum disorders (ASC)
- How long it takes to develop self-regulation skills
- Overview of Self-Regulation Program of Awareness and Resilience in Kids (**spark***)
    - Behavioral Self-regulation
    - Cognitive Self-regulation
    - Emotional Self-regulation

☑ Give an overview of **spark*** to parents & interested others.

The session will help parents and others understand the importance of self-regulation and how **spark*** approaches teaching. The issue of how self-regulation develops and refines over an extended period of time is vital for everyone to hear and understand – self-regulation isn't going to happen overnight; it takes time to learn and practice. They'll also have to start thinking about how to praise and prompt self-regulated behavior and then progressively stepping back to let the children use their new skills. This will be an issue that you'll have to revisit again and again.

The information sessions are ideal for handing out the first **spark*** newsletter. The Resource files contain all 18 of the **spark*** newsletters.

Read this book before starting intervention

I realize there's a lot of information in this book. Read the first four chapters for background information on executive functions, self-regulation, and where **spark*** comes from. If you really dislike science-y information, you can start with this chapter. Then read the introduction to the Behavioral Self-regulation unit before starting.

✔ Read all about self-regulation, executive functions, and **spark*** before starting.

Then read the lesson over carefully and think about how you can use materials and activities that will be interesting to the children. You need to understand what you're working on, why, how, and when you can introduce the next lesson. I worked with some smarty-pants grad students who told each other they didn't have to read the book before sessions with children. You could tell they didn't have a clue about why they were doing the activities or how. They were disorganized, didn't explicitly highlight key information and strategies, and didn't engage the children. You need to know the big picture of where you're heading and why, what self-regulation is, where executive functions fit, and how to interest children.

Each lesson is carefully laid-out, so you'll know what to expect and where to look. The sections important to lesson planning and implementation are:

- **Task structuring:** This give general organization and arrangement of the activity.

- **Objectives:** These are written as individual child goals with a description of the target behavior, accuracy or frequency expected and, in the Behavioral Self-regulation unit, the directness of adult involvement.

- **Materials:** This section suggests different activities and resources, many of which are included in the Resource files accessible through the **spark*** website.

- **Language of** spark* **to watch for and use in this lesson:** This highlights key words, phrases, concepts and vocabulary that need to be incorporated into interactions with the child.

- **Practice:** This section suggests ways in which you can engage the child to practice each activity, striving to solidify the skills and strategies.

- **Prompting:** This part provides verbal and nonverbal prompts that should be used to establish and solidify skills learned within the lesson.

- **Self-monitoring:** Because our goal is to help the child assume control over their own behavior, we need to teach them to judge their own performance. That way they can determine the accuracy and adequacy and self-correct as needed.

- **Solidifying:** Suggestions are made in this section about how to help them solidify their self-regulation skills.

- **Highlighting:** Suggestions are made in this section about how to highlight the child's use of appropriate self-regulation.

- **Additional comments:** Any features, skills and strategies that are critically important will be highlighted in this section. Suggestions for extension and generalization will also be provided.

Know as much as you can about the children before starting spark*

Seek and use input from families

You should know about the family composition: are there other children in the family, how old are they (this can be helpful information when figuring out ways to practice new skills and strategies), are two adults in the home (it's always important to know how readily skills can be fit into the schedule at home), do they have any pets?

Find out about other therapies the child has already been involved in and how effective they were. Ask the parents to give you some ideas about what worked and what didn't. This will help you figure out what to include in your sessions and what you might avoid.

A child background information form is included in the Resource files (FORM - Child background information file) accompanying this book.

☑ Know each child, their likes and dislikes.

The newsletters included in the **spark*** Resource files help keep parents informed about what you're doing. They also ask parents to provide information on situations that are priority areas for their children to develop better self-regulation skills. This ensures that each child has personalized target areas.

Make sure you know the child's interests and incorporate them in activities

If you want to engage the children and keep them interested, bring in their passions and affinities. Use the background information form included in the Resource files accessible through the **spark*** website. It asks families for information on videos or movies, games, TV shows, computer programs, books, toys, characters from videos, TV, games and/or books and music that the child likes and dislikes. This information lets you capture the child's attention by including their areas of interest and avoid turning them off or triggering reactions by bringing in topics that they dislike.

Be aware of each child's areas of challenge and make sure you don't 'exercise deficits'

Be aware of each child's strengths and areas of difficulty when planning activities. The background information form (included in the Resource files) asks families about areas of difficulty for the child, like reading, fine motor skills, and gross motor skills. It's really important to ensure that a creative and interesting activity isn't lost because a child has problems with motor skills or reading comprehension. I've seen therapists try to improve a child's speech and language skills using activities, like cutting or coloring, which are too challenging. The children spent more time, effort, and frustration on trying to do the cutting and coloring than on their speech and language goals. It probably would've been better to have the materials pre-colored and pre-cut so the children didn't waste so much mental and physical energy.

Problems with motor skills are common in children with autism. More than half have low muscle tone and about 9% have large muscle delays[249]. More than one-third have motor dyspraxia[250], or difficulty planning, coordinating, producing, and reproducing actions and movements with their bodies. This means the children have problems imitating gestures (such as waving or making thumbs up) and actions, and in using tools (such as pencils, scissors, toothbrushes). Because of dyspraxia, activities within spark* will need to be modified in terms of the amount, complexity, and accuracy of actions a child is asked to do. Consistency is a particular problem for children with dyspraxia. One of the hallmarks of it is being able to do an action on one occasion and not another. You'll have to adjust your standards and be alert to what's dyspraxia and what's lack of knowledge. Be sure to consult with occupational and/or physical therapists to determine each child's motor strengths and needs.

Decide on the format and setting

spark* can be offered in a number of different formats and settings - at home, in preschools, kindergartens, schools or in a clinic. Sessions can be individual or group. The focus of sessions can be on many different skills, with self-regulation as one component. spark* can also be used as the main emphasis in a group setting – the spark* group.

☑ Decide on format & setting for spark*.

If you're thinking of implementing spark* in a group setting, keep in mind that children's self-regulation skills are most highly challenged when working in pairs and small groups with peers[251]. For children with ASC, interaction with peers has to be planned and implemented carefully. But, it can provide an excellent testing ground for the emerging self-regulation skills.

Individual multi-focus therapy or teaching

spark* can be integrated into individual therapy or teaching sessions with a child. For example, you may be a speech-language therapist or occupational therapist who focuses on a number of different skills during your sessions. You can start each session with the **spark*** activity to help the child become calm and centered and more in control of their body, thinking, and emotions. This will likely help their learning during the other activities.

Classroom or multi-focus group setting

You can incorporate **spark*** activities into a classroom or other group setting. Start the day with **spark*** as this will help the children be more focused for other learning. Then, inject **spark*** practice sessions at different times during the day. For example, before starting a new topic or skill, have the children engage in a song or story from **spark*** as a warm-up. This will take just a few minutes but acts as a good reminder of their self-regulation skills.

Sole focus group intervention

Group therapy specifically focused on advancing participants' self-regulation skills, calls for different organization. Groups are more manageable when they include maximum 6 to 8 children with two or more leaders. It's critically important that you meet with each child and family to determine if the child is ready for a group setting. Some children may need individual sessions before being able to learn in groups. They may become over-stimulated by having other children so close or may shut down and become mute. These things can be worked on more effectively in a one-to-one setting before starting group sessions.

Implementing spark*

Be a model of self-regulation

When working with children on self-regulation, you need to act as an example for them. That means you have to model the skills and strategies you teach. At times, it's good to 'forget' to self-regulate and then show the children how to regain it.

Calm adults = calm children

Children with autism are like 'emotional sponges', they absorb emotions and feelings of others around them. They may not interpret what the feelings are or why. They'll likely just feel on edge and agitated. In this state, their learning isn't optimal, and the probability of behavior problems increases greatly.

☑ Model self-regulation for the children.

It's critical that before working on self-regulation, everyone involved calms and centers themselves. Learning and practicing mindfulness helps you help children remain calmer. To learn about mindfulness, check some of the resources in the Resource files accessible through the **spark*** website. Remember that mindfulness takes discipline and practice so don't expect mastery after just a few attempts.

Once you've experienced and practiced mindfulness, do a few minutes of focused breathing immediately before each **spark*** session. This can make a significant difference to how smoothly it proceeds. After watching some erratic self-regulation sessions conducted by grad students, we encouraged them do some mindful breathing. They remarked about how 'well behaved' the children were in those sessions.

OUR PLAN	
1	feet
2	music
3	snack
4	review
5	cool-down

Organize everything in advance for each lesson

It's critical to the child's learning that the environment and materials are well-organized. Put away any distracting or enticing things at least for your early sessions before the children learn to regulate their bodies and attention. Use visual support for plans, routines, and rules. A planning board that shows what will be done and in what order within your session is essential; see an example to the left. It shows that you're going to focus on self-regulation of your feet. This will be followed by musical activities related to foot self-regulation. Then will be snack, a review of what everyone learned and then a cool down before leaving.

Regardless of the children's abilities, having a visual helps them remain calmer because they know what to expect. Remember, children with autism often have difficulty with working memory. By having the information visible, they have won't overtax that executive function on non-essential things.

Assemble all the materials you'll need for the lesson. Place them in a "lesson box" so they're organized and close at hand but out of sight.

Transitions from activity to activity or topic to topic need to be as smooth as possible. A brief calming activity (like a little Turtle Breathing) or transition song between activities can help the children remain calm (see the Resource files for transition song resources).

Make sure the children are calm, alert and nourished before you start

Calm children learn better

☑ Make sure children are calm, alert, & nourished before expecting them to self-regulate.

Some amount of 'stress' is needed to keep the children alert and motivated to learn. It's when stress slips into distress that the impact on learning can be negative. Higher levels of stress can take over and the brain becomes overloaded "with powerful hormones and ignites a response that evolution designed for short-term duty in emergency situations only"[252]. Hormones are released that increase oxygen flow to the muscles (to help flee the situation if needed) and your heart and respiration system work harder. Stress can shut down your capacity to think, losing access to higher level thinking, creativity as well as normal cognitive capacities[253]. A stressed child will be considerably less likely to engage positively with others and to self-regulate.

Alert children learn better

Alertness comes from being well-rested. We know, however, that as many as two-thirds of children with ASC have atypical sleep patterns[254]. They tend to sleep less than other children and have poorer sleep quality. Autistic children with sleep problems are more likely to have behavior difficulties[255], including acting out, emotional reactivity, and anxiety.

Be alert to when children aren't well-rested. This'll help you be more sensitive to how far and how hard we can nudge them into learning. You may have to adjust your session that day. If the child is n't well-rested or feeling well, work on things that were successful in the past for that child. This means you're still practicing and staying positive.

Nourished children concentrate and learn better

Nourishment about every two hours is important to young children in order for them to learn. The types of foods should be balanced among vegetables, fruit, grain products, milk products, and meat, or alternatives[256]. More than three-quarters of children with ASC have atypical eating behavior[257,258,259]. They eat fewer vegetables and consume less calories, protein, and fiber and more carbohydrates than non-autistic children. There's a correlation between behavior and diet[260]. More behavior problems are seen in children who eat limited varieties of foods and have a lower intake of calories, protein, and fiber.

It's essential to understand the impact of nutrition on learning and behavior. Be sensitive to the status of a child's nutrition so you can know how much we can ask a child to do and how much 'pushing' might be appropriate.

Make sure the children are making progress in learning self-regulation

Assess progress made by each child

It's important to evaluate the child's skills before starting spark* and then re-assess them along the way. This helps you ensure your work is making a difference for the child.

As a rule of thumb, I <u>expect to see change within a few sessions</u>. If there isn't progress, change what you're doing or how you're presenting it.

☑ Regularly check each child's progress.

When looking at assessment of self-regulation skills, you can take two main approaches: (1) standardized measures and/or (2) non-standardized rating scales and informal observations. Both have merit and can be used together. Standardized assessments are appropriate when you want to compare the child to typical expectations in someone their age as well as look at change that's occurred. Description of some standardized measures is included in the Resource files.

Informal rating scales and observational approaches let you compare the child's performance before you start **spark*** with once you complete a unit. Descriptions of some information rating scales are in the Resource files accessible through the **spark*** website. Observational assessments are included in each of the three units. They let you sample some of the areas targeted within each unit and then compare gains once the unit's completed. Each observational assessment is included in the Resource files accessible through the **spark*** website.

Pay attention to lesson objectives

Move from lesson to lesson only after you have clear evidence that each child has met criterion of the current one. Watch the child carefully and decide if they meet the criterion shown in the objective of that lesson. It's critical that each child demonstrate fairly solid acquisition of skills before moving on. Remember, we're building a foundation.

A form for tracking the achievement of lesson objectives in each **spark*** unit is in the Resources. The form allows you to show when the child met the objectives for each lesson so you can report it in their individual educational or program plan.

Notice when self-regulation happens

Each lesson has instructions on ways to highlight when a child uses self-regulation. It's important to do this but It's not always easy. When a child self-regulates that means they're not doing something they used to. You have to think back at the possible ways they responded before. For example, maybe they used to strike out at anyone who took their toy but, this time, they didn't. That needs to be commented on in a positive way - "You really told your hands what to do when Bobby took your toy. Nice job!"

Be a model. Highlight your own use of self-regulation as well as failed attempts. If you find you forgot something for a session, comment on it - "Boy, I forgot to ..... I have to remember for next time. How can I help myself remember?". These comments can be powerful. They focus attention on the need for self-regulation as well as the fact that even adults forget sometimes.

Help the child check their own performance

During the session, ensure that child increasingly monitors their own behavior, thinking, and emotions and doesn't rely on you to tell them when to self-regulate. The self-monitoring section of each lesson of **spark*** is a reminder to ask the child, "How did you do?" and "Did you do okay?". This is an opportunity for them to look at what they did and evaluate it. Sometimes, you'll agree with the child's evaluation, sometimes you won't. You might end up telling them they did better than they thought. Other times, you might tell them their performance wasn't quite up to standard. Either way, be honest and clear about what they should do next time.

Use every opportunity to practice self-regulation

Every moment, including eating a snack, is a chance to use self-regulation. Snack is a time when children can self-regulate their hands and take one piece of food at a time. This should be discussed and highlighted before practicing – "How about we try eating one grape at a time?". Think about how you can weave self-regulation skills into other things you do, like walking in the hall or putting on their outdoor clothes. Be sure to include times when they can let loose, like on a playground.

Remember that developing self-regulation takes time

Learning is a process. Each child will child progressively improve their performance and solidify their knowledge. Remember that typically-developing children need at least the first two decades of life to develop self-regulation. Remind the child and everyone else in their life that it takes time and practice and some days will be easier than others. Within a few sessions, you should see progress in learning each small skill. If you don't, change how you're presenting it.

Generalization also doesn't occur right away. Help children learn skills solidly first and then work on applying them into everyday life. spark* is structured so the child has ample practice with skills before they're expected to use them in other settings. They'll need continuing support to use the skills and strategies consistently in everyday life.

The Language of spark*

A child's development can happen most effectively by being guided by a more caring, knowledgeable person. That person helps the child notice important things around them and new ways of thinking and acting. The relationship between the child and adult is critical. The adult needs to be tuned into the child by watching and listening to them. A trusted adult can open the child's mind to reasoning and perspectives. The adult must offer meaningful choices and minimize controlling language[261]. That means fewer orders and more suggestions. Also, things you ask of the child must be reasonably challenging but not overwhelming. The child needs to know that you'll help when needed and will encourage them to keep trying.

We need to help children feel capable of self-regulation. They need to have a sense of 'self-efficacy' or the belief that they can do what you're asking them to do. People with high self-efficacy are more likely to participate eagerly in activities, work harder and persist longer[262]. Developing self-efficacy takes more than just praising the child. They need chances to experience success. Children are more likely to engage actively in learning when[263]:

- They believe the material might be useful to them – it has purpose,

- The content of the material doesn't seem too difficult,

- Adults give them chances to try things out and don't give them too much help,

- Adults present the material in ways that are organized and understandable to the child, and

- Adults express confidence in the child's ability to enjoy the task and do well.

All of these are reflected in and supported by the language and interaction style used in **spark***.

Every interaction with a child has both cognitive and social-emotional goals that support their sense of self-efficacy (see Figure 7 below). There are three main cognitive goals for every child. The first ensures that they understand the meaning and purpose of skills and strategies we teach them. The second focuses on having them think on their own as much as possible. The third is for them to demonstrate their knowledge.

Figure 7. Important cognitive and social-emotional goals for enhancing self-efficacy in children

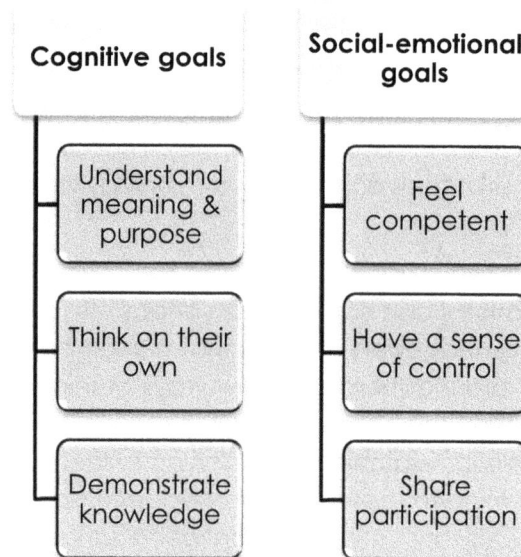

Three social-emotional goals need to be incorporated into this process. The child needs to be encouraged so they feel competent to do what's being asked of them. The second goal is to give each child a sense of control, a sense that they can have some say in what happens. The third component is making certain the child shares participation in each activity. That is, they're actively engaged and contributing along with the adult.

The words and actions presented in each **spark*** lesson are all intended to encourage these cognitive and social-emotional goals. The goals, actions, and words are discussed below.

Cognitive goals

1. ***Help each child understand the meaning and purpose of what they're doing***

In order for a child to 'buy in' to what we're doing, they need to understand the meaning and purpose. Think back on your own schooling: wouldn't it have been easier to study history or mathematics if you had had a clearer idea of how it might be useful in your day-to-day life?

The words and phrases used in **spark*** have been carefully crafted to provide simple descriptions of what each skill and strategy is and why we need to use them. These are important parts of the Language of **spark***.

2. ***Get children to think on their own***

Right from the outset, we prompt the child to think on their own. This promotes independence and decreases reliance on others.

Questions are the main way we encourage children to think on their own. Asking questions is more effective in getting them to move toward new learning. Ultimately, we want them to ask these questions of themselves - "What am I supposed to do here?", "How did I do?"

☑ Ask questions to activate learning

When interacting with the child, start with open-ended questions. Those are questions that don't have a simple "yes" or "no" answer. Ask, "What do you think we're going to do here?" or "What else could we do?".

If the child can't answer the question, follow these steps. First, rephrase the question; maybe the child didn't understand. Then, offer hints, but point ing out important features that may help them understand - "Look, that says 'Directions' so what do you think we should do?". If they still seem puzzled, give a little more information - "These words say ....., so what should we do now?" See Table 2 on the next page for some examples of how words and phrases in the Language of **spark*** are used to activate the child's thinking.

☑ Avoid telling the child what to do

Don't to <u>tell</u> them what to do. We want to activate their thinking. In general, we aim for our language to be at least 90% non-directive. That is, you ask questions and giving hints rather than giving direct commands.

3. ***Encourage each child to demonstrate their knowledge***

When you give children the freedom and confidence to try things on their own, you'll learn more about what they know and how they think. This process has at least three outcomes. First, you often learn that they know and can do more than you thought. Second, it enriches your understanding of that child and how they see the world. Third, it gives the child a sense of confidence and competence that you're willing to wait for them to respond.

☑ Give the child lots of time to respond & show you what he thinks

Children who are reticent to try a task or activity or to respond to our questions sometimes bring out a feeling that we need to protect them and not press them for responses[264]. Don't view the child's behavior negatively (they're just being lazy) or with sympathy (it's too difficult for them). Don't jump in to help them too quickly. Allow them to struggle a little with a task before assisting them. Do your best to lead them through a series of steps, like those shown in Table 2.

Because we want the child to feel comfortable in guessing and telling us what they're thinking, make every effort bolster their confidence. We avoid use of negative words, like "no", "not", and "don't". These words stop action and can decrease the child's confidence and cooperation. Always use positive language - rather than saying, "Don't do that", say "How about if we do it this way?"

Table 2. Example situations, open-ended first questions and subsequent questions that help prompt responses

Situation	Opening question ➡	Next steps
Introducing an activity	What do you think we're going to do here?	Have a look at this (focus their attention on an important signal, clue, or model).
	We're going to make this picture. What do you think we should do first?	How about we look at the biggest thing/shape?
Encountering a challenge	**Noise**: It looks like you're having a hard time thinking. What could you do to help yourself?	That noise is making it hard for your brain to think. What can you do to help yourself?
	Spilled juice on shirt: It looks like you've got a problem. What could you do to help yourself?	It looks like some juice got on your shirt and it's bugging you. What could you do to help yourself?
	Failure to wait turns: We need to think about ways to make sure everyone in our group gets a chance and it's fair for everyone.	How fair would it be if one person does all the talking? What could we do to make sure everyone gets a chance?
Introducing a topic	We're going to think about everything we know about dinosaurs. Can you tell me some things?	Let's make a picture of a dinosaur in our heads. What do you see?

☑ Guessing is encouraged & each child is supported to feel safe to guess.

Social-emotional goals

1. Help each child feel competent

A child's sense of competence comes from experiences of success. That's why we present tasks and activities that ensure the child has opportunities for high levels of success. The goal of all activities is first to ensure error-free learning before increasing the difficulty and complexity and asking for more. The language you use should be positive but honest. We want to encourage the child to keep trying but we need to give them feedback when they need to improve. For example, "I saw you really tried hard, but we still need to work on __. How about if we do it again and really watch out for that?"

2. Encourage each child to have a sense of control

Every child wants a sense of control in their life. It's our responsibility to teach them self-regulation skills and progressively allow them to exercise control where and when possible and reasonable. In spark*, the child develops control over their body, thinking, and emotions.

An effective process for encouraging children to gain a sense of control is to use 'distancing'. This means you teach children to mentally step away from the problem and look at it like an outsider would. This lets children view situations more objectively and with less emotion. An interesting study[265] was done to look at how distancing helped preschoolers self-regulate. Some were taught to talk to themselves by name ("Okay, Heather, what are you going to do now."). Others were taught to take the perspective of a favorite media character and ask themselves, "What would Batman do?" For experimental control, another group was left to do what they usually do. The results were clear: talking to yourself was pretty good at helping self-regulation. But, thinking like a media character was most helpful. They found, though, for children to benefit the most, they needed to have stronger Theory of Mind (that is, be able to think how someone else thinks).

> ☑ Each child becomes a 'master' of their brain & their body.

Autistic children are delayed in developing Theory of Mind[266] so I use distancing a little differently. Prompt children to talk to their brain, feet, hands, mouth, etc. as if they were separate entities. It started one time when a child ripped up a craft. I said, "Oh, look what you did." The child looked at me ready to cry. I felt horrid. My job was to teach them, not make them cry. I quickly corrected myself and said, "Look what your hands did. They forgot to be gentle. Let's teach those hands how to be gentle." It worked! The student looked at their hands and said, "Be gentle." They continued to work with a new sense of pride and command over their hands.

Distancing helps children see themselves as the commander of their body and their brain. It sets a boundary between the child and their behavior; they continue to be a strong and positive force in the world but their hands, feet, voice, whole body, and their brain sometimes forget how to do things. I often prompt children, "Tell your brain: don't get distracted, brain!" or "Tell your hands: you need to be gentle, hands!"

Tangible rewards are used very sparingly in spark*. This is because they can have an adverse effect on motivation and the sense of autonomy[267] we want each child to develop. Our task, as adults helping the child, is to identify, nurture, and build their inner intrinsic motivation. That is, their desire to exercise and stretch your abilities, challenge themselves, and look for chances to learn and explore.

3. Share participation with each child

☑ "We" is an important word for inspiring a sense of sharing.

One word used frequently in **spark*** is "we". This word signals shared participation between the adult and child. By saying, "We're going to ....", children get a sense of learning as a joint venture. It tells them that the adult is there to support and guide them. Other language forms that promote the feeling of sharing are "Let's ...." (inviting the child to engage in an activity) and "How about ...." (helping to focus the child on alternatives).

Work on yourself and with families and others to let go

The goal of self-regulation is for children to take over control of their own bodies, thinking, and emotions as much as possible. This means that other people have to let go. We have to allow them time and space to become more independent.

Our ultimate goal in teaching self-regulation is for children to make choices for themselves. They need to develop a sense of freedom. This means they become more autonomous and they don't need us so much.

First, we teach them how and when to regulate their bodies, thinking, and emotions. They need help to become aware of their ability to self-regulate, of when and where they need to use these skills, of how to be more resilient and how to advocate for themselves.

When working with children with autism, we become used to telling them what to do. We also help them a lot and do things for them. These are 'doing-to' and 'doing-for' approaches that ultimately keep children dependent on the adults around them. One study[268] found that education assistants spent 86% of every day within three feet of the child they were supporting. That doesn't allow the children wot learn to self-regulate and become more independent.

spark* is structured so we focus on doing activities with each child. We avoid doing things to them or for them. There's a time and place for telling children what to do (like, "Stay away from that dog!"). Some 'doing-for' are steps in the right direction. For example, when we set up visual schedules and streamline the environment, it's clearer to children what they're expected to do.

Progressively, we move children from our scaffold of support by 'doing-with' to doing things on their own. In order to move to 'do-it-yourself', you and others involved with the child have to focus on the end-goal of independence. We want children to plan and organize on themselves, inhibit unhelpful behaviors, remember what they plan to do, check their own progress, and change approaches if need be.

This means you and others involved with the child need to practice the following:

1. **Sit back and pretend you're in the passenger's seat** and the child is the driver. Trust yourself and trust the child.

2. **Use the inclusive 'we' of the Language of** spark*. It's a simple but powerful way to tell children you're in this together and you'll be there to support them if needed.

3. **Ask rather than tell.** Use words like "How about ...?", "What do you think if we do it this way?", "What'll happen if we do it this way?" when making suggestions.

4. **Give hints and encouragement.** Prompt children to think for themselves and figure things out. Ask them, "Did you notice this thing over here? Do you think that might help you?", "What do you need to do?" or "What could you do to help yourself?"

5. **Give them choices.** Choices can be about what to do, how, and/or when. This also includes giving a reason when choice is limited. Choice is powerful. It tells the children they're important and have some say. Choices can start out really simply. For example, you decide what things need to be done but the child determines the order for completing them. You offer milk and juice and the child selects one. Remember, once children make a choice, you have to respect it even if it's not what you had in mind.

6. **Invite and value their opinions.** Ask about what they'd like to do, how they'd like to do it, why they don't want to do it, etc. Listen to their ideas and respond to their suggestions. Acknowledge their outlook even if you disagree.

7. **Think out loud.** Explain in simple terms what you're thinking and the reason you want to do things in certain ways. You may not get your way, but the children will learn about other ways of doing things.

Key points in this chapter

Talk to families, preschool, schools, and other interested people about spark* so they understand what's being taught and why.

Read this book before starting intervention.

Know as much as you can about each child before starting spark* so you can engage them more easily.

Think about what format and setting for **spark*** might work best for the children and you.

Be a model of self-regulation for the child, staying calm and being organized.

Make sure each child is calm, alert and nourished before practicing self-regulation with them.

Monitor each child's progress toward achieving the goals and don't move on to the next lesson until they reach the objective.

Notice when the child tries to self-regulate and prompt them to be aware of their own responses.

Be patient and persistent when helping children learn self-regulation.

Use the Language of **spark*** to ensure you promote the cognitive and social-emotional goals.

Repetition is good; it helps solidify the child's knowledge of concepts, vocabulary, strategies and concepts. Don't worry about saying something too many times.

Avoid telling children what to do and doing things for them. Start by doing things with them and, progressively, encourage them to do it themselves. Families and others involved in the children's lives will need help and support to start letting go.

CHAPTER 6 - IMPROVING BEHAVIORAL SELF-REGULATION WITH spark*

In the **spark*** Behavioral Self-regulation unit, the child learns and practices conscious control for starting, modulating, and stopping actions with their body. This means that they learn to inhibit unimportant and/or undesirable actions in favor of a desired one. They'll modulate their physical responses and reactions, being gentle or firm when needed. They'll work toward being able to interrupt their current action in response to new or altered demands, such as stopping before crossing a road. The child also learns to continue a desired action even when faced with disruptions or interference.

It's critical that you don't confuse self-regulation with compliance. Our goal is to help the child learn to modulate their body movements and bring them under their voluntary control. It's NOT to bring the child under our control and have them simply do what we ask them.

Throughout the Behavioral Self-regulation unit, the child progressively learns to:

- Improve their awareness of the amount and types of control they have over their body.

- Be weaned from adult control and look more to peers and to themselves for direction.

- Know when and where they need to regulate their actions and when they can let go.

- Begin to calm and center themselves.

- Control their entire body.

Organization of the spark* **Behavioral Self-regulation unit**

Behavioral Self-regulation is divided into five different areas of focus:

1. Hands,
2. Breathing,
3. Feet,
4. Voice, and
5. Whole Body.

Each area of focus is practiced systematically in four different areas of skill development:

1. Awareness of Ability,
2. Awareness of Need,
3. Resilience and
4. Self-advocacy.

See Figure 9 below for an overview of these components and their relationships.

Figure 8. Diagram of the five areas of focus and four areas of skill development included in learning Behavioral Self-regulation.

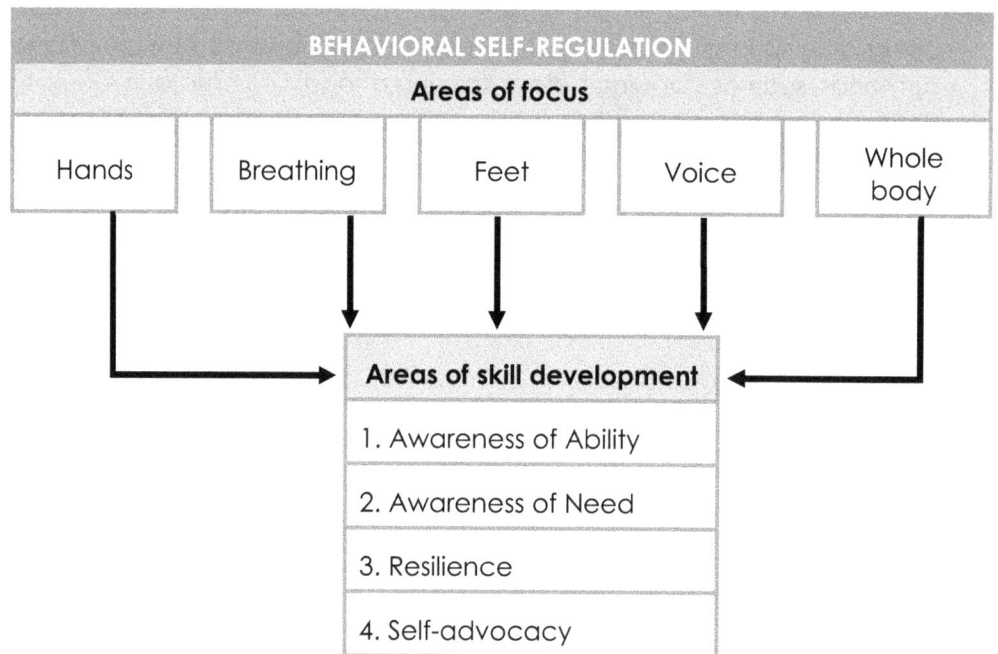

Behavioral Self-regulation is perhaps the most straightforward area of self-regulation to teach. It involves relatively simple actions. We start first with body parts and then progress to the whole body. It's much easier for children to focus on actions isolated to one body part at a time rather than their body as a whole. Also, the children can more easily watch their hands and feet in action.

Areas of focus

Five specific areas that receive attention in Behavioral Self-regulation including hands, breathing, feet, voice and the whole body as shown in Figure 9 on the previous page.

1. **Hands**. The first area of focus is the hands. It's generally the most straightforward area to start with because the adult can provide direct physical support to the child. Initially, actions done with the hands should involve only visible ones. That is, the actions can be seen by the child, like clapping your hands or touching your toes. Then invisible actions are introduced such as putting your hands behind your back. Action songs in the Resource files accessible through the **spark*** website are divided into visible and non-visible for your convenience.

2. **Breathing**. Children will learn to use "Turtle Breathing" to calm and center their bodies and brains. Turtle Breathing is slow and steady inhaling and exhaling through the nose or mouth. It helps children focus their attention on the here and now, not on what might or might not happen. This helps to reduce the child's level of anxiety which can allow them to be more open to changes and possibilities. Breathing will be used throughout **spark*** Cognitive and Emotional Self-regulation units as a means for the child to calm themselves and allow reflection.

3. **Feet.** Practice will follow a similar format to the hands but now we have a mobile (on their feet) child which lets us add more varied and interesting activities.

4. **Voice**. Many children with ASC have very powerful voices and some speak very quietly. In this section, we'll work on helping the child gain control over their voice volume so they can yell when appropriate as well as speak in a whisper. Voice volume will be emphasized again in the Emotional Self-regulation unit.

5. **Whole body**. The set of activities will have the child at their mobile best. At this point in the program, they're gained sufficient control over their body parts that we can work on helping them regulate movements of their body as a whole. This is when we introduce yoga so the children can learn slow easy stretching movements coordinated with their Turtle Breathing.

    Yoga helps children combine the calmness they discovered with Turtle Breathing with whole body self-regulation. It can help improve their concentration and attention by having them focus on breathing and the different body positions.

> **NOTE**: It's really important that you very clearly indicate to families that yoga is used within **spark*** as a helpful activity and there are **NO** connections to any religious beliefs..

Areas of skill development within each component of the spark* model

In the Behavioral Self-regulation unit, as well as the Cognitive and Emotional Self-regulation units, the child is taken through a series of steps toward independence and generalization (see Figure 9). The sequence includes:

1. Awareness of Ability
2. Awareness of Need
3. Resilience
4. Self-advocacy

Awareness of Ability

Awareness of Ability involves helping the child understand that they can voluntarily and consciously make different movements. They learn "I can do it!" They're helped to understand where their body is and how they can gain control over its location as well as the speed, intensity, and manner of movements. For example, at school, it's important to self-regulate in the hallways so you walk instead of running but you can run in the playground. At home, you can control your hands so you can wait your turn to take a cookie. The child learns to identify and recognize their body parts and the actions they can perform. We help them learn the vocabulary of self-regulation as well as the terms for body parts, locations, and actions.

Awareness of Need

During the Awareness of Need stage, the child is helped to understand where and when different actions are appropriate and possible. They learn "I need to do it here and here". This phase is included for two main reasons: first, it promotes generalization and, second, it helps highlight the usefulness of each skill for the child.

In order to adopt and use any new behavior, the child has to see that there's a need for it. They have to believe that it fulfills some need, otherwise they're taking on the behavior in obedience. If they're helped to appreciate the reasoning behind a form of self-regulation, they'll be more likely to adopt it. Once the child sees how a way of behaving and moving or using their body is connected with important events, people, and standards, they're also able to remember and embrace it more readily.

Resilience

Resilience entails helping the child use different skills and strategies, even in the presence of temptations, disruptions, or distractions. The child learns "I an do it even when ….". This is where we help them solidify their ability to regulate and modulate their behavior in everyday situations. Inhibitory control is strongly emphasized in this stage. The child must understand how to resist temptations and familiar behavior patterns. For example, if a child hits them, they learn not to strike back or, if they see a dog across the street, they don't dash out into traffic.

Typical advice for parents, teachers, and therapists dealing with children with ASC is to structure the environment and tasks, ensure a calm and quiet setting, and many more things. At some point, however, we need to help the child develop resilience in dealing with less structure, less-than-positive experiences, other people's motivations and interests, distractions, and reduced coherence. This is what they'll encounter in real life so we need to prepare them for it. Becoming resilient means that the child can continue their path toward a goal and not be deterred by disorganization, interruptions, or obstacles.

Self-advocacy

Self-advocacy involves the child's learning to speak out or act on behalf of themselves. They need to indicate or arrange what they need or want. The child needs to learn ways to help themselves cope and learn in daily settings. Even if they have increased their resilience, there will be situations and times when they aren't able to remain calm. At those times and in those settings, they need to help themselves in ways that are positive and socially acceptable.

We teach them to ask for help when needed and to arrange their environment so it's easier to function. This may mean that they put that plate of cookies away for right now, so it doesn't tempt them or that they move away from another child who's bothering them.

spark* Behavioral Self-regulation lesson content

The lessons that follow are formatted to help you work systematically through each body part and each area of skill development. Each figure below provides an example of the information shown in every lesson.

Executive functions

Each lesson shows which of the five main executive functions, presented in Chapter 2, is a primary focus and which ones are secondary. Brief explanations are provided about the rationale for designating some functions as primary and others as secondary (see the example on the next page).

At the beginning of the Behavioral Self-regulation unit, care is taken to emphasize only one or two executive functions at the same time, slowly adding more as the child exhibits greater facility.

Lesson identifying information: area of self-regulation, area of focus & area of skill development

Executive functions receiving primary and secondary focus, plus comments

Area of self-regulation 1: Behavior			
Area of focus 1: Hands			
Area of skill development 1: Awareness of Ability			
Primary executive functions:		**Secondary executive functions:**	
	Cognitive flexibility		Planning and organization
	Inhibitory control		Working memory
	Self-monitoring		

Comments on executive functions: This activity requires the child to control their impulses and begin to monitor their performance. There's little emphasis on planning and organization and working memory in the sense that only single actions are required each time and actions are done in direct imitation. The child must vary the location, speed, intensity and manner with which they perform different actions, so some degree of cognitive flexibility is needed. That is, they must move from doing the action ...

Inhibitory control is a major focus because it's the essence of Behavioral Self-regulation.

Self-monitoring is stressed throughout since the child will need to learn to evaluate the accuracy and quality of their responses and reactions. It is important to independent skill and strategy use as well as generalization.

The amount of focus on *planning and organization* and *working memory* will vary from lesson to lesson. *Cognitive flexibility* is increasingly emphasized but, initially, we use familiar activities when pressing the child to be more flexible. This is due to the fact that cognitive flexibility is a particularly challenging area for children with ASC.

Task variation

For each area of focus, actions are practiced using different variations (see the example below; the arrow denotes that some sections of the lesson plan were deleted so only pertinent information is highlighted). Since not all actions are appropriate to all variations, there will be exceptions. The four main variations include:

1. **Location or position**, including different places on the body (for example, hands on the knees) and in the environment (for example, feet on the floor).

2. **Speed or rate**, such as clapping quickly or breathing slowly, helping the child learn that they can act in fast, slow and in-between ways, not just full on.

3. **Intensity or force**, such as speaking quietly or stomping your feet, helping the child understand and sense gradations in the force with which they perform different actions.

4. **Manner** of movement concerns the style of movement, relating actions to different types of animals, like flitting like a butterfly or stomping like an elephant.

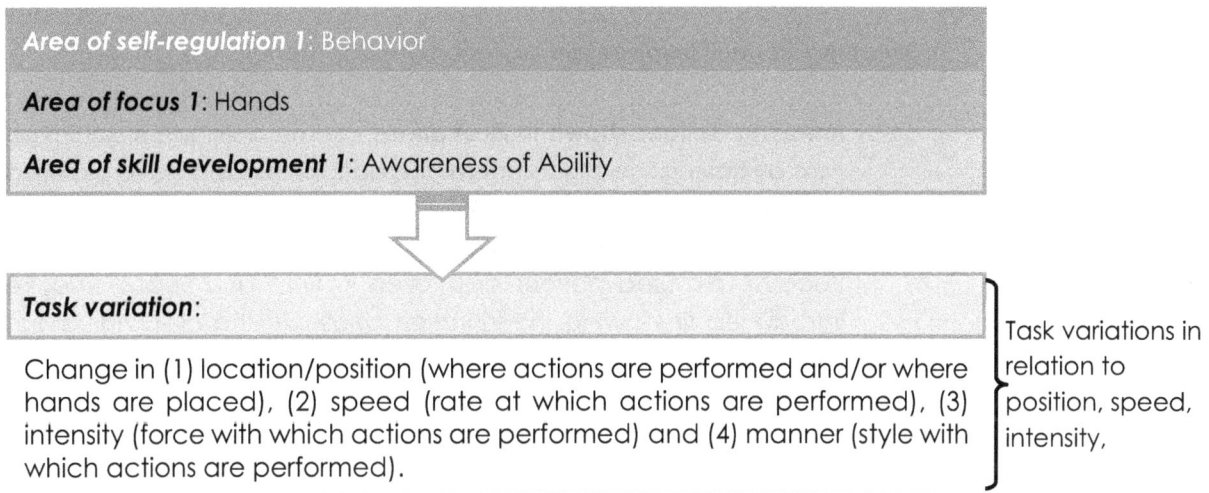

Area of self-regulation 1: Behavior

Area of focus 1: Hands

Area of skill development 1: Awareness of Ability

Task variation:

Change in (1) location/position (where actions are performed and/or where hands are placed), (2) speed (rate at which actions are performed), (3) intensity (force with which actions are performed) and (4) manner (style with which actions are performed).

Task variations in relation to position, speed, intensity,

These variations are introduced systematically so the child has experience with them one at a time. Location/position is targeted first because, as compared to speed/rate and intensity/force variations, it's less likely to cause over-excitement or over-stimulation in the child.

When working on Breathing, only speed differences will be presented and practiced. In addition, breathing through the mouth can be used because many children find it simpler. Some typically developing children don't master nose blowing until almost school age.

Activities involving voice will focus on intensity (loudness/softness) only.

Directness of adult involvement

Each action is practiced in five different contexts (see an example on the next page). These permit increasing distance from adult control and more reliance on verbal directions and on being able to self-regulate. The five contexts are:

1. **Imitating the adult** - Imitating an adult, especially when done side by side, is the least complex of the five contexts in terms of both cognitive and social factors. During this practice, the child is progressively introduced to the expectations for each activity, to the vocabulary for body parts and locations, and to the picture stimuli for each action.

Area of self-regulation 1: Behavior

Area of focus 1: Hands

Area of skill development 1: Awareness of Ability

Task structuring:

Directness of adult involvement

Directness of adult involvement: Imitation of adult model

---

2. **Imitating actions shown in illustrations** - Some distance is achieved next by having the child perform the actions in response to pictured models only. This increases the conceptual complexity by going from a live model to a two-dimensional, inanimate illustration. Because pictured actions are frozen in time and space, they're introduced first during the imitation phase so the child has direct experience with the movements cued by each illustration.

3. **Following verbal directions** – This involves the child's learning to follow directions from verbal information only. Children with ASC typically find verbal information more challenging to process and understand. That's why we use verbal directions first with familiar activities the children have already practiced.

4. **Imitating a peer** - The fourth stage is imitation of a peer which is important for future social learning. Children with ASC don't automatically imitate others and peers tend to be overlooked in most intervention programs. We want the children to learn how to imitate their peers as this is an important avenue for learning social skills.

5. **Self-direction** - The final step is for the child to internalize the skill and begin to monitor and adjust their own behavior. Clues and prompts from others will be progressively reduced as the children assume greater control of their behavior.

General organization and arrangement of the activity

In the Task structuring section of each lesson, there's advice about how to arrange and organize the activity (see an example below).

Area of self-regulation 1: Behavior

Area of focus 1: Hands

Area of skill development 1: Awareness of Ability

General organization and arrangement of the activity: You may wish to start work on imitation in a side-by-side position with the child, so they don't have to reverse/mirror your actions. Move on to face-to-face practice once the child successfully imitates actions.

For younger children, be sensitive to whether an action is visible or invisible to the child when first starting this lesson. Visible actions are those that they can see as they perform them. Invisible actions are out of the child's range of vision, such as on their head or behind their back. Some children may perform visible actions more readily at least in the initial stages so start there. Move on to invisible actions as the child's performance improves. Examples of songs/rhymes with visible and invisible actions can be found in the Resource files. ......

Suggestions for organizing activities & things to watch out for

Other suggestions are provided for optimizing learning; for example, high intensity activities, like making actions very quickly or with great force, can be over-stimulating for some children. It's important to arrange tasks so sufficient calmness is maintained. That means children can do stimulating and exciting activities, but then they're helped to return to an optimal level of calmness.

Objectives

Objectives are the level of accuracy or frequency a child must reach before moving to the next lesson (see an example on the next page). They're written as individual goals, with a description of the target behavior, accuracy or frequency expected, and directness of adult involvement.

The level of accuracy is typically 80% before a child should move on to the next lesson. Due to the nature of children with ASC and with life in general, achieving success on four out of five tries (80%) should be considered quite solid learning.

For activities that require extension into daily life, the accuracy levels are reduced to reflect the reality of challenges they'll likely encounter. For example, when the child is expected to advocate for themselves, the objective is set for 50% of the time.

> **Area of self-regulation 1**: Behavior
>
> **Area of focus 1**: Hands
>
> **Area of skill development 1**: Awareness of Ability

Objectives: level
of accuracy or
frequency of
use needed for
child to move to
the next lesson

> **Objectives**:
>
> The child will be able to imitate (1) location/position, (2) speed, (3) intensity and (4) manner variations in hand movements from an adult model with at least 80% accuracy each.

Materials

Materials needed for each lesson are outlined (see example below). Most are included in the Resource files accessible through the **spark*** website. Suggestions for both younger and older children are included in the files.

> **Area of self-regulation 1**: Behavior
>
> **Area of focus 1**: Hands
>
> **Area of skill development 1**: Awareness of Ability

Materials
suggested for
the lesson,
indicating those
available in the
Resources files

> **Materials:**
>
> - rhymes and songs and storybooks (see the Resource files – RESOURCES - *Internet sites coordinated with lesson activities* file for websites and examples of materials appropriate for both younger and older children) – incorporate favorites identified by the children and/or families
> - illustrations of action locations/positions, speed, intensities and manners (see examples in the Resource files – ILLUSTRATIONS – *Action intensity variation, Action speed variations, Action manner variations, Hand action and position variations*); for older children, incorporate ...

All activities in the Behavioral Self-regulation unit should be done to songs and rhymes, making them more fun and more memorable for the child. Be sure to ask families and children for favorite songs and rhymes so they can be incorporated into lessons. That can really help pique interest in the children. Sharing the songs and rhymes with the child's family can also help them to extend self-regulation activities into daily life. Songs like "*Head and Shoulders Knees and Toes*" or "'*If you're happy and you know it*" are good examples. Further examples can be found in the Resource files. Feel free to create or adapt other songs and rhymes.

Suggestions are also made in the Resource files for storybooks that can complement the lessons. Care has been taken to ensure that the suggested books don't suggest or model undesirable behavior. Children on the autism spectrum often pick up on these negative models and start using the behaviors. You can introduce books that model negative or naughty behavior once the children have progressed in self-regulation.

NOTE: If you incorporate technology in the lessons, be sure that it increases child participation and learning about self-regulation and doesn't interfere with learning or distract the child.

Language of spark* to use

For each lesson, key words and phrases for promoting the cognitive and social-emotional goals of each interaction are highlighted to help you remember to use them. In addition, important vocabulary and concepts are listed.

Area of self-regulation 1: Behavior
Area of focus 1: Hands
Area of skill development 1: Awareness of Ability

Language of spark to use in this lesson:*

Key words & phrases:

We're ...	We can ...
Let's ...	I need your help.
Did your hands ...?	Help me ...
How did your hands do?	Look how you made your hands ...
You really know how to ...	You did that all by yourself.

Language of spark* key words and phrases to use in the lesson

Vocabulary & concepts:

Positions: up, down	Locations: in, on, under, beside, behind, over, etc.
Body parts: hands,	Intensity: hard, soft(ly), in-between
Speed: fast, slow(ly), in-between	
Manner: animals, cartoon or video characters	

Language of spark* vocabulary and concepts to use in the lesson

Introduction

The Introduction section of each activity includes scripted instructions and explanations you give the child. The introduction is used to engage each child in the lesson and its objectives. See an example on the next page.

With all of these instructions, care has been taken to use the Language of **spark*** and provide clarity. Allowance is made also for each person using **spark*** to have some flexibility and to be creative. But it's critical that you use the specific words and phrases in the Language of **spark***.

Practice

The Practice section suggests ways in which you can engage the child to perform and repeat each activity, striving to solidify the skills and strategies. The Practice section is a chance to help the child explore the skills and strategies presented in the lesson. An example of lesson practice information is shown in the example below.

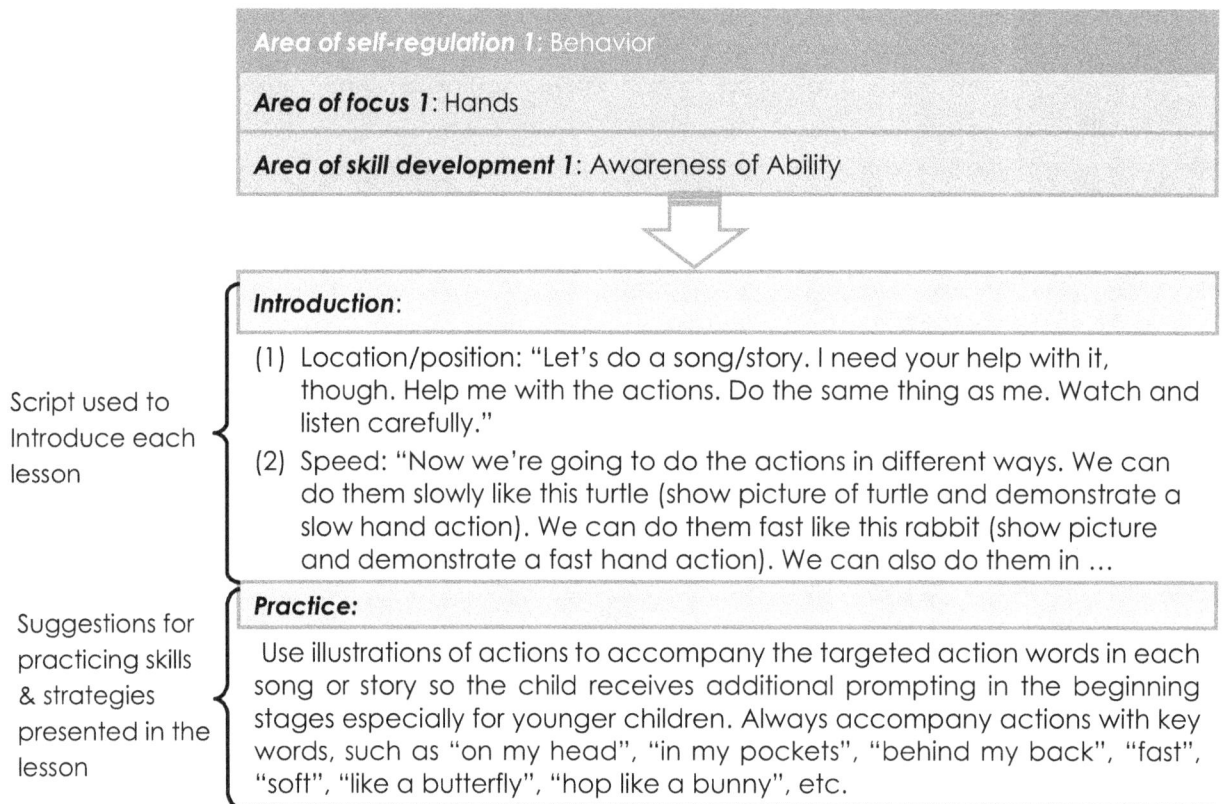

Area of self-regulation 1: Behavior
Area of focus 1: Hands
Area of skill development 1: Awareness of Ability

Script used to Introduce each lesson

Introduction:
(1) Location/position: "Let's do a song/story. I need your help with it, though. Help me with the actions. Do the same thing as me. Watch and listen carefully." (2) Speed: "Now we're going to do the actions in different ways. We can do them slowly like this turtle (show picture of turtle and demonstrate a slow hand action). We can do them fast like this rabbit (show picture and demonstrate a fast hand action). We can also do them in …

Suggestions for practicing skills & strategies presented in the lesson

Practice:
Use illustrations of actions to accompany the targeted action words in each song or story so the child receives additional prompting in the beginning stages especially for younger children. Always accompany actions with key words, such as "on my head", "in my pockets", "behind my back", "fast", "soft", "like a butterfly", "hop like a bunny", etc.

Prompting

This part provides verbal and nonverbal prompts that should be used to establish and solidify skills learned within the lesson. Strong emphasis is placed on the child's understanding that learning is a process. That means we help them understand that they won't reach perfection right away and will need to tolerate 'less-than-perfect' work until "Your brain and your body can practice".

An example of prompting information from a lesson plan is shown in example on the next page.

It's critically important that you don't <u>tell</u> the child what to do unless there's no alternative. Always prompt them to think for themselves by asking, "What could you do to help yourself?" By asking rather than telling, children have to think for themselves and not rely on adults.

The strategy of tapping on a picture or object is used to regain children's attention. It's effective and I've used it many times over the years. Initially, it seemed a little rude but it works. It gently refocuses the child's attention to the important object or picture so you can continue. The tapping is a quiet "I'll wait for you" that avoids stressing the child by bombarding them with words.

Area of self-regulation 1: Behavior

Area of focus 1: Hands

Area of skill development 1: Awareness of Ability

Prompting:

For children just learning to imitate others, say "I do this _____(position, speed, intensity, manner). Make your hands do the same". You can also just say "Do the same" and then make the action. Do an action and then say "You do" as you point to the child.....

Ways to prompt the child to practice

Self-monitoring

Because our goal is to help the child assume control over their own behavior, we need to teach them to judge their own performance from an early stage. That way they can determine the accuracy and adequacy of their own performance. An example of self-monitoring information is shown on the next page.

Solidifying

To help solidify learning from each lesson, children are helped to reflect on what they learned. They're prompted and helped to review (a) what they learned, (b) why it's important, and (c) what they noticed when they used the skills and strategies. Some children won't be able to verbalize this information, but every effort should be made to help them reflect on the lesson, whether they verbalize it. See the section on the next page.

Highlighting

Suggestions are made in this section about how to highlight the child's use of their appropriate self-regulation and how to help them solidify their skills in daily situations. Within each session, the child is also helped to reflect on what they learned, what it means, and what they might have noticed when they used the skills and strategies. An example is shown below.

Additional comments

Any features, skills and strategies that are critically important will be highlighted in this section on each lesson. Suggestions for extension and generalization will also be provided. Some optional supplemental activities to reinforce learning and awareness will be described in this section.

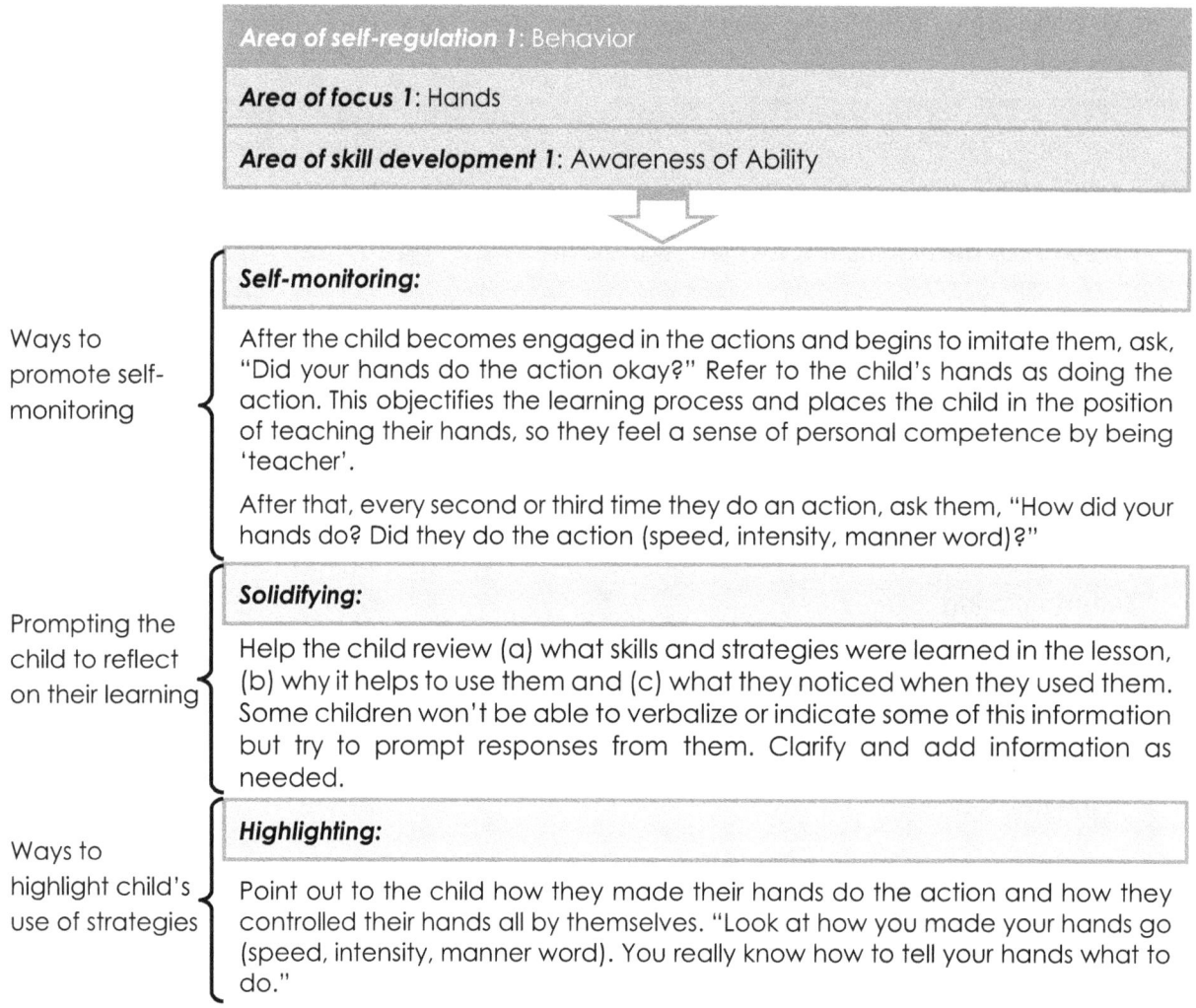

Area of self-regulation 1: Behavior
Area of focus 1: Hands
Area of skill development 1: Awareness of Ability

Ways to promote self-monitoring

Self-monitoring:

After the child becomes engaged in the actions and begins to imitate them, ask, "Did your hands do the action okay?" Refer to the child's hands as doing the action. This objectifies the learning process and places the child in the position of teaching their hands, so they feel a sense of personal competence by being 'teacher'.

After that, every second or third time they do an action, ask them, "How did your hands do? Did they do the action (speed, intensity, manner word)?"

Prompting the child to reflect on their learning

Solidifying:

Help the child review (a) what skills and strategies were learned in the lesson, (b) why it helps to use them and (c) what they noticed when they used them. Some children won't be able to verbalize or indicate some of this information but try to prompt responses from them. Clarify and add information as needed.

Ways to highlight child's use of strategies

Highlighting:

Point out to the child how they made their hands do the action and how they controlled their hands all by themselves. "Look at how you made your hands go (speed, intensity, manner word). You really know how to tell your hands what to do."

NOTE: Each component in this Behavioral Self-regulation unit takes small but important steps. Every step builds on the next, forming a solid foundation of self-regulation. **Don't skip any of the lessons**. Each lesson can be mere minutes in length and some children will meet criteria quickly and easily. Don't, however, skip any of the steps.

spark* **Observational Assessment**

In the observational assessment, evaluation is done by sampling the child's ability to imitate actions varying in location, speed, intensity, and manner; an excerpt is shown below. The complete form is in the Resource files (FORM - Observational Assessment – Behavioral Self-Regulation file).

Attempt each observational assessment task non-verbally to see if the child will imitate you with no further prompting. If they don't respond, use simple verbal prompts like "Do this" or "Put hands on your head", depending on the child and their language comprehension.

Do each action up to four times. Use nonverbal imitation first and, if they respond, encourage them to imitate the action three more times (total number of attempts is four). If they don't imitate your action on the first attempt, use verbal prompting up to three more times.

Figure 9. Excerpt from the **spark*** observational assessment for the Behavioral Self-regulation unit.

spark* *Observational Assessment – Behavioral Self-regulation*								
Child: Bobby			**Date:** Jan. 5					
Reporter: Heather								
Area of focus	**Imitates accurately:**							
	none of the trials		20% to 40% of the trials		60% to 80% of the trials		all of the trials	
Location/ Position differences:	no verbal prompt	verbal prompt	no verbal prompt	verbal prompt	no verbal prompt	verbal prompt	no verbal prompt	verbal prompt
place hands on head					✓			
put feet into the air while sitting				✓				
stand behind a chair				✓				

Then place a check mark (✓) in the box that corresponds to the accuracy of their responding:

- "none of the trials" if the child didn't respond to nonverbal and verbal prompts,
- "20% to 40% of the trials" if the child performed the action one to two of the five trials with nonverbal or verbal prompts,

- "60% to 80% of the trials" if the child performed the action three or four of the five trials with nonverbal of verbal prompts or

- "all of the trials" if they performed the action five out of five times with nonverbal or verbal prompts.

Do the Observational assessment actions in any order.

Documenting progress through spark* lesson objectives

To ensure progress toward program goals as well as for general accountability, each child's progress should be tracked over time. This ensures you've got a working document that shows when you started a lesson with the child, when they met the objective for that lesson, when you introduced the next lesson, and so on. In Figure 11 below is an excerpt of the **spark*** Achievement of Lesson Objectives form.

The complete form is in the Resource files (FORM - Achievement of Lesson Objectives – Behavioral Self-Regulation).

Figure 10. Excerpt from spark* Achievement of Lesson Objectives form for Behavioral Self-regulation.

spark* *Achievement of Lesson Objectives– Behavioral Self-regulation*							
Child: Bobby				**Time period:** June to December			
Reporter: Heather							
Areas of Focus	**Task Variation**	**Objective**		**Areas of skill develop-ment**	**Date started**	**Evaluation Date(s)**	
		The child will be able to:				June 7	
Control li-ing hands	Location, Speed, Intensity, Manner	B:H1 - imitate (1) location/position, (2) speed, (3) intensity and (4) manner variations in hand movements from an adult model with at least 80% accuracy each		Imitating the adult	June 1	D	

On the form is each major area of focus, task variation, and area of skill development included in the Behavioral Self-regulation unit, along with the objectives as stated in each lesson. The date on which the lesson was started is in the fifth column from the left. Then, after a period of time that's appropriate to the child and/or program, their progress is noted. The date of evaluation is entered into the column and a progress indicator is written into each appropriate row under that column. Progress toward the objective is marked as:

A – objective achieved,

D – skill developing but the child demonstrates it below the criterion level and

N - no discernible progress.

NOTE: space is left in each objective to add more specific information if required. For example, adding "across three samplings" to the objective below or adding a time span.

spark* **Behavioral Self-regulation Lesson Plan Users Guide**

On the next page is a table showing the overall organization of the spark* **Behavioral Self-regulation** unit. Information contained in each column of the table is described next.

Column	Information included

#1	Lesson Codes:
	    B – Behavioral Self-regulation plan
	    H – Hands
	    B – Breath
	    F – Feet
	    V – Voice
	    W – Whole body
	When you see the letter **N,** it means that a **Newsletter** is sent home at the beginning of this lesson.

#2	Pages - page numbers for that lesson
#3, 4, 5, 6	Area(s) of skill development — indicated with check mark (✔)
#7, 8, 9, 10	Task variations – indicated with a check mark (✔) Note: grey squares show variations not included for that body part
#11, 12, 13, 14, 15	Task structuring: – indicated with a check mark (✔)

Newsletters should be sent home at the start of these lessons:

Lesson	Newsletter #
Before starting spark*	1
B:H1	2
B:H2	3
B:H4	4
B:H5	5
B:F1	6
B:F3	7

Lesson	Pages	Area of Skill Development				Task Variations				Task structuring:				
		Awareness of Ability	Awareness of Need	Resilience	Self-advocacy	Location or position	Speed or rate	Intensity or force	Manner	Imitate adult model	Imitate pictured model	Follow verbal direction	Imitate peer	Self-directed
B:H1 N	77-81	✓				✓	✓	✓	✓	✓				
B:H2 N	82-84	✓				✓	✓	✓	✓		✓	✓	✓	
B:H3	85-90		✓			✓	✓	✓	✓					✓
B:H4 N	91-93			✓		✓	✓	✓	✓					✓
B:H5 N	94-97				✓	✓	✓	✓	✓					✓
B:B1	98-101	✓					✓			✓	✓	✓	✓	
B:B2	102-104		✓				✓							✓
B:B3	105-107			✓	✓		✓							✓
B:F1 N	108-111	✓				✓	✓	✓	✓	✓	✓	✓	✓	
B:F2	112-115		✓			✓	✓	✓	✓					✓
B:F3 N	116-119			✓	✓	✓	✓	✓	✓					✓
B:V1	120-122	✓						✓		✓	✓	✓	✓	
B:V2	123-126		✓					✓						✓
B:V3 N	127-130			✓	✓			✓						✓
B:W1	131-134	✓				✓	✓	✓	✓	✓	✓	✓	✓	
B:W2	135-138		✓			✓	✓	✓	✓					✓
B:W3	139-142			✓	✓	✓	✓	✓	✓					✓

Behavioral Self-regulation Lessons

NOTE: Hold a parent and preschool/school information session on **spark*** and self-regulation before starting. It'll help everyone understand the importance of self-regulation, how it develops over time, and the need for careful planning and sequencing of activities. See the Resource files (MATERIAL – *spark brochure* file) for the **spark*** brochure you can hand out.

Give out Newsletter #1 at the information session or send it home before starting the first lesson.

Review the lesson carefully before starting. You might want to copy the scripts, so you have the words close at hand when working with each child.

Follow the lessons exactly in terms of how information is presented, and the vocabulary and definitions used.

Lesson B:H1

Be sure to provide the parents and others involved with the child an overview of spark*, the spark* brochure and a copy of Newsletter #1 before starting this lesson. The brochure is in the Resources files – MATERIAL – **spark*** *brochure* file and the Newsletter is in the Resources files - NEWSLETTERS file.

Send home Newsletter #2 when starting this lesson.

Send home some songs and rhymes the child enjoys - you can print the songs and rhymes from the internet using the sites included in the Resources files – MATERIAL - *Suggested songs for the Behavioral Self-regulation* and RESOURCES - *Internet sites coordinated with lesson activities*.

NOTE: Always refer to the child's hands as doing the actions – not the children themselves. This 'compartmentalizes' their hands and places the child in the position of teaching their hands, so they feel a sense of personal competence by being 'commanders' and 'master's' of their own bodies.

The goal in this lesson is to help children learn they have control of their hands and can command them to move in different ways when imitating an adult.

Area of self-regulation 1: Behavior			
Area of focus 1: Hands			
Area of skill development 1: Awareness of Ability			
Primary executive functions:		**Secondary executive functions**:	
	Cognitive flexibility		Planning and organization
	Inhibitory control		Working memory
	Self-monitoring		

Comments on executive functions: This activity requires children to control their impulses and begin to monitor their performance. There's little emphasis on planning and organization and working memory in the sense that only single actions are required each time and actions are done in direct imitation. Children must vary the location, speed, intensity, and manner they perform different actions, so inhibitory control and some degree of cognitive flexibility are needed. That is, they must go from doing the action at one rate, intensity, or manner and then shift to another. When working on different manners of movement, associations are made between actions and animal or cartoon character movements so children's cognitive flexibility will receive a fairly significant 'stretch' during that task variation. Children will have to switch from the notion of a butterfly as a concrete thing and focus on its movement patterns.

Task variation:

Change in (1) location/position (where actions are performed and/or where hands are placed), (2) speed (rate at which actions are performed), (3) intensity (force with which actions are performed) and (4) manner (style with which actions are performed).

Task structuring:

Directness of adult involvement: Imitation of adult model

General organization and arrangement of the activity: You may wish to start work on imitation in a side-by-side position with the child, so they don't have to reverse/mirror your actions. Move on to face-to-face practice once the child successfully imitates actions.

For younger children, be sensitive to whether an action is visible or invisible to the child when first starting this lesson. Visible actions are those that they can see as they perform them. Invisible actions are out of the child's range of vision, such as on their head or behind their back. Some children may perform visible actions more readily at least in the initial stages so start there. Move on to invisible actions as the child's performance improves. Examples of songs/rhymes with visible and invisible actions can be found in the Resource files.

Using the dynamic of a group can help induce the child to engage in the activities more readily; they'll be side-by-side with peers and may be prompted by 'peer pressure'. Sometimes, however, being in a group can induce a lot of 'silliness' in some or all of the children. It's important to have strategies ready for dealing with group 'sillies' (see the Resource files).

Model actions so the positions/locations, three speeds (fast, in-between and slow), three intensities (hard, in-between, soft) and manners are clearly evident to the child. You may need to limit the amount of time spent doing higher speed and intensity actions as it can over-excite some children. Monitor them carefully.

It's usually best to use only one task variation for each song or story. At this stage, intermixing location, speed, intensity and manner may be overly complex for some children; for example, doing an action quickly, then switching to doing it softly and then doing it like a kangaroo within one song or rhyme. Be sure to try it out and see if the child can tolerate more than one variation. If they can, go ahead and include as many as possible,

It's important to use familiar songs and storybooks in the initial stages of this lesson so the new task requirements are used with known material. After the child's performance becomes more consistent, introduce new songs or stories.

Objectives:

The child will be able to imitate (1) location/position, (2) speed, (3) intensity and (4) manner variations in hand movements from an adult model with at least 80% accuracy each.

Materials:

- rhymes and songs and storybooks (see the Resource files – MATERIAL - Selected songs and rhymes for the Behavioral Self-regulation, RESOURCES - *Internet sites coordinated with lesson activities* and RESOURCES – *Storybooks coordinated with lesson target areas* files for websites and examples of materials appropriate for both younger and older children) – incorporate favorites identified by the children and/or families

- illustrations of action locations/positions, speed, intensities and manners (see examples in the Resource files – ILLUSTRATIONS – *Action intensity variation, Action speed variations, Action manner variations, Hand action and position variations*); for older children, incorporate manners of movement from the child's favorite TV and cartoon characters (see the Resource files – RESOURCES - *Internet sites coordinated with lesson activities*). For older children who are able to read, you may wish to use just the printed word as the animal associations may seem too young for them.

- drums and rhythm instruments (like tambourines, shakers, triangles) – all can be homemade (see the Resource files - RESOURCES - *Internet sites coordinated with lesson activities* for suggestions)

Language of spark* *to use in this lesson:*

Key words & phrases:

We're …	We can …
Let's …	I need your help.
Did your hands …?	Help me …
How did your hands do?	Look how you made your hands …
You really know how to …	You did that all by yourself.

Vocabulary & concepts:

Positions: up, down Body parts: hands, Speed: fast, slow(ly), in-between Manner: animals, cartoon or video characters	Locations: in, on, under, beside, behind, over, etc. Intensity: hard, soft(ly), in-between

Introduction:

(1) Location/position: "Let's do a song/story. I need your help with it, though. Help me with the actions. Do the same thing as me. Watch and listen carefully."

(2) Speed: "Now we're going to do the actions in different ways. We can do them slowly like this turtle (show picture of turtle and demonstrate a slow hand action). We can do them fast like this rabbit (show picture and demonstrate a fast hand action). We can also do them in

between – that's like how we usually do them (show picture and demonstrate a regular rate of action)."

(3) Intensity: "Now we're going to do the actions in even more ways. We can do them softly like a cloud (show picture of cloud and demonstrate performing an action softly). We can do them hard like this rock (show picture and demonstrate performing the action with force). We can also do them in between – that's like how we usually do it (show picture and demonstrate regular intensity of action)."

(4) Manner: "Now we're going to do the actions in even more ways. We can do them like a butterfly (show picture of butterfly and demonstrate 'fluttery' hand actions). We can do them like an elephant (show picture and demonstrate slow, forceful hand actions).

Practice:

Use illustrations of actions to accompany the targeted action words in each song or story so the child receives additional prompting in the beginning stages especially for younger children. Always accompany actions with key words, such as "on my head", "in my pockets", "behind my back", "fast", "soft", "like a butterfly", "hop like a bunny", etc.

Prompting:

For children just learning to imitate others, say "I do this ____(position, speed, intensity, manner). Make your hands do the same". You can also just say "Do the same" or "Do this" and then make the action. Do an action and then say "You do" as you point to the child.

Use the illustrations of actions to help clarify the meaning of words, especially for younger children. Typically, the pictures of the symbols of different action speeds (for example, the turtle) are the primary focus for visual prompting.

If the child becomes distracted from the activity, tap your finger on the picture repeatedly and wait for them to look. Remain silent while tapping, speaking only if the child hasn't responded after 20 seconds or more.

NOTE: There are no 'correct' ways to move your hands when practicing different manners. Allow the child a fair amount of latitude in performing actions so long as their interpretations are plausible as actions for that animal or character. They don't have to be identical to yours.

Self-monitoring:

After the child becomes engaged in the actions and begins to imitate them, ask, "Did your hands do the action okay.

After every second or third time they do an action, ask them, "How did your hands do? Did they do the action (speed, intensity, manner word)?" Wait for them to respond. Give them feedback about whether you agree or disagree and explain why.

Solidifying:

Help the child review (a) what skills and strategies were learned in the lesson, (b) why it helps to use them and (c) what they noticed when they used them. Some children won't be able to verbalize or indicate some of this information but try to prompt responses from them. Clarify and add information as needed.

Highlighting:

Point out to the child how they made their hands do the action and how they controlled their hands all by themselves. "Look at how you made your hands go (speed, intensity, manner word). You really know how to tell your hands what to do."

Additional Comments:

During these activities, avoid having the child touch other people until they gain consistent control of their body. This can avoid sensory and personal space issues.

Share with the child's family different songs and rhymes they're enjoyed so they can practice them while driving in the car and whenever they can fit them in.

Optional supplemental activities to increase each child's knowledge about their hands and what they can do: help the child make a "My Hands" book that shows in pictures or photos and words all the things that child can do with their hands in day-to-day life (for example, dressing themselves, eating, drawing, holding things).

Lesson B:H2

> **Send home Newsletter #3** at the beginning of this lesson.
>
> Now that we've established the child can imitate actions from an adult model, we want to help them be less focused on adults as their sole source of direction.

> **The goal in this lesson** is to help the child learn they have control of their hands and can command them to move in different ways when taking directions only from picture clues, verbal directions or when imitating a peer.

Area of Self-regulation *1*: Behavior			
Area of focus 1: Hands			
Area of skill development 1: Awareness of Ability			
Primary executive functions:		**Secondary executive functions:**	
	Cognitive flexibility		Planning and organization
	Inhibitory control		Working memory
	Self-monitoring		

Comments on executive functions: This activity requires the child to control their impulses and monitor their performance more carefully than the previous lesson since no adult modeling will be used. There's a little more emphasis on planning and organization and working memory but only single actions are required each time. Cognitive flexibility will be required because of the shift among the different task variations and among changes in adult involvement.

When the shift to verbal directions occurs, the child needs to control their impulses and listen carefully since only verbal information will be presented. This requires more self-monitoring of auditory information since the visual will be removed.

When peer modeling is introduced. The child will need to deal with the social element of having a peer lead the activity. Cognitive flexibility will be needed because of the change in 'teacher'.

Task variation:

Change (1) location/position, (2) speed, (3) intensity and (4) manner

Task structuring:

Directness of adult involvement: (1) Imitate pictured model, (2) follow verbal direction, (3) Imitate a peer model

General organization and arrangement of the activity: This is a time when we can stretch the children's flexibility even more by intermixing changes in location, speed, intensity and manner. For example, do an action quickly, then switch to doing it softly and then doing it like a kangaroo within one song or rhyme. Having to 'switch gears' like this from speed to intensity to manner can be difficult in the beginning but add variations over time.

It's important to use familiar songs and storybooks in the initial stages of this lesson so the new task requirements are used with known/familiar material. After the child's performance becomes more consistent, introduce a new song or story.

Special notes for peer modeling:

Before starting peer modeling, make sure the children know that one child at a time will be chosen to be 'teacher' and everyone will get a chance. Remind each child that they need to look and listen to the (peer) 'teacher'. You may wish to introduce the Role Reminder chart included in the Resource files.

In group situations, you need a clear and fair way of selecting the 'teacher'. You may have set up 'helper of the day' which rotates among the children one at a time, based on the calendar. You can also make the customizable dice (see Resource files) with each child's picture and/or name on each face of the dice; roll the die and whatever child appears at the top of the die is selected as the 'teacher'. This nicely incorporates the concept of 'being fair' while removing the adult from the selection process.

Be sure to have action pictures and the variation illustrations present so each 'teacher' can select what they wish to use. It's often too challenging to expect the child to recall them from memory.

Objectives:

The child will be able to perform hand movements (1) depicted in illustrations, (2) as stated in the verbal directions, and (3) as modeled by peers that vary by location, speed, intensity or manner at least 80% of the time for each.

Materials:

- rhymes and songs and storybooks (see the Resource files - MATERIAL - Selected songs and rhymes for the Behavioral Self-regulation, RESOURCES - *Internet sites coordinated with lesson activities* and RESOURCES – *Storybooks coordinated with lesson target areas*) – incorporate favorites identified for each child

- illustrations of action locations/positions, speed, intensities and manners (see examples in the Resource files - ILLUSTRATIONS – *Action intensity variation, Action speed variations, Action manner variations and Hand action and position variations*); for older children, incorporate manners of movement from the child's favorite TV and cartoon characters (see

Resource files - RESOURCES - *Internet sites coordinated with lesson activities* for suggested websites)

- drums and rhythm instruments (see Resource files - RESOURCES - *Internet sites coordinated with lesson activities*)
- Role Reminder chart (see Resource files – MATERIAL – *Role Reminder Chart*)
- customizable paper dice (see Resource files – TEMPLATE – *Customizable paper dice*)

Language of spark* *to use in this lesson:*

Key words & phrases:

We, we're …	We can …
Let's …	The pictures/the words might trick you.
Look/listen really carefully.	
Oops, what did the picture show/my words say?	It was pretty good, but I think your hands could do better.
How did you do?	You're right, your hands really did a great job!
Did you do the action okay?	
You really know how to …	Were you a good teacher?
Look at how you controlled your hands.	Did you help the other children do the action okay?
You really know how to tell your hands what to do.	You really listened and watched your friend (the 'teacher').
____ you really worked hard to be a good teacher.	(if using dice) That way it's fair for everyone and everyone gets a chance.

Vocabulary & concepts:

Positions: up, down	Locations: in, on, under, beside, behind, over, etc.
Body parts: hands,	Intensity: hard, soft(ly), in-between
Speed: fast, slow(ly), in-between	Teacher
Manner: animals, cartoon or video characters	

Introduction:

(1) Imitate pictured model: "Let's do a song/story. This time we won't use any words for the actions. You need to look really carefully. Do what the pictures show."

(2) Follow verbal directions: "We're going to listen and find out what to do. This time we won't use any pictures, just words. You need to listen really carefully. Do what the words say."

(3) Follow peer model: "First, ____ is going to be the teacher. They're going to tell us what to do and we have to watch and listen and do what they say."

Practice:

(1) Imitate pictured model: "Look really carefully. The pictures might trick you." Use a familiar song, rhyme or storybook and, when it comes time to perform the action, point to an illustration depicting the location,

speed, intensity or manner. Use drums and rhythm instruments as a means of practicing different speeds and intensities of hand movement, having the child imitate different patterns of drumming or sounding the instrument in ways shown in the illustrations.

(2) Follow verbal directions: "Listen really carefully. My words might trick you."

(3) Follow peer model: If a child is reluctant to be 'teacher', make a deal with them about what day they'll do it. Mark the date on a calendar so the child can see their upcoming obligation. That will place them back in control and also press them to make a commitment. You may wish to have a private one-to-one practice session with them before they're scheduled to be 'teacher' so they feel more comfortable.

When a peer leads, stand back and participate with the children. Let the 'teacher' take the lead.

Prompting:

(1) Imitate pictured model: If the child makes an error, simply say, "Oops, what did the picture show? Look carefully." Then model the action, saying, "I think the picture showed ___." If the child becomes distracted, tap your finger on the picture repeatedly and wait for them to look. Remain silent speaking only if the child hasn't responded within 20 seconds or more.

(2) Follow verbal directions: If the child doesn't respond accurately, say, "Oops, what did my words say? Listen carefully." Then repeat the direction with, "The words said ___." If the child doesn't respond accurately on the second attempt, show them the picture associated with the action or location, speed, intensity or manner.

(3) Follow peer model: Prompt the 'teacher' child only as necessary. If any of the other children are experiencing difficulty, direct your prompts to the 'teacher' so they can maintain their role and help the other children.

Self-monitoring:

Every second or third time the child performs an action, ask, "How did you do? Did you do the action okay?" Provide concise and honest information about their accuracy; for example, "It was pretty good, but I think your hands could do better." or "You're right, your hands really did a great job!"

For peer models: Every second or third time the 'teacher' child performs an action, ask, "How did you do? Were you a good teacher? Did you help the other children do the action okay?" Praise them for every bit of effort they make.

Solidifying:

Help the child review (a) what skills and strategies were learned in the lesson, (b) why it helps to use them and (c) what they noticed when they used them. Some children won't be able to verbalize or indicate some of this information but try to prompt responses from them. Clarify and add information as needed.

Highlighting:

(1) Follow pictured model: "Look at how you controlled your hands. You really know how to tell your hands what to do. You just looked at the pictures and knew what to do"

(2) Follow verbal directions: "Look at how you controlled your hands. You really know how to tell your hands what to do. You listened carefully and knew what to do"

(3) Follow peer model: To each child who followed the peer model: "Look at how you all controlled your hands. You really listened and watched your friend (the 'teacher') and knew how to tell your hands what to do."

To the child who was the 'teacher': "_____ you really worked hard to be a good teacher. Thank you."

Additional comments:

Whenever a child takes over the role of 'teacher', you're given a good opportunity to find out how you come across to the children. You'll find out how your voice sounds and what words and phrases you typically use. It's really effective feedback that lets you figure out if you need to change what you say or how you say it.

Lesson B:H3

Before starting this lesson, make sure you received feedback from families on times and places where each child needs to improve regulation of their hands from Newsletter #3.

We are now going to help the child think more about other settings and situations where their self-regulation skills need to be used. This is a critical step in promoting generalization. Tell the child about times and places in your life where you have difficulty controlling your hands. This helps let them know that they're not the only person who experiences these problems.

The goal in this lesson is to help the child learn where and when it's important to control their hands in everyday life as well as to continue practicing self-regulation of their hands.

Area of self-regulation 1: Behavior			
Area of focus 1: Hands			
Area of skill development 2: Awareness of Need			
Primary executive functions:		**Secondary executive functions**:	
👁 👁	Cognitive flexibility		
	Inhibitory control		
	Planning and organization		
	Self-monitoring		
	Working memory		

Comments on executive functions: This activity requires the child to control their impulses, monitor their performance and deal with the social variables of everyday life. There's more emphasis on planning and organization and working memory because the child is now expected to do more thinking ahead and to modulate their actions. Cognitive flexibility will be required because of the shift among the different activities and settings.

Task variation:

Use in daily settings

Task structuring:

Directness of adult involvement: Self-directed

General organization and arrangement of the activity: The tasks in this lesson center around helping the child identify where and/or when they need to regulate their hands. The places or times they identify are placed on a chart as they're discussed. The charts also act as commitments by the child since they helped construct it. Send the chart home, and ask the family to review it with the child. The chart should be posted at home in a central place, so it acts as a reminder for the whole family to self-regulate their hands.

Objective:

The child will be able to tell at least one specific important situation (times, places) per setting (at home, school/preschool, in the community) where self-regulation of their hands is important.

Materials:

- information from the parent's feedback on Newsletter #3 about times and places where the child needs improved regulation of their hands – prepare pictures or photos ahead of time or have the child draw pictures
- Awareness of Need chart. The chart has three main columns: home, school/preschool, community. There should be at least three boxes below each of these so pictures of specific events can be placed in them. See an example in the Resource files – EXAMPLE – *Awareness of Need chart for controlling hands*) and a template in the Resource files - TEMPLATE – *Awareness of Need chart* and ILLUSTRATIONS - *Topics for Awareness of Need charts - Behavioral self-regulation*.
- Books and games for practicing self-regulation (see the Resource files – RESOURCES – *Storybooks coordinated with lesson target areas* and MATERIAL – *Games for practicing self-regulation*)

Language of spark* to use in this lesson:

Key words & phrases:

We, we're …	I tell my hands …
How about …?	You can tell your hands …
What do you need to tell your hands?	You did a great job of controlling your hands!
Tell your hands, Hands, you need to _____.	How did your hands do?
	Did you control your hands?
You really know how to tell your hands what to do.	Where do you need to control your hands?
	How about when ….

Vocabulary & concepts:

Positions: up, down	Locations: in, on, under, beside, behind, over, etc.
Body parts: hands	Intensity: hard, soft(ly), in-between
Speed: fast, slow(ly), in-between	

Introduction:

"Today, we're going to think about places where it's important to control our hands. For me, it's sometimes hard to control my hands at lunch time. My hands want to pick up food. I need to tell my hands to use a fork or spoon. I'm going to put a picture of lunch right here (on chart) so'll remind me. How about you? Do your hands have a hard time at lunch too?" (this is from the information provided by the parents with you presenting the situation as if it's your issue)

Practice:

"Where do you need to control your hands? Let's put a picture on the chart for you."

Add more pictures, getting at least one idea for each main location. Be sure to describe the reason for hand self-regulation in each setting. For example, "We use slow hands at a restaurant, so nothing gets knocked on the floor."

Continue enjoying songs, rhymes and storybooks that incorporate action variations as a break from this more intense work.

Prompting:

If the child has difficulty coming up with ideas, suggest some from the parent's information ("How about when your brother ...?"). Use nonverbal prompts and verbal clues but don't to tell them. Get them to think and come up with some ideas – activate their thinking.

Catch them using self-regulation! Praise them more often than reminding them. Comment whenever you see them controlling their hands, especially in situations where they could have done something else, like grabbing.

If they do something with their hands that shows lack of self-regulation, like grabbing another child, intercede as quickly as possible with, stop them and ask: "What do you need to tell your hands?" Prompt the child to tell their hands: "Hands, you need to _____." DON'T just tell them what to do. We want the child to recall the information on their own. Then remind them that they can control their own hands and tell them you have confidence that they'll remember next time.

Self-monitoring:

Ask the child, "How can you help yourself remember to tell your hands what to do when you're (location or time you and the child added to their Awareness of Need chart)?" Help them think of ways they can remind themselves.

Solidifying:

Help the child review (a) what skills and strategies were learned in the lesson, (b) why it helps to use them and (c) what they noticed when they used them. Some children won't be able to verbalize or indicate some of this information but try to prompt responses from them. Clarify and add information as needed.

Highlighting:

Review all of the information on the child's Awareness of Need chart with them at the end of the session.

Comment whenever appropriate during other activities: "Look at how you controlled your hands. You really watched your hands and told them what to do."

Additional Comments:

Have the child's family review the chart on a frequent basis to help remind the child of their need to control their hands in those locations. Ask them to praise the child for any self-regulation they exercise, whether it happens in the targeted situations or not. If they forget to self-regulate their hands, have them ask them what they need to do.

Ask the child's family for feedback on how well the child does on a day-to-day basis.

Lesson B:H4

Send home Newsletter #4 at the beginning of this lesson.

This is an important step in helping the child overcome old habits and use their new skills even in tempting, distracting or anxiety-provoking situations. They need your help in becoming aware and noticing when they're being more resilient. Be sure to highlight instances and praise them.

The goal in this lesson is to help the child develop more resilience in being able to control their hands even when excited or tempted to do otherwise.

Area of self-regulation 1: Behavior		
Area of focus 1: Hands		
Area of skill development 3: Resilience		
Primary executive functions:	**Secondary executive functions:**	
Cognitive flexibility		
Inhibitory control		
Planning and organization		
Self-monitoring		
Working memory		

Comments on executive functions: This activity requires the child to control their impulses, monitor their performance and deal with the social variables of everyday life. There's more emphasis on planning and organization and working memory because the child is now expected to do more thinking ahead and self-modulation of their actions. Cognitive flexibility will be required because of application of the self-regulation skills to different activities and settings.

Task variation:

Regulation of location, speed, intensity and manner

Task structuring:

Directness of adult involvement: Self-directed

General organization and arrangement of the activity: Use games and everyday tasks that the child hasn't done with you.

Objective:

The child will be able to exhibit self-regulation of their hands at least 80% of the time when engaging in activities that are exciting or tempting to them.

Materials:

- tabletop games (like Don't Spill the Beans by Hasbro, Zoo Panic Game by Endless Games) that have an excitement element but require careful hand self-regulation
- exciting or tempting activities for practicing self-regulation (check each child's list for suggestions from parents)
- games for practicing self-regulation – especially the parachute games (see Resource files - MATERIAL – *Games for practicing self-regulation*)

Language of spark* *to use in this lesson:*

Key words & phrases:

We, we're ... How about ...? I think your hands forgot. What do you need to tell them? Hands, you need to _____.	You did a great job of controlling your hands! How did your hands do? You really know how to tell your hands what to do.

Vocabulary & concepts:

Positions: up, down Body parts: hands Speed: fast, slow(ly), in-between	Locations: in, on, under, beside, behind, over, etc. Intensity: hard, soft(ly), in-between

Introduction:

"You learned to control your hands so well. Now we're going to practice with things that are a bit more difficult. Let's see how we all do."

Practice:

Proceed with games and/or activities.

If possible, go for walks and visits in the community to practice.

Prompting:

Catch them using self-regulation! Praise them more often than reminding them. Comment whenever you see them controlling their hands, especially in situations that are more challenging for them.

If they do something with their hands that shows lack of self-regulation, stop them and say: "I think your hands forgot. What do you need to tell them?" Prompt the child to tell their hands: "Hands, you need to be _____." Then remind them that they can control their own hands and tell them you have confidence that they'll remember next time.

Self-monitoring:

Every second or third time the child performs an action, ask, "How did your hands do?" Then respond positively if at all possible; for example, "You bet, you did a great job of controlling your hands!"

Solidifying:

Help the child review (a) what skills and strategies were learned in the lesson, (b) why it helps to use them and (c) what they noticed when they used them. Some children won't be able to verbalize or indicate some of this information but try to prompt responses from them. Clarify and add information as needed.

Highlighting:

"Look at how you controlled your hands. You really watched your hands and told them what to do."

Additional Comments:

Ask the family to remind the child, before entering a targeted situation, about the need to tell their hands to be in control.

Lesson B:H5

Send home Newsletter #5 during this lesson to prepare the family for the next set of lessons.

This is the last step in building self-awareness, self-monitoring, and self-reliance. The child may need some prompting to advocate for themselves but be alert for their attempts and praise them.

The goal in this lesson is to help the child develop self-advocacy skills for when their hands are about to be or are becoming dysregulated (that is, when they feel out of control).

Area of self-regulation 1: Behavior		
Area of focus 1: Hands		
Area of skill development 4: Self-advocacy		
Primary executive functions:	**Secondary executive functions:**	
Cognitive flexibility		
Inhibitory control		
Planning and organization		
Self-monitoring		
Working memory		

Comments on executive functions: This activity requires the child to control their impulses, monitor their performance and deal with the social variables of everyday life. There's more emphasis on planning and organization and working memory because the child is now expected to do more thinking ahead and self-modulation of their actions. Cognitive flexibility is required because of the fact that the child must now determine the changes might help them exercise more self-regulation.

Task variation:

Use in daily settings

Task structuring:

Directness of adult involvement: Self-directed

General organization and arrangement of the activity: set up a few situations where the child will have to ask for assistance or change or make the change themselves in order to maintain control of their hands. For example, you may provide a delicate craft that requires gentle hands, an activity that requires strength to execute (e.g. opening a jar) or a game that's at too rapid a rate for the child. Don't jump in to help them too quickly. Let them struggle a little before you ask them what they could do. Don't promote the child's asking an adult for help immediately. We want them to become more self-reliant and to try things for themselves before asking for adult assistance. If they go directly to an adult for help, prompt them to think about what they could do to help themselves and to try something on their own first.

Objective:

The child will be able to ask for help or re-arrange a task or situation to facilitate their hand control at least 50% of the time in daily settings.

Materials:

- tabletop games (like Don't Spill the Beans by Hasbro, Zoo Panic Game by Endless Games) that have an excitement element but require careful hand self-regulation

- exciting or tempting activities for practicing self-regulation (check each child's list for suggestions from parents)

- games for practicing self-regulation – especially the parachute games (see Resource files - MATERIAL – *Games for practicing self-regulation*)

Language of spark* to use In this lesson:

Key words & phrases:

We, we're ... How about ...? Look at how you helped your hands. You really know how to tell your hands what to do. How did your hands do? What can you do to help your hands?	You did a great job of controlling your hands! You really know how to help yourself do things. That was a really smart/clever thing to do. Wow, it looks like your hands are having a hard time.

Vocabulary & concepts:

Positions: up, down Body parts: hands Speed: fast, slow(ly), in-between All by ourselves (point of pride: I did it all by myself!)	Locations: in, on, under, beside, behind, over, etc. Intensity: hard, strong, soft(ly), gentle, in-between

Introduction:

"From now on, we all need to control our hands by ourselves. If we need to use gentle hands, we can. If we need to use strong hands, we can. Sometimes, we can figure out ways to make it easier all by ourselves. Other times, we need help to make sure our hands can work well so we can ask for help. "If something gets in the way, what could you do to help yourself? See this (jar or other prop)? I need (strong) hands to (open it). What could I do to help myself?"

Use different materials and situations to model and promote self-advocacy.

Practice:

Proceed with games and/or activities. Set up situations where the child will encounter some challenges with self-regulating their hands. For example, difficult to open game parts or fast-paced activity that is hard for them to do. Wait for them to struggle a little bit before saying anything – see if they'll self-advocate.

Prompting:

If you see the child struggling with an object or situation involving their hands, wait a few seconds then ask them, "What could you do to help yourself?" Don't feel mean by not helping them – remember, we're helping them become more resourceful and self-reliant. If they seem uncertain, make a few suggestions and then have them enact one of the suggestions.

Be sure to praise them when they ask for help ("That's a smart thing to do. Sometimes adults can help you.") or uses some strategy to make it easier for them to control their hands or use them more effectively.

Self-monitoring:

Every second or third time the child performs an action, ask, "How did your hands do?"

I they encounter difficulties, wait, don't 'rescue them. Say, "Wow, it looks like your hands are having a hard time. What can you do to help your hands?"

Solidifying:

Help the child review (a) what skills and strategies were learned in the lesson, (b) why it helps to use them and (c) what they noticed when they used them. Some children won't be able to verbalize or indicate some of this information but try to prompt responses from them. Clarify and add information as needed.

Highlighting:

If they advocate for themselves, comment "Look at how you helped your hands. You really know how to help yourself do things."

Additional Comments:

Prompt the parents to let the child do (safe) activities on their own (with adult supervision) as much as possible and to count to at least 20 before saying or doing anything. Encourage them to ask the child, "What can you do to help yourself?" before offering any assistance or suggestions. Also, prompt them to comment whenever the child does something safe all by themselves, "Wow, look how you did that all by yourself. That's great!"

Lesson B:B1

Turtle Breathing is an important method for redirecting attention so the child can take a break and think only about the feel of breath come in and out of their nose. We are using it early in **spark*** so the child can experience what 'calm' feels like – that sensation of ease and quiet.

NOTE: Refer to the child's breath as doing the actions – not them. This 'compartmentalizes' their breathing and places the child in the position of teaching their breath, so they feel a sense of personal competence by being 'teacher'.

The goal in this lesson is to help the child learn to regulate their rate of breathing, with emphasis on a slower rate to help calm and center themselves.

Area of self-regulation 1: Behavior			
Area of focus 2: Breathing			
Area of skill development 1: Awareness of Ability			
Primary executive functions:		*Secondary executive functions*:	
	Inhibitory control		Planning and organization
	Self-monitoring		Working memory
	Cognitive flexibility		

Comments on executive functions: This activity requires the child to control their rate of breathing and begin to monitor their performance. Some cognitive flexibility is needed to perform the actions with less and less direction from an adult. There's little emphasis on planning and organization and working memory in the sense that only breathing is required each time and it's done in response to different models.

Task variation:

Change speed

Task structuring:

Directness of adult involvement: (1) Imitation of adult model, (2) imitation of pictured model, (3) verbal direction, (4) imitation of peer model

General organization and arrangement of the activity: Do three breaths in and out every time you practice slow Turtle Breathing.

Objectives:

The child will be able to use Turtle Breathing (1) by imitating the adult model, (2) by following a pictured model, (3) by doing as stated in the verbal directions, and (4) by imitating a peer model at least 80% of the time for each.

Materials:

- illustration of breathing (see Resource files – ILLUSTRATIONS – *Turtle Breathing*)

Language of spark* to use in this lesson:

Key words & phrases:

We, we're …	We can …
Let's …	The pictures/the words might trick you.
Look/listen really carefully.	
Oops, what did the picture show/my words say?	It was pretty good, but I think your Turtle Breathing could do better.
How did you do?	You're right, your Turtle Breathing really did a great job!
Did you do the Turtle Breathing okay?	
You really know how to do Turtle Breathing.	Did you help the other children do the Turtle Breathing okay?
Look at how you did your Turtle Breathing.	You really listened and watched your friend (the 'teacher').
You really know how to tell your breathing what to do.	____ you really worked hard to be a good teacher.

Vocabulary & concepts:

Turtle Breathing (slow)	*calm*
Teacher	

Introduction:

(1) "Now we're going to do breathing in a new way. We can breathe slowly like this turtle (show picture of turtle and demonstrate slow breathing through your mouth or nose). Feel the air come into your nose 1-2-3 and then out very slowly 1-2-3. This helps your brain and your body feel calm". Use the Turtle Breathing picture. "When we use our

Turtle Breathing, it helps our brains and our bodies feel calm. Do the same thing as me."

(2) "Let's practice our Turtle Breathing. This time we're going to do what the picture says. We won't use any words for the Turtle Breathing. You need to look carefully. Do what the picture shows."

(3) "This time we won't use any pictures, just words. You need to listen really carefully. When you hear me say "Turtle Breathing", do what the words say."

(4) "Today, one child is going to be the teacher. They're going to show us and tell us when to do our Turtle Breathing and other actions. We have to watch and listen and do what they say."

Practice:

(1) Do a fairly vigorous song or read an exciting story and at the end of every verse or book-page, model three slow Turtle Breaths for the children to do. Say, "Feel the air come into your nose and then out very slowly. This helps your brain and your body feel calm". Intersperse other actions.

(2) "Look really carefully. The pictures might trick you." Do the same as #1 above but hold up the Turtle Breathing card when you want them to use it.

(3) "Listen really carefully. You might miss something." Do the same as in #1 above but just say "Turtle Breathing" when you want the child to start doing it. Don't model it yourself. Only use verbal directions.

(4) Stand back and participate with the children. Let the 'teacher' take the lead. Use the same procedures as #1 above.

Prompting:

(1) "I can breathe really slowly. Make your breathing do the same". Feel the air come into your nose and then out very slowly. This helps your brain and your body feel calm. Use the Turtle Breathing picture.

(2) If the child makes an error, simply state "Oops, what did the picture show? Look carefully." Then model the action, saying, "I think the picture showed ___. Feel the air come into your nose and then out very slowly. This helps your brain and your body feel calm."

(3) If the child doesn't respond accurately, say, "Oops, what did my words say? Listen carefully." Then repeat the direction with, "The words said ___." If the child doesn't respond accurately on the second attempt, show them the picture associated with Turtle Breathing and model it if needed. Say, "Feel the air come into your nose and then out very slowly. This helps your brain and your body feel calm".

(4) Prompt the 'teacher' child only as necessary. If any of the other children are experiencing difficulty, direct your prompts to the 'teacher' so they can maintain their role.

Self-monitoring:

Every second or third time the child does Turtle Breathing practice, ask, "Did you do your Turtle Breathing okay?

Provide concise and honest information about their accuracy, for example, "It was pretty good, but I think your Turtle Breathing could be slower." or "You're right, your Turtle Breathing was really good!"

Solidifying:

Help the child review (a) what skills and strategies were learned in the lesson, (b) why it helps to use them and (c) what they noticed when they used them. Some children won't be able to verbalize or indicate some of this information but try to prompt responses from them. Clarify and add information as needed.

Highlighting:

"Look at how you made your breathing go slow. You really know how to do Turtle Breathing."

Additional Comments:

Lesson B:B2

Before starting this lesson, make sure you received feedback from families on times and places where each child needs to improve regulation of their calmness by using their Turtle Breathing.

Tell the child about times and places in your life where you need to use Turtle Breathing to help calm and center yourself. This helps let them know that they're not the only person who experiences these problems.

The goal in this lesson is to help the child learn where and when using their Turtle Breathing can help them calm their brain and body in day-to-day life.

Area of self-regulation 1: Behavior			
Area of focus 2: Breathing			
Area of skill development 2: Awareness of Need			
Primary executive functions:		*Secondary executive functions:*	
👁 👁	Cognitive flexibility		
	Inhibitory control		
	Planning and organization		
	Self-monitoring		
	Working memory		

Comments on executive functions: This activity requires the child to control their impulses, monitor their performance and deal with the social variables of everyday life. There's more emphasis on planning and organization and working memory because the child is now expected to do more thinking ahead and self-modulation of their breathing. Some cognitive flexibility will be required because of the shift among the different activities and settings.

Task variation:

Use in daily settings

Task structuring:

Directness of adult involvement: Self-directed

General organization and arrangement of the activity: The tasks in this lesson center around helping the child identify where and/or when they need to regulate their breathing. The places or times they identify are placed on the chart as they're discussed. Then each child will take the chart home to act as a reminder for them as well as a commitment.

Objective:

The child will be able to tell at least one specific important situation (times, places) per setting (home, pre-/school, community) where Turtle Breathing is important.

Materials:

- Awareness of Need chart (see Resource files - TEMPLATE – *Awareness of Need chart*) and ILLUSTRATIONS - *Topics for Awareness of Need charts - Behavioral self-regulation*.

- information from the parent's feedback on Newsletter #5 about times and places where the child needs improved calming – prepare pictures ahead of time

- storybooks where the character can use Turtle Breathing to help themselves stay calm and make good decisions (see Resource files - RESOURCES – *Storybooks coordinated with lesson target areas*)

Language of spark* to use in this lesson:

Key words & phrases:

We, we're … Did you use your Turtle Breathing? Look at how you used your Turtle Breathing.	Let's do Turtle Breathing so our brains and bodies can be calm. You really helped your body and your brain.

Vocabulary & concepts:

Turtle Breathing (slow)	calm

Introduction:

"Today, we're going to think about places where it's important to use our Turtle Breathing. Turtle Breathing can help our brains and bodies work better. For me, I need to use Turtle Breathing when I've got to think really hard. It helps me to make my body and my brain calm. I'm going to put a picture of an activity on my chart so will remind me to do my Turtle Breathing. Sometimes, when I get upset, my Turtle Breathing can help me stay calm. How about you? When can you do Turtle Breathing to help your brain and your body be calm?"

Practice:

Emphasize situations where doing a Turtle Breath can help the child give themselves a chance to self-regulate. Use ideas from the parents but also add things you've noticed. "Where do you need to use your Turtle Breathing? Where can you breathe really slowly to help your brain and your body? Let's put a picture on the chart for you." Add more pictures, getting at least one idea for each main location.

Read storybooks that show one or more of the characters or the reader in a dilemma or frustrating or annoying situation. Demonstrate use of Turtle Breathing and have the child join in to help the character/reader calm them/herself to deal more effectively with the problem.

Prompting:

If the child has difficulty coming up with ideas, suggest some from the list the family sent in and from your experience with them. You might want to start with less emotionally-charged, fairly innocuous situations. By the end of the session, be sure to have at least one or two more challenging situations for the child, like when they typically have a 'meltdown'.

Praise them more often than reminding them. Comment whenever you see them using Turtle Breathing.

Self-monitoring:

Ask the child, "How can you help yourself remember to use your Turtle Breathing when you're (location or time you and the child added to their Awareness of Need chart)?" Help them think of ways they can remind themselves.

Solidifying:

Help the child review (a) what skills and strategies were learned in the lesson, (b) why it helps to use Turtle Breathing and (c) what they noticed when they used it. Some children won't be able to verbalize or indicate some of this information but try to prompt responses from them. Clarify and add information as needed.

Highlighting:

If you see them using their Turtle Breathing, even if you prompted them to use it, highlight it. Say, "Look at how you used your Turtle Breathing. You really helped your body and your brain."

Additional Comments:

Prompt the child's family and others involved with them to use Turtle Breathing themselves in daily situations. Make sure they praise the child for any self-regulation they exercise. If they forget to use their Turtle Breathing, have them ask them what they should do. Have them use the prompting like that outlined above.

Lesson B:B3

In this lesson we use Turtle Breathing not only to redirect the child's attention but also as a chance to 'cool' down their emotions and thinking by focusing on pleasurable things and ridding themselves of other things and may be bothering them.

Before starting this lesson, be sure to get information from the family about the child's favorite objects, animals, people, smells, feels and tastes. This will help you complete the "I am calm" book with them.

The "I am clam" book is intended to be a fun activity that helps the child summarize the things they're learned to this point about things they can do while they do their Turtle Breathing. The focus with the 'visualizing' of favorite things and people is to cool down and stress, anxiety or emotion they're experiencing. This book is meant to be like a social story for the child to take home, and review on a frequent basis. You should make a copy of the book so you can review it with the child. It'll be helpful when you reach the Emotional Self-regulation unit.

The goal in this lesson is to help the child develop resilience and self-advocacy skills for when they need to calm themselves with Turtle Breathing.

Area of self-regulation 1: Behavior		
Area of focus 2: Breathing		
Area of skill development 3 & 4: Resilience and Self-advocacy		
Primary executive functions:	**Secondary executive functions**:	
Inhibitory control		
Cognitive flexibility		
Planning and organization		
Self-monitoring		
Working memory		

Comments on executive functions: This activity requires the child to control their impulses, monitor their performance and deal with the social variables of everyday life. There's more emphasis on planning and organization and working memory because the child is now expected to do more thinking ahead and spontaneous use of Turtle Breathing. Some cognitive flexibility will be required because of application of the self-regulation skills to different activities and settings.

Task variation:

Regulation of speed

Task structuring:

Directness of adult involvement: Self-directed

General organization and arrangement of the activity: Complete the "I am Calm" book so they increase the number of strategies available to them for remaining calm. Then use daily tasks that are challenging and exciting and give many opportunities for using Turtle Breathing to calm and center themselves.

Objective:

The child will be able to use Turtle Breathing and other calming strategies at least 50% of the time in appropriate situations.

Materials:

- *"I am Calm"* book (see Resource files - TEMPLATE - *I am calm book*)
- games and activities for practicing Turtle Breathing (see Resource files - RESOURCE - *Games for practicing self-regulation* and RESOURCES - *Internet sites coordinated with lesson activities*)

Language of spark* *to use in this lesson:*

Key words & phrases:

When we use our Turtle Breathing, it helps our brains and our bodies feel calm and work better.	You really know how to make your brain and your body be calm.
What are some other things you put in your book that can help you?	Let's make a picture in our heads of our favorite things/people.
How did you do?	Let's make some things float away from our brains.
What can you do to help yourself?	What did you do to help yourself be calm?
What do you want to float away?	

Vocabulary & concepts:

Turtle Breathing (slow)	Calm
	Making a picture in our heads

Introduction:

"You've learned to use your Turtle Breathing so well. Now we're going to practice every day. To help you make your body and your brain calm, we're going to make a special book together. It's for you to take home, and read with your family. The book gives us some more ways to help your body and your brain be calm and work better."

Practice:

Complete the *"I am Calm"* book with the child.

Do an exciting and/or challenging activity and prompt them to use the ideas and images from *their "I am Calm"* book to help themselves.

Prompting:

Make sure you remind the child every so often about why we use Turtle Breathing: "When we use our Turtle Breathing, it helps our brains and our bodies feel calm and work better. What are some other things you put in your book that can help you?"

Remind the child about the images they put in their *"I am Calm"* book. Help them make those same images in their head.

Catch them using Turtle Breathing. Praise them more often than reminding them. Comment whenever you see them using their Turtle Breathing or other strategy, especially in situations where they need to calm themselves.

Self-monitoring:

While playing a game or doing an activity, when you see the child remaining calm, ask them how they did. Say, "You look nice and calm. What did you do to keep yourself calm?" Then respond positively if at all possible; for example, "You bet, you did a great job!" If they start to become anxious or excited, ask them, "What can you do to help yourself?"

Solidifying:

Help the child review (a) what skills and strategies were learned in the lesson, (b) why it helps to use them and (c) what they noticed when they used them. Some children won't be able to verbalize or indicate some of this information but try to prompt responses from them. Clarify and add information as needed.

Highlighting:

"Look at how you used your Turtle Breathing. You really helped your body and your brain be calm. I bet you made a really cool picture in your head of things and people you like."

Additional Comments:

Prompt the child's family and others involved with them to use Turtle Breathing and other strategies from the *"I am Calm"* book. Also, make sure they praise the child for any self-regulation they exercise, whether it involves their hands, Turtle Breathing or other calming strategies. If they forget, have them ask them what they should do. Have them use the prompting outlined in the lessons.

Ask them for feedback on how well the child does.

The Autistic Child's Guide

Lesson B:F1

Before starting this lesson, be sure to check each child's background information form to make sure they have no restrictions in relation to physical activity.

Send home Newsletter #6 which explains the current focus and requests suggestions for situations where the child needs to improve their foot self-regulation (important for the next lesson).

Send home any new songs or rhymes as well as some games they can play in the yard or park.

NOTE: Refer to the child's feet as doing the actions – not them. This 'compartmentalizes' their feet and places the child in the position of teaching their feet, so they feel a sense of personal competence by being 'teacher'.

The goal in this lesson is to help the child learn to regulate how fast, how hard and in what way they use their feet.

Area of Self-regulation 1: Behavior

Area of focus 3: Feet

Area of skill development 1: Awareness of Ability

Primary executive functions:		*Secondary executive functions*:	
	Cognitive flexibility		Planning and organization
	Inhibitory control		Working memory
	Self-monitoring		

Comments on executive functions: This activity requires the child to control their impulses and begin to monitor their performance. There's little emphasis on planning and organization and working memory in the sense that only single actions are required each time. Since a number of different variations as well as different models (adult, picture, peer) are used, the child's cognitive flexibility will receive a fairly significant 'stretch'.

Task variation:

Change (1) speed (2) intensity and (3) manner of actions

Task structuring:

Directness of adult involvement: (1) Imitation of adult model, (2) Imitation of pictured model,(3) follow verbal directions, and (4) imitate a peer.

General organization and arrangement of the activity: We continue stretching the child's flexibility by working on a new body part and introducing all task variations. Introduce the variations one at a time, adding more as you see the child successfully do it. Intermix the variations, challenging the child but also assuring success and fun.

Objective:

The child will be able to produce foot movements varying in speed, intensity and manner from (1) adult models, (2) illustrated variations, (3) verbal directions, and (4) peer models with at least 80% accuracy each.

Materials:

- rhymes and songs (see Resource files - MATERIAL - Selected songs and rhymes for the Behavioral Self-regulation)
- illustrations of foot movements (see Resource files - EXAMPLE - *Foot or body movements*)
- illustrations of symbols of different speeds, intensities, manners (see Resource files - ILLUSTRATIONS – *Action intensity variation, Action speed variations and Action manner variations*)

Language of spark* to use in this lesson:

Key words & phrases:

We're …	We can …
Let's …	Look how you made your feet …
Did your feet …?	You did that all by yourself.
How did your feet do?	Did my feet do okay?
You really know how to …	

Vocabulary & concepts:

Body parts: feet,	Intensity: hard, soft(ly), in-between
Speed: fast, slow(ly), in-between	Manner: animals, cartoon or video
Teacher	characters

Introduction:

(1) "Now we're going to make our feet move in different ways. We can make them move fast, slowly, and in between, softly, hard, and in between or like a kangaroo, elephant or (animé or cartoon character)". Show pictures of each variation and demonstrate). "First,

I'll be the model and show you which one to do. You do the same thing as me."

(2) Imitate pictured model: "This time, we're going to use just pictures to tell us what to do. Look really carefully. The pictures might trick you." Use a familiar song, rhyme or storybook and, when it comes time to perform the action, point to an illustration depicting the speed, intensity or manner.

(3) Follow verbal directions: "This time only words will tell you what to do. Listen really carefully. My words might trick you."

(4) Follow peer model: Now you're going to be the model and show me what I'm supposed to do. You be the teacher this time."

Practice:

Use illustrations of different rates of speed, intensities or manners. Allow the child to choose different speeds by selecting or pointing to one of the pictures.

As the child becomes more flexible in switching among variations, you can challenge them more by combining variations. For example, move like an elephant going softly/quietly or move your feet fast and hard. ·

Prompting:

There are no 'correct' ways to move your feet. Allow the child a fair amount of latitude in performing actions so long as their interpretations are plausible as actions for that concept or animal/character. They don't have to be identical to yours.

If the child makes an error, simply state "Oops, what did I do/the picture show/the words say/your friend do?" Then have the direction or model repeat and ask the child to try again.

Self-monitoring:

Every second or third time the child performs an action, ask, "How did your feet do?"

You can also ask them about your actions. Ask, "Did my feet do okay?" If they say "no", prompt them to explain what needs improvement and to show you how to do the action. You can do an action imprecisely to give the child a chance to correct you. This lets them know that it takes practice to teach your feet and also others can make mistakes.

Solidifying:

Help the child review (a) what skills and strategies were learned in the lesson, (b) why it helps to use them and (c) what they noticed when they used them. Some children won't be able to verbalize or indicate some of this information but try to prompt responses from them. Clarify and add information as needed.

Highlighting:

"Look at how you controlled your feet. You really know how to tell your feet what to do."

Additional Comments:

Lesson B:F2

Before starting this lesson, make sure you received feedback from families on times and places where each child needs to improve regulation of their feet.

Tell the child about times and places in your life where you have difficulty controlling your feet. This helps let them know that they're not the only person who experiences these problems.

The goal in this lesson is to help the child learn where and when they need to regulate the speed, intensity and manner of their foot movements.

Area of self-regulation 1: Behavior		
Area of focus 3: Feet		
Area of skill development 2: Awareness of Need		
Primary executive functions:	**Secondary executive functions:**	
Cognitive flexibility		
Inhibitory control		
Planning and organization		
Self-monitoring		
Working memory		

Comments on executive functions: This activity requires the child to control their impulses, monitor their performance and deal with the social variables of everyday life. There's more emphasis on planning and organization and working memory because the child is now expected to do more thinking ahead and self-modulation of their actions. Cognitive flexibility will be required because of the shift among the different activities and settings.

Task variation:

Use in daily settings

Task structuring:

Directness of adult involvement: Self-directed

General organization and arrangement of the activity: The tasks in this lesson center around helping the child identify where and/or when they need to regulate their feet. The places or times they identify are placed on the Awareness of Need chart as they're discussed. Then the child takes the chart home, and shares it with their family. The chart can act as a reminder for them as well as a commitment.

When playing exciting games, be sure to do some Turtle Breathing with the child between rounds of the game and/or between games. This will help them stay centered and calmer.

Objective:

The child will be able to tell at least one specific important situation (times, places) per setting (home, pre-/school, community) where self-regulation of their feet is important.

Materials:

- Awareness of Need chart (see Resource files - ILLUSTRATIONS - *Topics for Awareness of Need charts - Behavioral self-regulation*)

- information from the parent's feedback on Newsletter #6 about times and places where the child needs improved control – prepare pictures ahead of time

- games for practicing self-regulation (see Resource files - MATERIAL - *Games for practicing behavioral self-regulation*)

Language of spark* to use in this lesson:

Key words & phrases:

We're …	Look how you made your feet …
How did your feet do?	You really know how to …
	Feet, you need to ….

Vocabulary & concepts:

Body parts: feet	Intensity: hard, soft, in-between
Speed: fast, slow, in-between	Manner: animals, cartoon or video characters

Introduction:

"Today, we're going to think about places where it's important to control our feet. For me, it's sometimes hard to control my feet when I walk down the stairs. My feet want to go fast and sometimes I fall down and hurt myself. I need to tell my feet to walk slowly on the stairs. I am going to put a picture of stairs right here (on chart) so will remind me."

Practice:

"Where do you need to control your feet? Let's put a picture on the chart for you." Add more pictures, getting at least one idea for each main location. Be sure to provide the child with a reason why they should move differently in each situation. For example, we use our quiet, slow feet at the library so we're quiet and don't distract anybody from their reading. At the end of the practice session, review the chart with the child.

Play some exciting stop-and-go type games (see Resource files) at first indoors. If at all possible, play the games outdoors but only where it's safe, preferably a fenced area. This outdoor space or a large indoor space can really 'test' the child's self-regulation.

Prompting:

If the child has difficulty coming up with ideas of where and when they need to self-regulate their feet, suggest some from the family's list and from your experience with them. By the end of the session, be sure to have at least one or two more challenging situations on the child's chart.

During all activities, catch them using self-regulation. Praise them more often than reminding them. Comment whenever you see them controlling their feet, especially in situations where they could have done something else.

If they're about to attempt some action (like running where it's not appropriate), intercede as quickly as possible with: "What do you need to tell your feet?" Prompt the child to say: "Feet, you need to _____." Then remind them that they can control their own feet and tell them you have confidence that they'll remember next time.

Self-monitoring:

Ask the child, "How can you help yourself remember to tell your feet what to do when you're (location or time you and the child added to their Awareness of Need chart)?" Help them think of ways they can remind themselves.

Solidifying:

Help the child review (a) what skills and strategies were learned in the lesson, (b) why it helps to use them and (c) what they noticed when they used them. Some children won't be able to verbalize or indicate some of this information but try to prompt responses from them. Clarify and add information as needed.

Highlighting:

Review all of the information on the child's Awareness of Need chart at the end of the session to help remind the child of their need to control their feet.

Whenever possible, comment: "Look at how you controlled your feet. You really watched your feet and told them what to do."

Additional Comments:

Inform the parents and other people involved with the child of the areas you and they identified for foot control. Prompt them to model regulating their own feet. Ask them to remind the child before entering a targeted situation about the need to tell their feet to be in control. Also, make sure they praise the child for any self-regulation they exercise. If they forget to self-regulate their feet, have them ask them, "What can you do to help yourself?" Have them use the prompting outlined above.

Ask them for feedback on how well the child does.

Lesson B:F3

Send home Newsletter #7 during this lesson to prepare the family for the next set of lessons.

The goal in this lesson is to help the child develop resilience and self-advocacy skills for when they need to regulate their feet.

Area of self-regulation 1: Behavior		
Area of focus 3: Feet		
Area of skill development 3 & 4: Resilience and Self-advocacy		
Primary executive functions:		**Secondary executive functions:**
	Cognitive flexibility	
	Inhibitory control	
	Planning and organization	
	Self-monitoring	
	Working memory	

Comments on executive functions: This activity requires the child to control their impulses, monitor their performance and deal with the social variables of everyday life. There's more emphasis on planning and organization and working memory because the child is now expected to do more thinking ahead and self-modulation of their actions. Cognitive flexibility will be required because of application of the self-regulation skills to different activities and settings.

Task variation:

Regulation of speed, intensity and manner

Task structuring:

Directness of adult involvement: Self-directed

General organization and arrangement of the activity: Use challenging activities, like tag and other chase or stop-and-go games, to help them develop more resilience and be able to self-regulate even when tempted or excited. Vary the action for each turn by specifying or having the child specify which movement variation to use (such as fast, loud, like a dinosaur). Practice outdoors but make sure it's in a safe, fenced area. Outdoor spaces can really 'test' the child's self-regulation.

Set up a few situations where the child will have to ask for assistance/change or make the change themselves in order to help themselves control their feet. For example, you may introduce them to an open area that normally tempts them to run or a game that's set at too rapid (or slow) a rate.

If possible, go for walks and visits in the community to practice – just make sure they're sufficiently safe and you have an adequate child-to-staff ratio.

Objective:

The child will be able to exhibit self-regulation of their feet at least 80% of the time in their typical learning environment and to ask for help or arrange a task or situation to facilitate their foot control at least 50% of the time in daily settings.

Materials:

- Storybooks about characters who have difficulty regulating their feet (see Resource files - RESOURCES – *Storybooks coordinated with lesson target areas*)
- games for practicing self-regulation (see Resource files - MATERIAL - *Games for practicing self-regulation*)

Language of spark* to use in this lesson:

Key words & phrases:

We're ...	We can ...
How did your feet do?	Look how you made your feet ...
You really know how to ...	You did that all by yourself.
What could you do to help yourself?	

Vocabulary & concepts:

Body parts: feet	Intensity: hard, soft, in-between
Speed: fast, slow, in-between	Manner: animals, cartoon or video characters

Introduction:

"You learned to control your feet so well. Now we're going to practice and make it a little bit harder. Let's see how we all do. If we need to use slow feet, we can. If we need to use fast feet, we can. Sometimes, we can tell our feet what to do. Sometimes, other people need to help us. Remember to use your Turtle Breathing to help your brain and your body be calm."

Describe different problems and ask the child how they could help themselves or ask for help: "If something gets in the way, what could you do to help yourself? If I go to walk upstairs, I need slow feet. What could I do to help myself?"

Practice:

Read storybooks about characters who have difficulty self-regulating their feet. Prompt the child to act out the story.

Play tag and other chase or stop-and-go games. Vary the action for each turn by specifying or having the child specify which movement variation to use. Practice outdoors if a safe, fenced area is available.

Set up a few situations where the child will have to ask for assistance/change or make the change themselves in order to help themselves control their feet.

If possible, go for walks and visits in the community to practice, especially in locations where the child had difficulties in the past. Ensure that the child-to-adult ratio is sufficient to make sure every child is safe.

Prompting:

Catch the child using self-regulation. Praise them more often than reminding them. Comment whenever you see them controlling their feet, especially in situations where they could have done something else.

If they do something with their feet that shows lack of self-regulation, stop them and ask: "What do you need to tell your feet?" Prompt the child to tell their feet: "Feet, you need to _____." Then remind them that they can control their own feet and tell them you have confidence that they'll remember next time.

Self-monitoring:

Every second or third turn in a game, ask the child how they did. Ask, "How did your feet do?" Then respond positively if at all possible; for example, "You bet, you did a great job of controlling your feet!"

Solidifying:

Help the child review (a) what skills and strategies were learned in the lesson, (b) why it helps to use them and (c) what they noticed when they used them. Some children won't be able to verbalize or indicate some of this information but try to prompt responses from them. Clarify and add information as needed.

Highlighting:

"Look at how you controlled your feet. You really watched your feet and told them what to do."

If they advocate for themselves, comment "Look at how you helped your feet. You really know how to help yourself do things."

Additional Comments:

Prompt the child's family to model and comment on control of their own feet. It's helpful if they 'forget' sometimes and then self-correct while commenting out loud. For example, they might start running up the stairs then stop and remind themselves to use normal speed because they might hurt themselves (giving a reason is very important). This lets the child see that other people forget sometimes but they can fix things up.

Make sure they praise the child for any self-regulation they exercise. If they forget to self-regulate their feet, have them ask them what they should do. Have them use the prompting outlined above.

Encourage the family and others to take the child to locations where they can practice their self-regulation. Remind them to prompt and praise their efforts.

Ask them for feedback on how well the child does.

Lesson B:V1

NOTE: Refer to the child's voice as doing the actions – not them. This 'compartmentalizes' their voice and places the child in the position of teaching their voice, so they feel a sense of personal competence by being 'teacher'.

The goal in this lesson is to help the child develop the ability to regulate the volume of their voice.

Area of Self-regulation *1*: Behavior			
Area of focus 4: Voice			
Area of skill development 1: Awareness of Ability			
Primary executive functions:		*Secondary executive functions*:	
	Inhibitory control		Cognitive flexibility
	Self-monitoring		Planning and organization
	Working memory		

Comments on executive functions: This activity requires the child to control their impulses with regard to voice loudness and begin to monitor it. Working memory is involved somewhat because the child is expected to recall songs and stories used to practice voice regulation. There's little emphasis on planning and organization or cognitive flexibility since only single actions are required each time.

Task variation:

Change intensity

Task structuring:

Directness of adult involvement: (1) Imitation of adult model, (2) Imitation of pictured model, (3) follow verbal directions and (4) imitate a peer.

General organization and arrangement of the activity: We continue stretching the child's flexibility by working on a new body part and introducing all variations. Introduce the variations one at a time, adding more as you see the child successfully do it. Intermix the variations, challenging the child but also assuring success and fun.

Objective:

The child will be able to produce different voice volumes from (1) adult models, (2) illustrated variations, (3) verbal directions, and (4) peer models with at least 80% accuracy each.

Materials:

- rhymes and songs (see Resource files - MATERIAL - Selected songs and rhymes for the Behavioral Self-regulation and RESOURCES - *Internet sites coordinated with lesson activities*) and storybooks (see Resource files - RESOURCES – *Storybooks coordinated with lesson target areas*)

- picture stimuli of different voice intensities (see Resource files - ILLUSTRATIONS - *Voice intensity variations*)

Language of spark* to use in this lesson:

Key words & phrases:

We're …	We can …
Let's …	Look how you made your voice …
Did your voice …?	You did that all by yourself.
How did your voice sound?	Did my voice sound okay?
You really know how to …	

Vocabulary & concepts:

Body parts: voice	Intensity: loud, quiet, normal
Teacher	

Introduction:

(1) "Now we're going to make our voices do different things. We can make our voice quiet (show picture of quiet voice and demonstrate whispering). We can make a loud voice (show picture of loud voice and demonstrate speaking loudly). We can make a normal voice (continue speaking at your normal volume). First, I'll be the model and show you which one to do. You do the same thing as me."

(2) Imitate pictured model: "This time, we're going to use just pictures to tell us what to do. Look really carefully. The pictures might trick you." Use a familiar song, rhyme or storybook and, when it comes time to change loudness, point to an illustration depicting the intensity.

(3) Follow verbal directions: "This time only words will tell you what to do. Listen really carefully. My words might trick you."

(4) Follow peer model: Now you're going to be the model and show me what I'm supposed to do. You be the teacher this time."

Practice:

During a song or rhyme, select loudness level for sections of it. Use illustrations of the different intensities. Allow the child to choose different loudness levels by selecting or pointing to one of the pictures.

Always accompany voice loudness with key intensity words so the child becomes familiar with them.

Prompting:

"Does my voice sound (loud/soft/normal)? Make your voice sound like mine (for adult modeling)/the picture (for picture models)/what the words said (for verbal directions)/like your friend showed (for per modeling)? You're right. You did a great job telling your voice how to sound."

Have the child judge how you did. Ask them, "Did my voice sound okay?" If they say "no", prompt them to explain what needs improvement and to show you how to make the voice. You can also use a voice loudness that's not appropriate to give the child a chance to correct you. This lets them know that it takes practice to teach your voice and also others can make mistakes.

Self-monitoring:

After the child has a chance to change their voice volume, ask, "How did your voice do? Was it loud/soft/normal?"

Solidifying:

Help the child review (a) what skills and strategies were learned in the lesson, (b) why it helps to use them and (c) what they noticed when they used them. Some children won't be able to verbalize or indicate some of this information but try to prompt responses from them. Clarify and add information as needed.

Highlighting:

"Look at how you made your voice go loud sometimes, soft sometimes and then normal again. You really know how to tell your voice what to do."

Additional Comments:

Lesson B:V2

Before starting this lesson, make sure you received feedback from families on times and places where each child needs to improve regulation of their feet from Newsletter #7.

Tell the child about times and places in your life where you have difficulty controlling your voice. This helps let them know that they're not the only person who experiences these problems.

The goal in this lesson is to help the child learn where and when they need to regulate the volume of their voice.

Area of self-regulation 1: Behavior			
Area of focus 3: Voice			
Area of skill development 2: Awareness of Need			
Primary executive functions:		**Secondary executive functions:**	
	Cognitive flexibility		
	Inhibitory control		
	Planning and organization		
	Self-monitoring		
	Working memory		

Comments on executive functions: This activity requires the child to control their voice volume, monitor their performance and deal with the social variables of everyday life. There's more emphasis on planning and organization and working memory because the child is now expected to do more thinking ahead and self-modulation of their voice. Cognitive flexibility will be required because of the shift among the different activities and settings.

Task variation:

Use in daily settings

Task structuring:

Directness of adult involvement: Self-directed

General organization and arrangement of the activity: The tasks in this lesson center around helping the child identify where and/or when they need to regulate their voice. The places or times they identify are placed on the Awareness of Need chart as they're discussed. Then the child takes the chart home, and shares it with their family. The chart can act as a reminder for them as well as a commitment.

When playing exciting games or songs/rhymes, be sure to do some Turtle Breathing with the child between rounds and/or between games/songs/rhymes. This will help them stay centered and calmer.

Objective:

The child will be able to tell at least one important situation (times, places) per setting (home, pre-/school, community) where self-regulation of their voice is important.

Materials:

- Awareness of Need chart (see Resource files - TEMPLATE – *Awareness of Need chart*) and topic picture (see Resource files - ILLUSTRATIONS - *Topics for Awareness of Need charts - Behavioral self-regulation*)

- information from the parent's feedback on Newsletter #7 about times and places where the child needs improved control – prepare pictures ahead of time

- games and songs/rhymes for practicing self-regulation (see Resource files - MATERIAL – *Games for practicing self-regulation*, RESOURCES - *Internet sites coordinated with lesson activities* and MATERIAL - *Selected songs and rhymes for the Behavioral Self-regulation*)

- pictures of different voice intensities (see Resource files - ILLUSTRATIONS - *Voice intensity variations*)

Language of spark* to use in this lesson:

Key words & phrases:	
We're …	Look how you made your voice …
How did your voice do?	You really know how to …
How was your voice?	Voice, you need to ….

Vocabulary & concepts:	
Body parts: voice	Intensity: loud, quiet, normal

Introduction:

"Today, we're going to think about places where it's important to control our voices. For me, it's sometimes hard to control my voice when I'm angry at home. My voice wants to go really loud and sometimes I forget and really scare other people. I need to tell my voice to be quieter. I am going to put a picture of angry me right here (on chart) so will remind me."

Practice:

"Where do you need to control your voice? Let's put a picture on the chart for you." Add more pictures, getting at least one idea for each main location. At the end of the practice session, review the chart with the child.

"Now let's sing some songs and pretend we are singing them in different places." Use situations from each child's Awareness of Need chart as well as places where it's okay to use a loud voice. Sing sections of songs pretending you're in the different locations. For example, "Let's pretend we're at the library/playground, how would we sing our song?"

Prompting:

If the child has difficulty coming up with ideas of where and when they need to self-regulate their voice, suggest some from the family's list and from your experience with them. By the end of the session, be sure to have at least one or two more challenging situations for the child.

During all activities, catch them using self-regulation! Praise them more often than reminding them. Comment whenever you see them controlling their voice, especially in situations where they could have done something else.

If they start using an inappropriate voice volume (too loud or too soft), intercede as quickly as possible with: "What do you need to tell your voice? This is a place for a normal voice." Prompt the child to say: "Voice, you need to be normal." Then remind them that they can control their own voice and tell them you have confidence that they'll remember next time.

Self-monitoring:

Ask the child, "How can you help yourself remember to tell your voice what to do when you're (location or time you and the child added to their Awareness of Need chart)?" Help them think of ways they can remind themselves.

Solidifying:

Help the child review (a) what skills and strategies were learned in the lesson, (b) why it helps to use them and (c) what they noticed when they used them. Some children won't be able to verbalize or indicate some of this information but try to prompt responses from them. Clarify and add information as needed.

Highlighting:

Review all of the information on the child's Awareness of Need chart at the end of the lesson.

During any activity, comment: "Look at how you controlled your voice. You really listened to your voice and told it what to do."

Additional Comments:

Inform other people involved with the child of the areas you and they identified for voice control. Prompt them to model regulating their own voice. Ask them to remind the child before entering a targeted situation about the need to tell their voice to be in control. Also, make sure they praise the child for any self-regulation they exercise. If they forget to self-regulate their voice, have them ask them what they should do. Have them use the prompting outlined above.

Ask them for feedback on how well the child does.

Lesson B:V3

Send home Newsletter #8 during this lesson to prepare the family for the next set of lessons. Be sure to include pictures of yoga positions and information on yoga resources and children's games (like tag) so parents and the whole family can become more involved.

The goal in this lesson is to help the child develop resilience and self-advocacy skills for when they need to regulate their voice.

Area of self-regulation 1: Behavior

Area of focus 3: Voice

Area of skill development 3: Resilience and Self-advocacy

Primary executive functions:		Secondary executive functions:	
	Cognitive flexibility		
	Inhibitory control		
	Planning and organization		
	Self-monitoring		
	Working memory		

Comments on executive functions: This activity requires the child to control their voice volume, monitor it and deal with the social variables of everyday life. There's more emphasis on planning and organization and working memory because the child is now expected to do more thinking ahead and self-modulation of their voice. Cognitive flexibility will be required because of application of the self-regulation skills to different activities and settings.

Task variation:

Use in daily settings

Task structuring:

Directness of adult involvement: Self-directed

General organization and arrangement of the activity: Use challenging activities, like tag and other chase or stop-and-go games, to help them develop more resilience and be able to self-regulate even when tempted or excited. Vary the action for each turn by specifying or having the child specify which voice volume to use (such as loud, quiet, normal). Practice outdoors making sure it's in a safe, fenced area. In outdoor spaces, they can use their loud voice.

Read storybooks about characters who have difficulty self-regulating their voice. Prompt the child to act out the story.

Set up a few situations where the child will have to ask for assistance/change or make the change themselves in order to help themselves control their voice. For example, you may introduce them to an open area that normally tempts them to use a loud voice or an exciting game that's indoors. Prompt them to use Turtle Breathing to calm themselves.

If possible, go for walks and visits in the community to practice – just make sure they're sufficiently safe for them and you have an adequate child-to-adult ratio.

Objective:

The child will be able to exhibit self-regulation of their voice at least 80% of the time in their typical learning environment and to ask for, arrange a task or situation to facilitate their voice control at least 50% of the time in daily settings.

Materials:

- storybooks with characters having difficulty self-regulating their voices (see Resource files - RESOURCES – *Storybooks coordinated with lesson target areas*)
- games for practicing self-regulation (see Resource files - MATERIAL – *Games for practicing self-regulation* and RESOURCES - *Internet sites coordinated with lesson activities*)

Language of spark* to use in this lesson:

Key words & phrases:

We're ...	We can ...
How did your voice do?	Look how you made your voice ...
You really know how to ...	You did that all by yourself.
What could you do to help yourself?	

Vocabulary & concepts:

Body parts: voice	Intensity: loud, quiet, normal

Introduction:

"You learned to control your voice so well. Now we're going to practice and make it a little bit harder. Let's see how we all do. If we need to use quiet voice, we can. If we need to use loud voice, we can. Sometimes, we need help to make sure our voice isn't too loud or too quiet. Sometimes, other people need to help us. Remember to use your Turtle Breathing to help your brain and your body be calm."

"If your voice is too loud or too quiet, what could you do to help yourself? If I go to the library, I need a quiet voice. What could I do to help myself?" Use different situations to model and promote self-advocacy.

Practice:

Read storybooks about characters who have difficulty self-regulating their voice. Prompt the child to act out the story but bring themselves back into self-regulation, such as by using Turtle Breathing.

Play tag and other chase or stop-and-go games. Vary the voice volume for each turn by specifying or having the child specify which loudness to use or locations associated with different voice loudness. Practice outdoors where loud voices are okay but quiet voices are difficult to hear.

If possible, go for walks and visits in the community to practice, especially in locations where the child had difficulties in the past.

Prompting:

Catch them using self-regulation. Praise them more often than reminding them. Comment whenever you see them controlling their voice, especially in situations where they could have done something else.

If they start using an inappropriate voice volume (too loud or too soft), intercede as quickly as possible with: "What do you need to tell your voice? This is a place for a normal/quiet voice." Prompt the child to say: "Voice, you need to be normal/quiet." Then remind them that they can control their own voice and tell them you have confidence that they'll remember next time.

Self-monitoring:

Every second or third turn in a game, ask, "How did your voice do?" Then respond positively if at all possible; for example, "You bet, you did a great job of controlling your voice!"

Solidifying:

Help the child review (a) what skills and strategies were learned in the lesson, (b) why it helps to use them and (c) what they noticed when they used them. Some children won't be able to verbalize or indicate some of this information but try to prompt responses from them. Clarify and add information as needed.

Highlighting:

"Look at how you controlled your voice. You really listened to your voice and told it what to do."

If they advocate for themselves, comment "Look at how you helped your voice. You really know how to help yourself do things."

Additional Comments:

Prompt the child's family to model and comment on control of their own voice volume. It's helpful if they 'forget' sometimes and then self-correct while commenting out loud on it. This lets the child see that other people forget sometimes but they can fix things up.

Make sure they praise the child for any self-regulation they exercise. If they forget to self-regulate their voice, have them ask them what they should do. Have them use the prompting outlined above.

Encourage the family and others to take the child to locations where they can practice their self-regulation. Be sure to remind them to prompt and praise their efforts.

Lesson B:W1

Before starting this lesson, be sure to check each child's background information form to make sure they have no restrictions in relation to physical activity.

In this set of lessons, we use yoga as a means to experience whole body calm. This is intermixed with high energy activities so each child experiences the differences in activities that involve higher speed and intensity and those that emphasize calm.

NOTE: Refer to the child's body as doing the actions – not them. This 'compartmentalizes' their body and places the child in the position of teaching their body, so they feel a sense of personal competence by being 'teacher'.

The goal in this lesson is to help the child develop a stronger understanding of their ability to make their body calm and centered as well as make it move at different speeds and intensities.

Area of self-regulation 1: Behavior		
Area of focus 5: Whole body		
Area of skill development 1: Awareness of Ability		
Primary executive functions:	**Secondary executive functions:**	
Cognitive flexibility		
Inhibitory control		
Planning and organization		
Self-monitoring		
Working memory		

Comments on executive functions: This activity requires the child to control their impulses and monitor their own performance. There's some emphasis on planning and organization and working memory since more complex movement patterns are being requested of them. Since a number of different variations as well as different models (adult, picture, peer) are used, the child's cognitive flexibility will receive a fairly significant 'stretch'.

Task variation:

Change location/position, speed, intensity, manner

Task structuring:

Directness of adult involvement: (1) Imitation of adult model, (2) Imitation of pictured model (3)follow verbal directions, and (4) imitate a peer.

General organization and arrangement of the activity: We continue stretching the child's cognitive flexibility by working on the whole body and introducing all variations – we'll also work on their body flexibility with the yoga exercises. Intermix the variations, challenging the child but also assuring success and fun.

Yoga uses a calm slow pace with careful coordination between breathing (asanas) and body positions (pranayamas). A session usually starts with a warm-up and centering on breathing and loosening the body, then on to a range of movements for the spine and finally to relaxation once again at the end. These different movements are done in a gentle, slow, flowing manner, allowing the body to experience each state and keeping breathing steady and not rushed.

When doing yoga, prompt the child to take a Turtle Breath before assuming a pose and then take another one once they're attained the position.

Be sure to incorporate breathing with each slower-paced activity as well as for the yoga positions. It should also be used in between faster or more vigorously paced activities. We're aiming toward having the child use breathing to help calm and center themselves.

Objective:

The child will be able to produce whole body movements varying in speed, intensity and manner from (1) adult models, (2) illustrated variations, (3) verbal directions, and (4) peer models with at least 80% accuracy each.

Materials:

- rhymes and songs (see Resource files - MATERIAL - Selected songs and rhymes for the Behavioral Self-regulation and RESOURCES - *Internet sites coordinated with lesson activities)*

- illustrations of action speeds, intensities and manners (see Resource files - ILLUSTRATIONS – *Action intensity variation, Action speed variations and Action manner variations)*

- illustrations of yoga positions (see Resource files - ILLUSTRATIONS - *Yoga positions* for the illustrations and RESOURCES - Commercially available books and materials) as well as suggestions for developing a yoga program or sequence (SEE Resource files - MATERIAL - *Designing a yoga program)*

Language of spark* *to use in this lesson:*	
Key words & phrases:	
We're ...	We can ...
Let's ...	I need your help.
Did your body ...?	Look how you made your body ...
How did your body do?	You did that all by yourself.
You really know how to ...	Did my body do okay?
Vocabulary & concepts:	
Body parts: body, hands, feet, voice	Intensity: hard/loud,
Speed: fast, slow(ly), in-between	soft(ly)/quiet(ly), in-between
Teacher	Names of yoga positions

Introduction:

(1) "Now we're going to make our body move in different ways. We can make them move fast, slowly, and in between, softly, hard, and in between or like a mountain or a dog. First, I'll be the model and show you which one to do. You do the same thing as me." For the yoga positions, associate the appropriate labels with each pose so the child can learn to assume it just by name.

(2) Imitate pictured model: "This time, we're going to use just pictures to tell us what to do. Look really carefully. The pictures might trick you." Use a familiar song, rhyme or storybook and, when it comes time to perform the action, point to an illustration depicting the location, speed, intensity or manner. You can also use pictured models with familiar yoga poses.

(3) Follow verbal directions: "This time only words will tell you what to do. Listen really carefully. My words might trick you." For the yoga positions, associate the appropriate labels with each pose so the child can learn to assume it just by name.

(4) Follow peer model: Now you're going to be the model and show me what I'm supposed to do. You be the teacher this time."

Practice:

As needed during games, use illustrations of different rates of speed, intensities or yoga positions. Allow the child to choose different speeds, intensities or positions by selecting or pointing to one of the pictures.

Prompting:

If the child makes an error, simply state "Oops, what did I do/the picture show/the words say/your friend do? Look carefully." Then repeat the direction. If the child doesn't respond accurately on the second attempt, point out the position in the picture and help them put their body in the position.

Self-monitoring:

Every second or third time the child performs an action, ask, "How did your body do?" Provide concise and honest information about their accuracy, for example, "It was pretty good, but I think your body could do better." or "You're right, your body really did a great job!"

You can also ask the child to give you feedback. Ask them, "Did my body do okay?" If they say "no", prompt them to explain what needs improvement and to show you how to do the action. You can do an action imprecisely to give the child a chance to correct you. This lets them know that it takes practice to teach your body and also others can make mistakes.

Solidifying:

Help the child review (a) what skills and strategies were learned in the lesson, (b) why it helps to use them and (c) what they noticed when they used them. Some children won't be able to verbalize or indicate some of this information but try to prompt responses from them. Clarify and add information as needed.

Highlighting:

"Look at how you controlled your body. You really know how to tell your body what to do."

"Look at how you controlled your body. You really know how to tell your body what to do. You just listened (and watched) carefully and knew what to do"

Additional Comments:

Lesson B:W2

Before starting this lesson, be sure to have copies of the *"I can control my body"* comic book ready.

The comic is intended to be a fun activity that helps the child summarize the things they're learned to this point about controlling their hands, feet, voice and body. There's also an opportunity for the child to identify when and where they don't have to self-regulate. This book is meant to be like a social story for the child to take home, and review on a frequent basis. You should make a copy of the book so you can review it with the child also.

NOTE: the comic 'explosions' included in the comic book were selected carefully to be non-violent. If you wish to add any 'explosions' of your own, please ensure that they're positive and non-violent.

During this lesson, tell the child about times and places in your life where you have difficulty controlling your body. This helps let them know that they're not the only person who experiences these problems.

The goal in this lesson is to help the child recall where and when they need to regulate their hands, breathing, feet, voice and learn more about when and where to regulate their whole body as well as when and where they can let loose.

Area of self-regulation 1: Behavior			
Area of focus 5: Whole body			
Area of skill development 2: Awareness of Need			
Primary executive functions:		**Secondary executive functions:**	
	Cognitive flexibility		
	Inhibitory control		
	Planning and organization		
	Self-monitoring		
	Working memory		

Comments on executive functions: This activity requires the child to control their impulses and old ways of doing things, monitor their performance and deal with the social variables of everyday life. There's more emphasis on planning and organization and working memory because the child is now expected to do more thinking ahead and self-modulation of their whole body. Cognitive flexibility will be required because of the shift among the different body parts, activities and settings.

Task variation:

Use in daily settings

Task structuring:

Directness of adult involvement: Self-directed

General organization and arrangement of the activity: The tasks in this lesson center around helping the child recall where and when they need to regulate their hands, feet and voice and learn where and when they can 'let loose' with their whole body. The information is placed in the *"I can control my body"* comic book – directions for completing this book are attached to it.

Objective:

The child will be able to tell at least one important situation (times, places) per setting (at home, school/preschool, in the community) where self-regulation of their hands, feet, and voice is important and places where they can let loose.

Materials:

- *"I can control my body"* comic book (see Resource files - TEMPLATE - *I can control my body comic book*).
- information from the parent's feedback on Newsletter #8 about times and places where the child needs improved control – prepare pictures ahead of time
- markers, scissors, pencils
- games for practicing self-regulation (see Resource files - MATERIAL – *Games for practicing self-regulation* and RESOURCES - *Internet sites coordinated with lesson activities*)
- illustrations of yoga positions (see Resource files - ILLUSTRATIONS - *Yoga positions*)

Language of spark* to use in this lesson:

Key words & phrases:	
I can control my hands, feet, voice, whole body. We're ... How did your body do?	Look how you made your body ... You really know how to ... Hands, feet, voice, body, you need to ....

Vocabulary & concepts:	
Body parts: hands, breathing, feet, voice, whole body	Control Fast, loud, stomp

Introduction:

"Today, we're going to make a really cool comic book for you to take home. The comic book even has 'explosions' for us to use to make it even cooler.

Let's look at it. Here's the cover – you can color it and decorate it. Here's the first page – it has places for us to put times when it's important to control your hands at home, at school and in one other place that you can decide. The next page is about controlling your feet and the next page is about controlling your voice. On the last page, we're going to think of places where you can make your body go fast, stomp your feet, and use a loud voice. Let's start by decorating the cover."

Practice:

Complete the comic book with the child. Encourage them to do as much as possible on their own. Activate their thinking. Provide guidance and prompting but have the child do as much as possible.

At the end of the practice session, review the comic book with the child.

Prompting:

If the child has difficulty coming up with ideas, suggest some from the family list and from your experience with them. Complete the comic book by the end of the session but you may wish to take breaks or complete it another time if the child begins tiring.

Catch them using self-regulation. Praise them more often than reminding them. Comment whenever you see them controlling their body, especially in situations where they could have done something else.

If they do something with their body that shows lack of self-regulation, stop them and ask: "What do you need to tell your hands, feet, voice, body?" Prompt the child to tell their body or body part: "_____, you need to be _____." Then remind them that they can control their own body and tell them you have confidence that they'll remember next time.

Self-monitoring:

Ask the child, "How can you help yourself remember to tell your body what to do when you're (location or time you and the child added to their Awareness of Need chart)?" Help them think of ways they can remind themselves.

Solidifying:

Help the child review (a) what skills and strategies were learned in the lesson, (b) why it helps to use them and (c) what they noticed when they used them. Some children won't be able to verbalize or indicate some of this information but try to prompt responses from them. Clarify and add information as needed.

Highlighting:

Whenever possible and appropriate, comment "Look at how you controlled your body. You really watched your body and told it what to do."

Additional Comments:

Make sure their comic book is reviewed with the child at home with great pride and pleasure from their family.

Ask the family to remind the child, before entering a targeted situation, about the need to tell their body to be in control.

Prompt them to encourage Turtle Breathing at home, and in other places to help the child calm and center themselves.

Encourage the family to model and comment on their own body control. Also, make sure they praise the child for any self-regulation they exercise. If they forget to self-regulate their body, have them ask them what they should do. Have them use the prompting outlined above.

Always be sure the family continues to give the child times when they can be totally dysregulated. They'll need consistent breaks from self-regulation.

Ask them for feedback on how well the child does.

Lesson B:W3

Send home Newsletter #9.

Before this lesson, copy and complete the Certificate of Completion (see Resources files – Certificate of completion - Behavioral self-regulation unit) and have it ready to give to the child. The Certificate of Completion is an opportunity to celebrate all the skills and strategies the child has learned to use in this unit. Be sure to present it to them with sincerity and respect.

The goal in this lesson is to help the child develop resilience and self-advocacy skills for when they need to regulate their hands, breathing, feet, voice and whole body.

Area of self-regulation 1: Behavior

Area of focus 5: Whole body

Area of skill development 3 & 4: Resilience and Self-advocacy

Primary executive functions:		**Secondary executive functions**:	
	Cognitive flexibility		
	Inhibitory control		
	Planning and organization		
	Self-monitoring		
	Working memory		

Comments on executive functions: This activity requires the child to control their impulses, monitor their performance and deal with the social variables of everyday life. There's more emphasis on planning and organization and working memory because the child is now expected to do more thinking ahead and self-modulation of their actions. Cognitive flexibility will be required to apply the self-regulation skills to different activities and settings.

Task variation:

Regulation of location, speed, intensity and manner

Task structuring:

Directness of adult involvement: Self-directed

General organization and arrangement of the activity: Use a variety of activities the child enjoys and finds exciting. Don't hold back on new experiences as much as in the past because, by now, the child should have fairly solid self-regulation skills.

Continue enjoying songs, rhymes and storybooks that incorporate different actions, especially ones that are exciting and require more self-regulation.

Objective:

The child will be able to exhibit self-regulation of their body at least 60% of the time in their everyday environments and will be able to ask for, arrange a situation or use self-talk to facilitate their whole body control at least 50% of the time in daily settings.

Materials:

- rhymes and songs that are stimulating and exciting and require stop-go actions (see Resource files - MATERIAL - Selected songs and rhymes for the Behavioral Self-regulation and RESOURCES - *Internet sites coordinated with lesson activities*)
- Stop and Go signs (see Resource files - ILLUSTRATIONS - *Stop and Go signs*)
- storybooks about characters that are dysregulated (see Resource files - RESOURCES – *Storybooks coordinated with lesson target areas*)
- illustrations of yoga positions (see Resource files - ILLUSTRATIONS - *Yoga positions*)
- Take a rest and Stop-think songs (see Resource files MATERIAL - *Songs to help regain Self-regulation*)
- games for practicing self-regulation (see Resource files - MATERIAL – *Games for practicing self-regulation* and RESOURCES - *Internet sites coordinated with lesson activities*)

Introduction:

"You learned to control your body so well. Now we're going to practice every day. Let's see how we all do. Remember to use your Turtle Breathing to help your brain and body."

"I've got a special song that helps me control my body. It's called Stop and Think. Let's give it a try."

"From now on, we all need to help our bodies so they can work well for us. If we need to use a quiet and slow body, we can. If we need to use fast body, we can. Sometimes, we need help to make sure our bodies can work well. Sometimes, other people need to help us. Remember to use your Turtle Breathing to help your brain and body be calm."

"If something gets in the way, what could you do to help ourselves? See this (balloon or other tempting prop)? I want to go and touch it and maybe pop it. I don't think I'm supposed to. What could I do to help myself?" Demonstrate use of Turtle Breathing and show how to put the prop away.

Practice:

Read storybooks about characters who have difficulty self-regulating any of their boy parts. Prompt the child to act out the story.

Play tag and other chase or stop-and-go games. Vary the action for each turn by specifying or having the child specify which movement variation to use. Practice outdoors.

Set up a few situations where the child will have to ask for assistance/change or make the change themselves in order to help themselves control their body.

If possible, go for walks and visits in the community to practice, especially in locations where the child had difficulties in the past.

Prompt the child to take a Turtle Breath before entering and while in challenging settings so they can calm and re-center themselves. You can sing the Stop-Think song quietly with them to help them regain equilibrium.

Continue practicing yoga and Turtle Breathing.

Continue enjoying rhymes, songs and storybooks that incorporate different action variations.

Prompting:

Catch them using self-regulation. Praise them more often than reminding them. Comment whenever you see them controlling their body, especially in situations where they could have done something else.

Prompt the child to sing the Stop-Think song to themselves and do their Turtle Breathing in stimulating situations.

If they're about to attempt some action, intercede as quickly as possible with: "What do you need to tell your (body part)?" Prompt the child to tell their body or body part: "_____, you need to be _____." Then remind them that they can control their own body and tell them you have confidence that they'll remember next time.

If you see the child struggling with an object or situation involving their self-regulation of their body, ask them, "What could you do to help yourself?" Don't feel mean by not helping them – remember, we are helping them become more resourceful and self-reliant. If they seem uncertain, make a few suggestions and then have them enact one. Remember, we want to prompt them to be more resourceful and independent.

Self-monitoring:

Every second or third round of an activity or song, ask the child, "How did your body do?" Then respond positively if at all possible; for example, "You bet, you did a great job of controlling your body! You're a star!"

Solidifying:

Help the child review (a) what skills and strategies were learned in the lesson, (b) why it helps to use them and (c) what they noticed when they used them. Some children won't be able to verbalize or indicate some of this information but try to prompt responses from them. Clarify and add information as needed.

Highlighting:

"Look at how you controlled your body. You really watched your body and told it what to do."

If they advocate for themselves, comment "Look at how you helped your body. You really know how to help yourself do things."

Additional Comments:

Prompt the child's family to model and comment on their own body self-regulation. Also, make sure they praise the child for any self-regulation they exercise. If they forget to self-regulate their body, have them ask them what they should do. Encourage them to take the child to locations where they can practice their self-regulation

Make sure the family gives the child times when they can be totally dysregulated. This self-regulation stuff is a lot of hard work! They'll need consistent breaks from self-regulation so introduce them to appropriate settings where they can run and yell or whatever they wish to do.

Ask the child's family for feedback on how well the child does. Also,

CHAPTER 7 - IMPROVING COGNITIVE SELF-REGULATION WITH spark*

Cognitive Self-regulation involves helping the child learn how to make the best use of their thinking. We want them to learn how to modulate and control how they take in, put together, and explain information.

In the Behavioral Self-regulation unit, they gained conscious control over their body and attention and are now in a better position to regulate their thinking.

In this unit, children are helped to decide what to pay attention to and how to prevent other unimportant and irrelevant information from invading their thoughts. They learn to think about the information they're heard and seen, decide if they understand it, and get more information when they're not sure. They also learn to organize their ideas and explain them to other people in ways they can understand.

Organization of spark* Cognitive Self-regulation unit

Cognitive Self-regulation is divided into three different areas of focus as shown in Figure 12 on the next page. Each area of focus is made up of a number of major subskills. Each of these is discussed below.

There are three main areas of focus for Cognitive Self-regulation. They correspond to taking in information, interpreting it, and then deciding how to respond to it. There's an almost infinite number of subskills that could be included within these. Subskills in **spark*** lessons were selected based on their importance to children with ASC, their value to future cognitive development, and their feasibility with young children.

The importance of the subskills shown in Figure 12 on the next page becomes clearer when you envision a child confronted by a task. They need to look carefully at the task and focus on its important features. Then they picture it in their mind and ask themselves, "Hmm, what am I supposed to do here?" While this is happening, they put the various pieces of information together and decide what the expectations might be. They need to check their understanding of the task and of any directions they received to make sure that what they're doing makes sense to them. They then put all of this together to think ahead to how it might end up. Now it's time to figure out how to talk about their ideas, making sure other people will understand what they're communicating.

Figure 11. Diagram of the three areas of focus and four areas of skill development included in learning Cognitive Self-regulation.

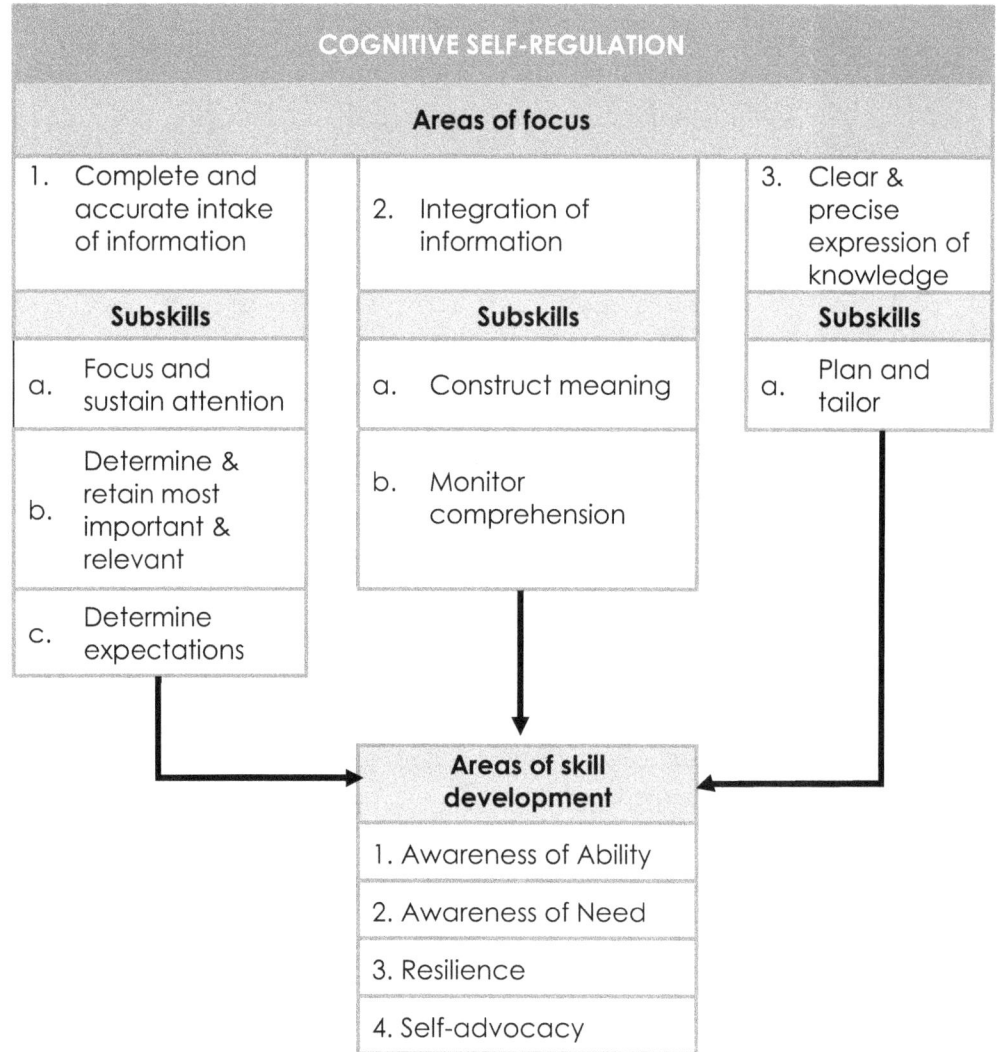

COGNITIVE SELF-REGULATION		
Areas of focus		
1. Complete and accurate intake of information	2. Integration of information	3. Clear & precise expression of knowledge
Subskills	**Subskills**	**Subskills**
a. Focus and sustain attention	a. Construct meaning	a. Plan and tailor
b. Determine & retain most important & relevant	b. Monitor comprehension	
c. Determine expectations		

Areas of skill development
1. Awareness of Ability
2. Awareness of Need
3. Resilience
4. Self-advocacy

Areas of focus and subskills

Complete and accurate intake of information

Intake requires careful consideration of ideas and features of both the task and the situation. spark*'s three major subskills include the child's ability to (a) focus and sustain their attention, (b) decide which is the most important and relevant information at this point in time and (c) hang on to that information in their working memory long enough to figure out what they're supposed to do with it.

We work with the child to approach tasks systematically and to use physical self-prompting (the child uses their 'finder finger') to focus their attention. Then the child is helped to figure out which information is important to what they're doing. They're taught to use rehearsal ("say it over in your brain") to help them hang on to the key information. The third subskill involves teaching the child to notice signals, clues, and models that help them figure out what they should do. These are signals, clues, and models we all use on a daily basis: we know to park our cars in locations where signs show it's okay, we notice the "wait to be seated" sign at a restaurant, and we watch a game to figure out how to play it.

Integration of information

Once the child has learned to take in all of the important pieces of information, we need to teach them how to make sense of them. They're taught strategies for combining pieces of information into a whole image or story and deciding if they understand the information. We help the child "make a picture in your brain" as they listen to information. This prompts them to integrate the ideas into a coherent picture and not just move from detail to detail in a string of ideas. We then help them think about the information to make sure they understand it and it makes sense to them.

Clear and precise expression of knowledge

This subskill involves helping the child plan what they want to communicate. The goals is to help them explain their thinking and ideas more clearly and completely so others can understand it.

The ultimate goal of this progression of skill development is the child taking both responsibility and control of their thinking. They'll learn to become aware of how to use strategies to monitor their thinking and knowledge and reflect on information and ideas. This process lets the child become more aware of their thinking and manage it more effectively.

Areas of skill development within each component of the spark* model

In the Cognitive Self-regulation unit, as with Behavioral Self-regulation, the child taken through a series of steps toward independence and generalization. Within each area of focus, we'll work toward the child is assuming more control and responsibility using this sequence (1) Awareness of Ability, (2) Awareness of Need, (3) Resilience, and (4) Self-advocacy.

Awareness of Ability

This involves helping the child become aware of each cognitive subskill and that they have control over it.

Awareness of Need

After the subskill is identified and practiced, the child is helped to identify when and where to use these skills and strategies in everyday life. With input from parents, they identify situations at school, home, and in the community when self-regulation of their thinking is important. For example, at school, it's important to self-regulate their attention in the classroom when other children are making noise.

Resilience

The child is helped to solidify their use of the skills and strategies so they're more resilient and less readily affected by disruptions around them. We want to help 'toughen' them cognitively so they can deal with more distractions, interruptions, and changes like those that occur in the real world.

Self-advocacy

In this stage, the child is prompted to use their self-awareness, resilience, and knowledge of place and time to support themselves. They're prompted to ask for help when needed and/or to arrange their environment so it's easier for them to function. Primary emphasis placed on the child's being able to keep from becoming dysregulated.

spark* Cognitive Self-regulation lesson content

The lessons that follow are formatted to help you work systematically through each subskill. Each figure below provides an example of the information shown in every lesson.

With all instructions in the lessons, care has been taken to provide clarity while still allowing for flexibility and creativity in the individual practitioner. Lessons are laid out and sequenced so the child is progressively placed in a position where they can assume increasing control over their thinking.

Executive functions

Each lesson shows which of the five main executive functions, presented in Chapter 2, is a primary focus and which ones are secondary. Brief explanations are provided about the rationale for designating some functions as primary and others as secondary (see the example on the next page).

Throughout the activities, care is taken to progressively add more executive functions as the child exhibits greater facility. *Self-monitoring* is stressed throughout this unit, with the child being asked to evaluate the accuracy and quality of their performance. *Inhibitory control* continues to be an important focus because of the need for selective, sustained, and shifting attention. Increasingly, *planning and organization* and *working memory* are needed to succeed with each activity. *Cognitive flexibility* will enter incrementally into all activities, particularly when the emphasis is placed on generalization of skills.

Area of self-regulation 2: Cognitive			
Area receiving focus 1: Complete and accurate intake of information			
Subskill a: Focus and sustain attention			
Area of skill development 1: Awareness of Ability			
Primary executive functions:		*Secondary executive functions*:	
	Inhibitory control		Working memory
	Planning and organization		Cognitive flexibility
	Self-monitoring		

Lesson identifying information: area of self-regulation, area of focus, subskills & area of skill development

Executive functions receiving primary and secondary focus, plus comments

Comments on executive functions: This activity requires the child to control their impulses and monitor their performance. There's strong emphasis on using an organized approach with some advance planning needed for them to figure out how to proceed. Little emphasis is placed on working memory in the sense that they don't at this point have to recall any of the information, only approach it systematically. Some cognitive flexibility is needed to move from one piece of information to another but it's not a central factor.

Task structuring

The Task structuring section of each lesson provides information about the general organization and arrangement of the activity (see examples on the next page). We worked systematically on directness of adult involvement in the Behavioral Self-regulation unit and the child has learned to be less dependent upon adults for learning. Because of this, it's no longer a central focus in the Cognitive Self-regulation unit.

Objective

Objectives are written as individual child goals with a description of the target behavior and accuracy or frequency expected (see an example on the next page). The level of accuracy is typically 80%. Due to the nature of children with ASC and with life in general, achieving success on four out of five tries should be considered quite solid learning. For activities that require extension into daily life, the accuracy levels are reduced to reflect the reality of the challenges they'll likely encounter.

Area of self-regulation 2: Cognitive
Area receiving focus 1: Complete and accurate intake of information
Subskill a: Focus and sustain attention
Area of skill development 1: Awareness of Ability

Suggestions for organizing activities & things to watch out for

Task structuring:

Set up tasks so the child is easily guided to work left to right and/or top to bottom. For example, you can make up a grid of twelve two-inch squares on a sheet of paper where there's one object or picture in each square. In the beginning, since the emphasis is on learning to be systematic, tasks should be relatively simple and contain at least some familiar information....

Objectives: level of accuracy or frequency of use needed for child to move to next lesson

Objective:

The child will be able to work systematically (left to right and top to bottom) at least 80% of the time with adult support.

Materials suggested for the lesson, indicating those available in the Resources files

Materials:

- any worksheet or picture with multiple pictures and/or words on it (see examples and sources in the Resource files - RESOURCES - *Commercially available books and materials* and RESOURCES - *Internet sites coordinated with lesson activities* files) ....

Materials

Materials for each lesson are outlined (see example above). Most are included in the Resource files accessible through the **spark*** website. Suggestions for both younger and older children are included in the files.

Suggestions are made for storybooks that complement the lessons. Great care has been taken to ensure that the suggested books don't suggest or model undesirable behavior. Children on the autism spectrum often pick up on these negative models and start using the behaviors. An exception to the book selection occurs once the children have made significant progress in their self-regulation.

Effort has been made to either include materials in the Resource files or require only a few other items to implement each lesson.

You'll notice quite a few of the activities involve worksheets. Some people object to using worksheets, but they're used for a number of good reasons. Worksheets make the examples concrete. Lesson objectives can be isolated, and work can be reviewed. Once the child understands the concepts presented, we move on to other types of activities.

Throughout **spark***, the main options presented won't incorporate technology, but the meaningful use of technology is encouraged. If you decide to integrate technology, be sure that it increases child participation and interest and doesn't take time away from interacting with them. Sometimes, the child can become so over-focused on the technology that meaningful interactions with others become almost impossible. Technology can provide us with many excellent options and learning games but needs to be carefully planned.

Language of spark*

For each lesson, key words and phrases for promoting the cognitive and social-emotional goals of each interaction, discussed in Chapter 5, are highlighted to help you remember to use them. In addition, important vocabulary and concepts you will be using are listed. An example is shown below.

Area of self-regulation 2: Cognitive

Area receiving focus 1: Complete and accurate intake of information

Subskill a: Focus and sustain attention

Area of skill development 1: Awareness of Ability

Language of spark* *to use in this lesson*:

Key words & phrases:	
We're ... You can .... Looking with your eyes Did your work systematically?	Let's uh oh, we don't want to miss anything. Did you remember to be systematic?

Vocabulary & concepts:	
Systematic(ally) Finder finger	Brain Green means 'go'

Language of spark* key words and phrases to use in the lesson

Vocabulary and concepts to use in the lesson

Introduction

The Introduction section of each activity is a script of the instructions and explanations that are to be provided to the child. The introduction is used to engage each child in the lesson and its objectives. An example is shown on the next page.

With all of these instructions, care has been taken to use the Language of **spark*** and provide clarity. Allowance is made also for each person using **spark*** to have some flexibility and to be creative but it's critical that you keep in mind that the words have been carefully crafted.

Practice

The Practice section suggests ways you can engage the child to perform and repeat each activity, striving to solidify the skills and strategies. The Practice section is a chance to help the child explore the skills and strategies presented in the lesson. An example of lesson practice information is shown in the example below.

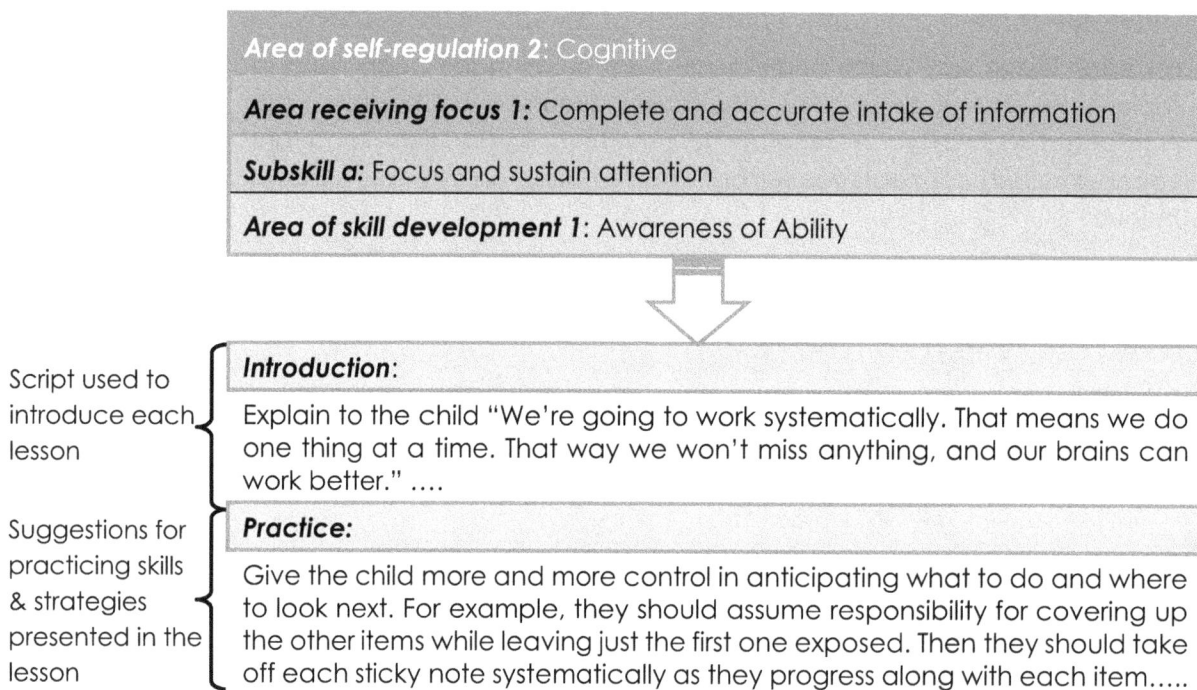

Area of self-regulation 2: Cognitive

Area receiving focus 1: Complete and accurate intake of information

Subskill a: Focus and sustain attention

Area of skill development 1: Awareness of Ability

Script used to introduce each lesson

Introduction:

Explain to the child "We're going to work systematically. That means we do one thing at a time. That way we won't miss anything, and our brains can work better." ....

Suggestions for practicing skills & strategies presented in the lesson

Practice:

Give the child more and more control in anticipating what to do and where to look next. For example, they should assume responsibility for covering up the other items while leaving just the first one exposed. Then they should take off each sticky note systematically as they progress along with each item.....

Metacognition, or thinking about what you're thinking and doing, is emphasized throughout the Cognitive Self-regulation unit. The child is guided to develop metacognitive strategies that will help them monitor and optimize their thinking. For example, they'll learn to use self-talk ("I need to tell my brain: don't get distracted"). Initially, the child is prompted to think out loud when using self-talk. This will give you a chance to monitor what they're saying to themselves and it's an opportunity to help shape and prompt their thinking. Over time, they need to learn to internalize this self-talk and say it quietly to themselves. Once it's fully established, encourage them to "just say it in your brain".

Be sure to prompt the child to use Turtle Breathing before and during tasks to help them be calm and centered. Model the use of Turtle Breathing, reminding them that helps your brain and your body work better.

Prompting

This part provides verbal and nonverbal prompts that should be used to establish, solidify, and extend skills learned within the lesson. Strong emphasis is placed on the child's understanding that learning is a process. That means we help them understand they won't reach perfection right away and will need to tolerate 'less-than-perfect' work until "Your brain and your body can practice". An example of prompting information is shown below.

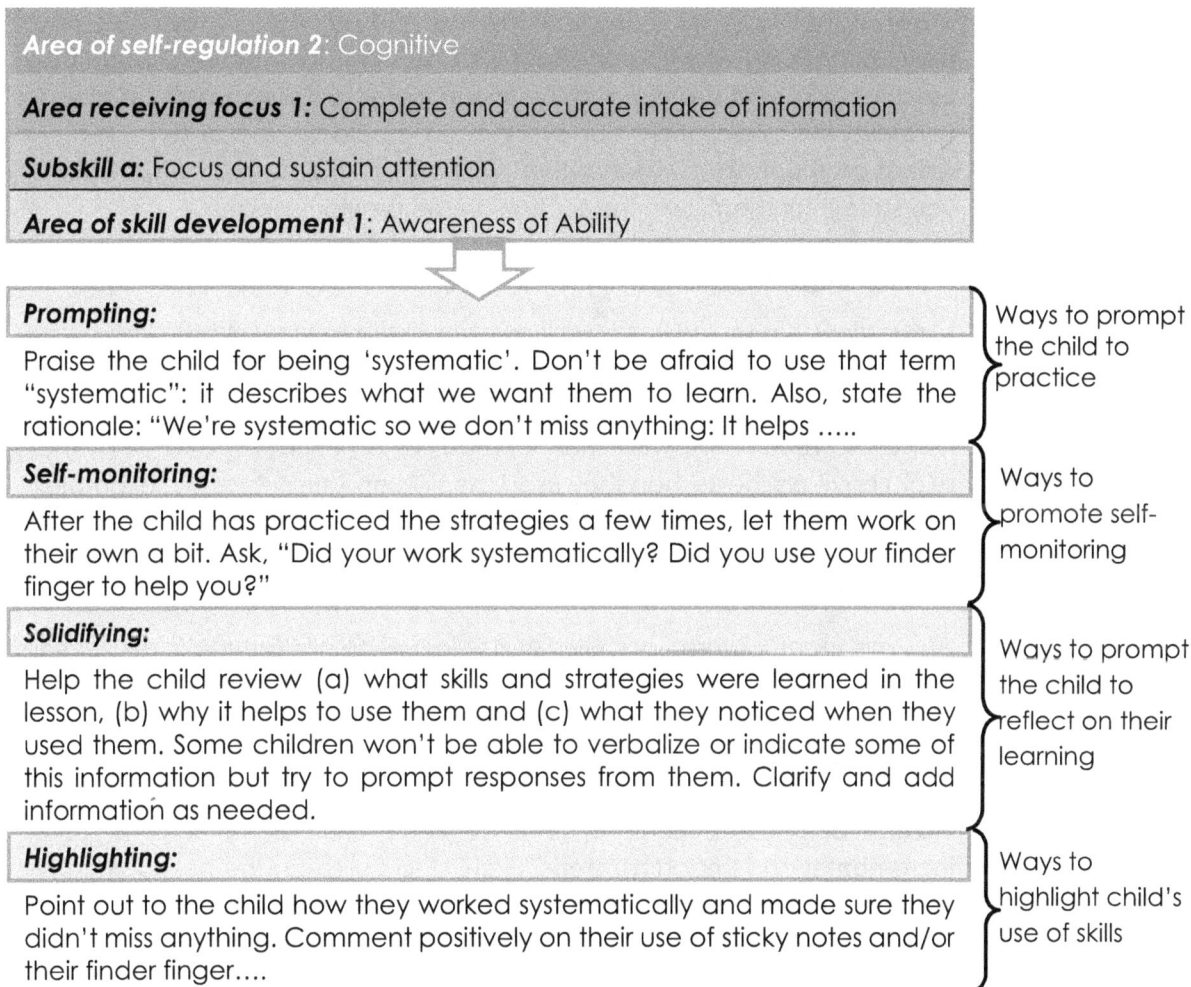

Area of self-regulation 2: Cognitive
Area receiving focus 1: Complete and accurate intake of information
Subskill a: Focus and sustain attention
Area of skill development 1: Awareness of Ability

Prompting:

Praise the child for being 'systematic'. Don't be afraid to use that term "systematic": it describes what we want them to learn. Also, state the rationale: "We're systematic so we don't miss anything: It helps ....." — *Ways to prompt the child to practice*

Self-monitoring:

After the child has practiced the strategies a few times, let them work on their own a bit. Ask, "Did your work systematically? Did you use your finder finger to help you?" — *Ways to promote self-monitoring*

Solidifying:

Help the child review (a) what skills and strategies were learned in the lesson, (b) why it helps to use them and (c) what they noticed when they used them. Some children won't be able to verbalize or indicate some of this information but try to prompt responses from them. Clarify and add information as needed. — *Ways to prompt the child to reflect on their learning*

Highlighting:

Point out to the child how they worked systematically and made sure they didn't miss anything. Comment positively on their use of sticky notes and/or their finder finger.... — *Ways to highlight child's use of skills*

It's critically important that you don't <u>tell</u> the child to use their self-regulation unless there's no alternative. Always prompt them to think for themselves by asking, "What could you do to help yourself?" By asking rather than telling, the child is encouraged to think for themselves and not rely on adults to direct them.

The child must consistently be given positive messages about their ability to reason and problem-solve. Telling the child occasionally, "You've got a good brain" will take them a long way in learning.

Self-monitoring

Because our goal is to help the child assume control over their own thinking, we need to teach them to judge their own performance from an early stage. That way they can determine the accuracy and adequacy of their own performance. An example is shown on the previous page.

Solidifying

To help solidify learning from each lesson, the children are helped to reflect on what they learned. They're prompted and helped to review (a) what they learned, (b) why it's important and (c) what they noticed when they used the skills and strategies in the lesson. Some children won't be able to verbalize this information, but every effort should be made to help them reflect on the lesson, whether they verbalize it, indicates it nonverbally or you state it for them. See the section on the previous page.

Highlighting

Suggestions are made in this section about how to highlight the child's use of their appropriate self-regulation in day-to-day life and how to help them solidify their skills in daily situations. Within each session, the child is also helped to reflect on what they learned, what it means, and what they might have noticed when they used the skills and strategies. An example is shown on the previous page.

Additional comments

Any important features, skills and strategies will be highlighted in this section of each lesson. Suggestions for extension and generalization will also be provided. Some optional supplemental activities to reinforce learning and awareness will be described in this section.

NOTE: Each component in this Cognitive Self-regulation unit takes incremental and important steps. Every step builds on the next, forming a solid foundation of self-regulation. Don't skip any of the lessons. Each lesson can take just a few minutes and some children will meet criteria quickly and easily. Remember, we're developing skills that will serve the child throughout their life, not just today.

spark* **Observational Assessment**

In the observational assessment, an excerpt is shown in Figure 13 on the next page, you sample the child's ability to spontaneously use the cognitive subskills. The complete form is in the Resource files (FORM - Observational assessment - Cognitive Self-regulation file).

In the observational assessment, watch the child in daily settings and look at their use of the cognitive subskills. Watch them during a variety of activities, particularly ones that have some natural order or structure, like a sorting task, a puzzle, or a paper and pencil activity. An excerpt from the list of questions to ask yourself during observations is presented in Figure 14 on the next page. These will help clarify the intent of the observation category. The complete list of questions is in the Resource files accessible through the **spark*** website.

spark* Observational Assessment - Cognitive Self-regulation			
Child: *Bobby*	**Date:** *June 12*		
Reporter: *Heather*			
Areas of focus and subskills	Exhibits independently in everyday settings:		
	Never	Sometimes	Most of the time
Complete & accurate intake of information			
focuses and sustains attention on tasks			
determines and retains most important and relevant information in tasks			
determines expectations of a task or situation without being			

Figure 12. Example spark* observational assessment for the Cognitive Self-regulation unit.

Then place a check mark (✔) in the box that corresponds to the frequency of use of each subskill: Never, Sometimes (more than 0% but not more than 75% of the time) or Most of the time (more than 75% of the time).

Documenting progress through spark* **lesson objectives**

To ensure progress toward program goals as well as general accountability, each child's progress should be tracked over time. This ensures you've got a working document that shows when you started a lesson with the child, when they met the objective for that lesson, when you introduced the next lesson and so on. On the next page, in Figure 14, is an excerpt of the **spark*** Achievement of Lesson Objectives form. The complete form is in the Resource files (FORM - Achievement of lesson objectives - Cognitive self-regulation file).

Figure 13.
Excerpt from the sample of questions for the spark* Cognitive Self-regulation observational assessment.

Area of focus	Questions to ask during observations
Information intake:	
Focus and sustain attention	Do they look carefully and specifically at the task or event, keeping themselves from becoming distracted by other irrelevant information and events?
Determine and retain most important and relevant information	Do they home in on the critical pieces of information or figure out what's important right now? Do they have to keep returning to material to remind themselves of what it is, or do they ask for information to be repeated?
Determine expectations	Do they use a model or prototype to guide them or do they always have to wait to be told what to do?

On the Achievement of Lesson Objectives form is each major area of focus, task variation, and area of skill development included in the Cognitive Self-regulation unit, along with the objectives as stated in each lesson. See the example on the next page.

The date on which the lesson was started is noted in the fifth column from the left. Then, after a period of time that's appropriate to the child and/or program, the child's progress is noted.

The date of evaluation is entered into the column and a progress indicator is written into each appropriate row under that column. Progress toward the objective is marked as:

A – objective achieved,

D – skill developing but the child demonstrates it below the criterion level and

N - no discernible progress.

NOTE: space will be left in each objective to add more specific information is this is required. For example, adding "across three samplings" to the objective below or adding a time span.

spark* Achievement of Lesson Objectives– Cognitive Self-regulation						
Child: Bobby			**Date:** June to December			
Reporter: Heather						
Areas of focus and subskills	**Objective** The child will be able to …	**Areas of skill development**	**Date started**	**Evaluation Date(s)**		
				07/6		
Intake of information						
Focus and sustain attention	C:la1 - work systematically (left to right and top to bottom) at least 80% of the time with adult support	Awareness of Ability	*June 1*	D		
	C:la2 - indicate at least one example of when it's important to be systematic and organized for each of the three targeted settings with adult support	Awareness of Need				

Figure 14. Example excerpt from **spark*** Achievement of Lesson Objectives form for Cognitive Self-regulation.

spark* **Cognitive Self-regulation Lesson Plan Users Guide**

On the next pages are tables showing the spark* **Cognitive Self-regulation Scope and Sequence.**

Column	Information included

#1	Lesson Codes:
	
	    C – Cognitive Self-regulation plan
	    I – Intake of information
	        a – focus and sustain attention
	        ir – determine and retain most important/relevant information
	        e – determine expectation
	    N – Integration of information
	        c – construct meaning
	        m – monitor comprehension
	    E – Expression of thinking
	        pt – plan and tailor
	
	When you see the letter **N,** it means that a **Newsletter** is sent home at the beginning of this lesson.

#2	Pages - page numbers for that lesson
#3	Area of focus
#4	Subskills
#5, 6, 7, 8	Areas of skill development – indicated with a check mark (✔)

Newsletters should be sent home at the start of these lessons:

Lesson	Newsletter #
C:Ia1	9
C:Iir1	10
C:Ie1	11
C:Nc1	12
C:Nm1	13
C:Ept1	14

Rhymes, songs, storybooks and illustrations appropriate for each lesson included the Resource files are referenced in the Materials section of each lesson plan.

Just a reminder: Each component in the spark* Cognitive Self-regulation unit takes small but important steps. Each step builds on the next. To form a solid foundation, please don't skip any lesson.

Lesson	Pages	Area of Focus	Subskill	Areas of skill development			
				Awareness of Ability	Awareness of Need	Resilience	Self-advocacy
C:la1 N	159-162	Intake	focus and sustain attention	✔			
C:la2	163-166	Intake	focus and sustain attention		✔		
C:la3 –	167-171	Intake	focus and sustain attention			✔	✔
C:lir1 N	172-175	Intake	determine and retain most important and relevant	✔			
C:lir2	176-179	Intake	determine and retain most important and relevant		✔		
C:lir3	180-184	Intake	determine and retain most important and relevant			✔	✔
C:le1 N	185-188	Intake	determine expectation	✔			
C:le2	189-191	Intake	determine expectation		✔		
C:le3 –	192-195	Intake	determine expectation			✔	✔
C:Nc1 N	196-199	Integration	construct meaning	✔			
C:Nc2	200-202	Integr-ation	construct meaning		✔		
C:Nc3	203-205	Integr-ation	construct meaning			✔	✔
C:Nm1 N	206-209	Integr-ation	monitor comprehension	✔			
C:Nm2	210-212	Integrat-ion	monitor comprehension		✔		
C:Nm3	213-216	Integrat-ion	monitor comprehension			✔	✔

Lesson	Pages	Area of Focus	Subskill	Areas of skill development			
				Awareness of Ability	Awareness of Need	Resilience	Self-advocacy
C:Ept1	217-223	Express-ion	plan and tailor	✔			
C:Ept2	224-226	Express-ion	plan and tailor		✔		
C:Ept3	227-230	Express-ion	plan and tailor			✔	✔

Cognitive Self-regulation Lessons

Review the lesson carefully before starting. You might want to copy the scripts, so you have the words close at hand when working with each child. Use the exact terms, definitions and reasons presented in the lesson. For example, the term "systematic" is used and defined as "doing one thing at a time" and the reason is "so we don't miss anything".

Follow the lessons exactly in terms of how information is presented, vocabulary used, and definitions presented.

NOTE: Turtle Breathing should be used on a consistent basis to help both you and the child calm and center yourselves. Model Turtle Breathing before activities and during them, especially when extra effort is required. Prompt the child to use their Turtle Breathing by asking, "What could you do to help yourself calm your body and your brain?" If they don't respond by doing their Turtle Breathing, prompt them more directly with, "Let's do our Turtle Breathing to help calm our brains and our bodies."

Lesson C:Ia1

Send home Newsletter #9 when starting this lesson.

In this lesson, we help the child use strategies to isolate pieces of information so they're not overwhelmed. Then we work with them in dealing with more and more information. By using sticky notes and their index finger as the 'finder finger', we give them tools for helping to isolate information to keep it from being overwhelming – important to self-advocacy. Also, we start on the path to learning 'to look where the finger points' which is an important social clue that we'll introduce in the Emotional Self-regulation unit.

Tip: to reduce the amount of paper waste and copying of materials, you can either laminate coloring pages and worksheets or put them inside sheet protectors and have the child use washable (non-permanent) markers. The laminate and sheet protectors can be wiped clean after each use.

The goal in this lesson is to help the child learn to look at one thing at a time, organize materials before starting and view each systematically so nothing is missed.

Area of self-regulation 2: Cognitive			
Area receiving focus 1: Complete and accurate intake of information			
Subskill a: Focus and sustain attention			
Area of skill development 1: Awareness of Ability			
Primary executive functions:		**Secondary executive functions:**	
	Inhibitory control		Cognitive flexibility
	Planning and organization		
	Self-monitoring		
	Working memory		

Comments on executive functions: This activity requires the child to control their impulses and monitor their performance. There's strong emphasis on using an organized approach with some advance planning needed for them to figure out the materials needed and how to proceed. Emphasis is placed on working memory because we ask the child to anticipate what materials they'll need to complete each task. Some cognitive flexibility is needed to move from one piece of information to another but it's not a central factor.

Task structuring:

Set up tasks so all materials are present and available. Use activities that let the child to work left to right and/or top to bottom. For example, you can make up a grid of twelve two-inch squares on a sheet of paper where there's one object or picture in each square. In the beginning, since the emphasis is on learning to be systematic, tasks should be relatively simple so the child can focus on the new process they're learning.

Initially, place a visual reminder of where to start. For example, place a green 'go' dot, sticker or other marker in the upper left hand corner of the worksheet. Also, cover up all of the other items on the sheet with sticky notes so they don't become distractions.

NOTE: Use of Turtle Breathing before and during tasks should be encouraged.

Objective:

The child will be able to work systematically (left to right and top to bottom) at least 80% of the time with adult support.

Materials:

- any worksheet or picture with multiple pictures and/or words on it (see examples and sources in the Resource files - EXAMPLE - *Worksheets for using systematic approach*, RESOURCES - *Commercially available books and materials* and RESOURCES - *Internet sites coordinated with lesson activities* files)
- sticky notes the same size as pictures, words or objects used
- markers, crayons/colors

Language of spark* to use in this lesson:

Key words & phrases:

We, we're …	Let's
You can ….	Uh oh, we don't want to miss anything.
Look with your eyes	
Did you work systematically?	Did you remember to be systematic/organized?
Did you use your finder finger to help you?	How did you do?

Vocabulary & concepts:

Systematic(ally) – do one thing at a time so we don't miss anything	Brain
Finder finger	Green means 'go'
Organized – we've got everything we need	Distracted

Introduction:

Explain to the child "We're going to organize our work. That way we make sure we've got everything we need. Then, we're going to work systematically. That means we do one thing at a time. That way we won't miss anything, and our brains can work better."

Put out all the materials you will need. Name each as you put it out and then say, "There, we're organized. We've got everything we need. That makes it easier to work." Ask them, "Where should we start?" If they point to the upper left-hand corner, say, "You're right! How did you know that?" If they point to another location or isn't sure where to start, explain, "green means go so's where we start." Tap your finger in the first box or on the first item and tell them "the green dot tells us this is where we start".

Then tell them, "Sometimes it's hard for my brain to look at all of these things so I cover them up. Do you want to try covering them up too? It might make it easier for your brain?" If they seem to agree that it'd be okay to try, say, "Let's put these sticky notes on the rest of the things so your brain doesn't get distracted." Have the child help you cover up all of the other items. Once they're covered, say, "There it's all organized. That makes it easier." Then, you can start.

Once the child shows you they can isolate one piece of information at a time and work systematically, introduce the notion of the 'finder finger'. Tell them that they have something on their own body that can help them look at one thing at a time. Then help them isolate the index finger of their right hand and tell them "That's your finder finger. It helps you find things. If you use your finder finger, you may not need the sticky notes anymore. Let's try."

Practice:

Give the child more and more control in anticipating what to do and where to look next. Ask them, "What do we need so we'll be organized?" You can begin naming things and try to prompt the child to join in: "Okay, we've got the sheet of paper, what else do we need?" Also, give them responsibility for covering up some of the items with sticky notes. Then they should take off each sticky note systematically as they progress along with each item.

When first practicing with the finder finger, if necessary, hold the child's hand with extended index finger and help them point to the first item on the worksheet or display. Note for them, "See, you can look where your finger points." Then let them proceed with the task, interceding only if necessary. Even if the child is reticent to use their finder finger, press to do so. It's an important skill to develop. Visual scanning alone will develop with time, but every child should practice careful scanning using their finder finger first.

Prompting:

Praise the child for being 'systematic' and 'organized'. Don't be afraid to use that terms "systematic" and "organized": they describe what we want them to learn. Also, state the rationale frequently: "We're systematic and organized so we don't miss anything: It helps our brains work better."

Be sure to praise the child for looking carefully at one item at a time: "Wow, you really know how to look with your eyes!" Careful visual scanning are important skills to develop in children with ASC.

If the child's performance isn't systematic or organized, remind them gently with "Uh oh, we don't want to miss anything. Did you remember to be systematic/organized?" This may suggest also they're rushing so help them take a Turtle Breath before starting again. If they're unable to self-correct their behavior, model a systematic approach and then let them try.

Self-monitoring:

After the child has practiced the strategies a few times, let them work on their own a bit. Ask after each item, "Did you work systematically? Did you organize everything before starting? Did you use your finder finger to help you?"

Solidifying:

Help the child review (a) what skills and strategies were learned in the lesson, (b) why it helps to use them and (c) what they noticed when they used them. Some children won't be able to verbalize or indicate some of this information but try to prompt responses from them. Clarify and add information as needed.

Highlighting:

Point out to the child how they worked systematically, organized the material before starting and made sure they didn't miss anything. Comment positively on their use of sticky notes and/or their finder finger.

Be sure to highlight the child's use of a systematic/organized approach with any task or activity. Remind them how it helps make sure they don't miss anything, so they're reminded of the reason for being systematic and organized: "That way you don't miss anything, and it makes it easier for your brain."

Additional Comments:

Sticky notes are suggested as a way to cover up potentially distracting elements on worksheets. When presented as tools to make it easier to think and focus, children rarely if ever play or fiddle with the sticky notes. If they do, just remind them "The notes are to help our brains, so they need to stay on the worksheet".

Lesson C:la2

> **Before starting this lesson**, make sure you received feedback from families on times and places where each child needs to work systematically and be organized from Newsletter #9.
>
> During this lesson, be sure to tell the child about times and places in your life where you have difficulty being systematic and organized and what happens because of it. This helps let them know that they're not the only person who experiences these problems.

> **The goal in this lesson** is to help the child identify when and where they need to do one thing at a time, be organized and work systematically in day-to-day life.

Area of self-regulation 2: Cognitive			
Area receiving focus 1: Complete and accurate intake of information			
Subskill a: Focus and sustain attention			
Area of skill development 2: Awareness of Need			
Primary executive functions:		**Secondary executive functions:**	
	Cognitive flexibility		Working memory
	Inhibitory control		
	Planning and organization		
	Self-monitoring		

Comments on executive functions: This activity requires the child to control their impulses and monitor their performance. There's strong emphasis on using an organized approach with advance planning about how to proceed. Little emphasis is placed on working memory since the child doesn't have to recall any of the information, only approach it systematically and in an organized manner. Cognitive flexibility is needed to identify different situations where systematic approaches are important.

Task structuring:

When focusing on Awareness of Need, we structure the task, so the child is helped to think of where else they need to be systematic and focused. Examples should be drawn from the child (and from the child's family via the newsletter) that encompass their life (a) at school, (b) at home, and (c) in the community. All three settings must be addressed so extension and generalization receive specific focus.

Objective:

The child will be able to indicate at least one example of when it's important to be systematic and organized for each of the three targeted settings with adult support.

Materials:

- Awareness of Need chart (see Resource files - EXAMPLE - *Awareness of Need chart for systematic approach*, TEMPLATE – *Awareness of Need chart* and ILLUSTRATIONS - *Topics for Awareness of Need chart - Cognitive self-regulation*)
- information from the parent's feedback on Newsletter #9 about times and places where the child needs improved control – prepare pictures ahead of time
- activities that require a systematic, organized approach – for example, building/construction toys, putting on clothes (doll with clothing), paper airplane construction, Where's Waldo/Wally books (see Resource files - RESOURCES - *Internet sites coordinated with lesson activities and*)

Language of spark* *to use in this lesson:*

Key words & phrases:

We, we're …	Let's …
You can ….	Uh oh, we don't want to miss anything.
Look with your eyes	Did you remember to be systematic/organized?
Did you work systematically?	
Did you use your finder finger to help you?	How did you do?

Vocabulary & concepts:

Systematic(ally) – do one thing at a time so we don't miss anything	Brain
	Distracted
Organized – we've got everything we need	

Introduction:

Explain to the child that you want them to help you think of times when we need to work systematically. Tell them: "We're going to think of things at school, at home, and in other places. Can you think of one thing we do at school/home/other places where we need to be systematic and do one thing at a time?"

Practice:

If the child cannot come up with any ideas, take out one of the activities suggested in the Materials section. Say, "Okay, let's try this. What should we do first?" If they're not sure, remind them, "We've got to organize it to make sure we've got everything we need. You go ahead." Let the child work organize the material, giving them help as needed. Then comment, "Wow, that's a time when you need to organize things .... when you play with toys. That makes sure you have all the parts you need. Let's put that one on your chart."

Do some of the activities, like dressing a doll, assembling a toy, making paper airplanes or looking at a book, doing them systematically and also haphazardly so the child can see what happens when they're contrasted.

Add more pictures, getting at least one idea for each main location. School examples of the need to (a) organize things include getting all your craft supplies ready or pens and pencils ready and (b) be systematic include anything where there's a left-to-right order, such as following schedules and plans, starting to print/write your name on the right-hand side of a page or skipping pages in a book. Home examples for (a) be organized can include putting clothes in drawers and (b) being systematic can include putting on clothes, following a recipe or assembling toys. In the community, examples for (a) being organized can include getting all of the things you'll need for swimming or other sports and (b) being systematic might be following your grocery list or a map or getting ready for your swimming lesson by putting your bathing suit on without removing your clothes.

Prompting:

If the child has difficulty coming up with ideas, suggest some from the family information and your experience with them. You might want to start with simple, familiar things, like putting clothes on someone else's hook or in someone else's cubbie. By the end of the session, be sure to have at least one challenging situation for the child.

Catch them organizing themselves and being systematic. Praise them more often than reminding them. Comment whenever you see them working or playing systematically/in an organized way, especially in situations where they could have done something else.

Enact an event or do an activity where you don't work systematically or in an organized way and prompt the child to notice and correct you.

Self-monitoring:

Ask the child, "How can you help yourself remember to be systematic/organized when you're (location or time you and the child added to their Awareness of Need chart)?" Help them think of ways they can remind themselves.

Solidifying:

Help the child review (a) what skills and strategies were learned in the lesson, (b) why it helps to use them and (c) what they noticed when they used them. Some children won't be able to verbalize or indicate some of this information but try to prompt responses from them. Clarify and add information as needed.

Highlighting:

Point out to the child how they organized themselves and worked or played systematically and how that helped make sure they didn't miss anything. Also point out when you organize your work and/or do something systematically and comment, "Look, I organized everything before I started. That really helped me." Or "Look how I did one thing at a time and didn't miss anything! Good for me."

Additional Comments:

Share information with the family and other people involved with the child. Prompt them to model and comment when they use an organized, systematic approach. Also, make sure they praise the child for being organized and/or systematic. If they forget to be systematic/organized, have them ask them what they should do to help themselves.

Ask them to remind the child before entering a situation targeted on the Awareness of Need chart. Have them comment about the need to be systematic so they don't miss anything.

Ask them for feedback on how well the child does.

Lesson C:la3

In this lesson, we want to simulate some distractions and noises from day-to-day life to help the child become more used to dealing with them. We try to simulate those conditions so They find that they can continue doing what they're doing and not let them bother them.

It's helpful to pre-record background noises so you aren't distracted from your work with the child. These activities should be fun so make sure you use noises that are acceptable to the child - at least in the beginning. If noxious sounds are used, they may upset them to the point where they can't use the targeted skills and strategies (check the Child Background information form to see which sounds may bother them). You want to simulate real-life situations that child has to learn to deal with but introduce challenging sounds only after the child has shown good facility in using the skills and strategies from this lesson.

The goal in this lesson is to help the child become resilient and continue to use an organized and systematic approach, doing one thing at a time, even when distracted by other things. They will also change things around them or use other self-advocacy strategies to help themselves stay on task and undistracted.

Area of self-regulation 2: Cognitive

Area receiving focus 1: Complete and accurate intake of information

Subskill a: Focus and sustain attention

Area of skill development 3 & 4: Resilience & Self-advocacy

Primary executive functions:		Secondary executive functions:	
	Cognitive flexibility		
	Inhibitory control		
	Planning and organization		
	Self-monitoring		
	Working memory		

Comments on executive functions: This activity requires the child control their impulses and attention and monitor their performance. There's strong emphasis on using an organized approach with advance planning about how to proceed. Working memory is needed in order for the child to keep in mind what they're working on and not to allow distractions to sway them. Some cognitive flexibility is needed to move from one piece of information to another and across different settings.

Task structuring:

Increasingly, provide the child with more visually complex ('busy') and disorganized material. At this Resilience stage, we want to increase their tolerance for material that's distracting for them. We need them to learn how to ignore unimportant information and focus solely on the key ideas.

When focusing on Self-advocacy, we introduce activities and events that aren't completely organized so the child has to focus their attention, figure out a systematic way of doing it and ignore distractions.

Encourage the child to use Turtle Breathing so they can keep themselves calm and focused.

Objectives:

The child will be able to organize their work and work systematically at least 80% of the time independently.

The child will be able to organize their own tasks and ignore distractions at least 50% of the time so they're able to work systematically.

Materials:

- any worksheet or picture with multiple pictures and/or words on it – pictured scenes with a lot of detail and activity can be very effective (see Resource files for ideas)
- you might add your own visual distractions to an activity or work area such as by putting a drop of paint on the page
- sticky notes should be available to the child so they can choose to use them to help themselves
- recorded sound effects and environmental sounds, music, noises (see Resource files - RESOURCES - *Internet sites coordinated with lesson activities* for internet sources of background noise) – make sure the sounds aren't ones that can trigger anxiety or distress in the child.
- pre-recorded activities with varying types of background noise at different intensities (see Resource files - RESOURCES - *Commercially available books*)
- activities that require a systematic, organized approach – for example, building/construction toys, putting on clothes (doll with clothing), paper airplane construction, Where's Waldo/Wally books (see Resource files - RESOURCES - *Internet sites coordinated with lesson activities* and RESOURCES – *Storybooks coordinated with lesson target areas*)

Language of spark* *to use in this lesson:*	
Key words & phrases:	
We, we're ...	Let's ...
You can	Uh oh, we don't want to miss anything.
We do one thing at a time, so we don't miss anything	Did you remember to be systematic/organized?
Did you work systematically/in an organized way?	How did you do?
I can ignore that.	I can tell my brain, don't get distracted, brain.
That's not important right now.	
Vocabulary & concepts:	
Systematic(ally)	Brain
Organized	Distracted, Ignore

Introduction:

To increase their resilience and ability to remain on task, introduce the concept of ignoring. Tell them, "We can ignore things that aren't important. That can help our brains think better." Model some examples for them: drop an object while you're working, play a sound effect or music, indicate that one of the pictures on your worksheet is bugging you or place a favorite toy on the table. Say, "I can ignore that. It's not important right now. I can tell my brain, don't get distracted, brain."

To work on Self-advocacy, tell the child that you know they can organize themselves, work systematically and ignore distractions all by themselves. Now you want them to help their brain by making sure their work is organized before they start and then they work systematically. Tell them, "When something is organized, then it's easier to be systematic and use your good brain." Remind them to tell their brain "Don't get distracted".

Practice:

Introduce some minor distractions while the child is working. Point out the distraction and ask them what they could do to help themselves. Prompt them to tell their brain to ignore it because "it's not important right now". Introduce more visually complex information and images and then add distracting sounds again.

You should add distracting sounds occasionally and model telling yourself "Don't get distracted, brain" and keep working.

Prompting:

If the child chooses to use sticky notes, praise them for helping their brain. If they ask for or puts a starting (green) dot on the worksheet, praise them and let them do it. These are both forms of Self-advocacy.

If the child's performance isn't systematic or organized, just say "Oops, I think you missed something. What can you do to help yourself?" If they're unable to self-correct their behavior, gently remind them of the approach you presented and then let them try.

If they become distracted by a sound or sight, remind them, "We can just ignore that. It's not important." and continue with the task. As the child becomes more automatic in using an organized and systematic approach and ignoring distractions, ask them how they did.

Prompting at the Self-advocacy stage involves the least amount of direction or suggestion. Watch the child carefully and don't be tempted to 'rescue' them. Let them make mistakes. When they encounter difficulties, ask, "What could you do to help yourself?" Prompt them to think on their own, giving them suggestions only as needed.

Self-monitoring:

After a sound or other distraction, ask the child how they did. Ask, "Did you organize your work, do it systematically and ignore distractions?" Then respond positively if at all possible; for example, "You bet, you did a great job of being organized/systematic/ignoring distractions! You really helped your brain." If they don't organize their work or work systematically, prompt them to look at what they're doing and figure out a way to help themselves, so they don't miss anything.

When working on Self-advocacy, after the child becomes engaged in an activity, ask them how they're doing. Ask, "Are you being organized/systematic/ignoring distractions? Remind yourself so you can help your brain."

Solidifying:

Help the child review (a) what skills and strategies were learned in the lesson, (b) why it helps to use them and (c) what they noticed when they used them. Some children won't be able to verbalize or indicate some of this information but try to prompt responses from them. Clarify and add information as needed.

Highlighting:

After prompting and reinforcing the child's attempts, start asking them to explain, "Why do you think it's important to be organized/systematic/ignore distractions?" Do this just occasionally so they don't feel like you're interrogating them. Accept any reasonable answer, like "that way I won't miss anything." You can also present them with visual options to point to if they have problems with verbal explanations. The options could be "I just like it", "It helps my brain" or "I don't know". Having them express their reasoning will help solidify the rationale for looking for and thinking about only what is important.

Be sure to highlight the child's focusing their attention on or ignoring objects and events while performing tasks so they begin to understand how this information can assist them. Say, "Look at how you were /organized/systematic/ignored distractions. You really helped your brain."

Comment positively on their use of any strategy to help themselves, including Turtle Breathing, self-talk as well as props like sticky notes and green starting dots.

"Look at how you organized your work/worked systematically/ignored the ____. You didn't miss a thing. You really know how to help your brain."

Additional Comments:

Prompt the child's family to model and comment on being organized/systematic and/or ignoring distractions. Ask them not to set tasks up too carefully so the child has to organize some things themselves before starting. Also, make sure everyone praises them for any self-regulation they exercise. If they forget to be organized/systematic or ignore distractions, have them ask them, "What can you do to help yourself?"

Ask them for feedback on how well the child does.

Lesson C:lir1

> **Send home Newsletter #10 at the end of this lesson.**
> The strategies taught in this lesson are very important for future work. When dealing with visual information, they learn to remain focused on the features and events important and relevant to the present situation and not become distracted. When dealing with verbal information, the child learns about 'topic' - that will help them with conversational skills later on. We need to prompt them more and more to say things over to themselves as a way to improve their focus of attention and their working memory.

> **The goal in this lesson** is to help the child identify and focus on just the most important information that is relevant to the task they're working on. This means ignoring some things, even if they're interesting to them.

Area of self-regulation 2: Cognitive			
Area receiving focus 1: Complete and accurate intake of information			
Subskill b: Determine and retain most important and relevant information			
Area of skill development 1: Awareness of Ability			
Primary executive functions:		**Secondary executive functions:**	
	Cognitive flexibility		
	Inhibitory control		
	Planning and organization		
	Self-monitoring		
	Working memory		

Comments on executive functions: This activity requires the child to control their attention, monitor their performance and keep information in their working memory. There's also emphasis on planning and organization in that they're required to work systematically and to begin to identify the most important and relevant information. Cognitive flexibility is emphasized somewhat in these activities because the child must shift from item to item while maintaining their focus on the 'most important thing'.

Task structuring:

Depending on the child's skills, you can start off with simple matching tasks. Move on to more visually-complex tasks and those involving verbal directions as they show progress. The materials must give clear clues about the object to be matched as that will be identified as "the most important thing". It will need clear visual referencing by having clear outlining to make it stand out (see an example in the Resource files)

For most children, verbal directions should, in the beginning, be simple, using short phrases. Then move to complete and more complex sentences once the child's successful. The material should include a variety of objects on a page. The verbal directions should state an action the child should do to one of the objects (e.g. color the boy's hair purple."). (see an example in the Resource files)

NOTE: Use of Turtle Breathing before and during tasks should be encouraged.

Objective:

The child will be able to determine and label the most important and relevant information at least 80% of the time with adult support.

Materials:

- visual matching tasks with increasing number of distracter items (see Resource files - EXAMPLE - *Visual matching worksheet for determining most important and relevant information* for an example)
- worksheets and other activities (e.g. coloring pages) that have a visual component with verbal directions (see Resource files - RESOURCES - *Internet sites coordinated with lesson activities*)
- books where key objects/characters are hidden (see Resource files - RESOURCES – *Storybooks coordinated with lesson target areas* for suggestions)
- markers, crayons/colors, sticky notes

Language of spark* to use in this lesson:

Key words & phrases:

We, we're ...	Let's ...
You can	Let's think
You're right ...	That's the most important thing.
Where should we start looking?	Is that important right now?
We start on the left side at the top	That's interesting but we're not thinking about that right now.
That helps your brain remember.	
That's important because we're looking at ... and that's a	Can you find something that's important right now?
What can you do to help yourself?	Say it over in your head.
Sometimes it makes it easier for our brains.	That'll help your brain remember.
	How did you do?
I can tell my brain, don't get distracted, brain.	Where do we go next?
	That's not important right now.
Find something important.	Just ignore it.
What should I do to help myself?	

Vocabulary & concepts:	
Systematic(ally)	Brain
Same	Finder finger
Topic – most important thing	Important
Name (as in the name of something depicted in a drawing)	Distracted
	Ignore

Introduction:

Point out the main item of focus or the 'topic': "See this (tap your finger on the item), we're going to work systematically to find one the same. Where should we start looking?" If the child points to the box on the upper left side, praise them: "You're right, we start on the left side at the top. Good thinking!" If the child points to some other place or shows uncertainty, ask them: "Where do we start so we can work systematically? Let's think." As need be, point where to start and prompt the child to do the same and then acknowledge them, "You're right. We start on the left side at the top." Place a green dot at the upper left corner as a reminder if need be.

For matching activities: "Now, let's find ones the same as this (tap on the picture) one. That's the topic. That's the most important thing. Every time you put your finder finger on a picture, say the name of that thing. That helps your brain remember."

For activities involving verbal direction following: "Now, we're going to do some listening. I'm going to say something, and I want you to find a picture that goes with those words. Listen carefully and say the words over to yourself. That helps your brain remember."

Practice:

For matching activities: As the child is scanning and labeling each object and action, ask them: "Is that important right now?" Then give them feedback like, "That's right, that's important because we're looking at trucks/numbers/letters and that's a truck/number/letter."

If the child becomes distracted by something that isn't relevant or central to the task, respond positively by saying "that's interesting but we're not thinking about that right now. Can you find something that's important right now?"

If the child seems distracted by the multiple pictures on the page, ask them what they could do to help themselves. Remind them not to get distracted and that sticky notes can help them. Indicate, "Sometimes it makes it easier for our brains."

Let the child work at their own pace so long as they're smoothly moving from one item to the next, pointing to and naming each.

For verbal direction following activities: prompt the child, "Say it over in your head. That'll help your brain remember." Model putting your finger on the first picture, saying the direction out loud and then deciding if the picture and words match the instruction.

Prompting:

If the child hesitates while looking at each item, prompt them: "Where do we go next?" Put your finger on the next image if they appear uncertain. Then let them proceed.

After the child has consistent success, select something 'silly' or absurd and model how to redirect your thinking. For example, "Oh, look, there's a number two on the paper. Oh-oh, brain, that's not important right now. Just ignore it. Find something important." After modeling this, do a 'silly' thing again, stop and ask the child, "What should I do to help myself?" Prompt them to help you.

Self-monitoring:

After the child has practiced the strategies a few times, let them work on their own a bit. Ask after every second or third item, "How did you do? Did you find the most important thing? Did you say it over to yourself to help your brain?"

Solidifying:

Help the child review (a) what skills and strategies were learned in the lesson, (b) why it helps to use them and (c) what they noticed when they used them. Some children won't be able to verbalize or indicate some of this information but try to prompt responses from them. Clarify and add information as needed.

Highlighting:

Point out to the child how they figured out and remembered what was most important. Comment positively on their use of any strategy to help themselves. Be sure to highlight when the child purposefully focuses their attention while performing tasks.

Additional Comments:

Lesson C:lir2

Before starting this lesson, make sure you received feedback from families on times and places where each child needs to improve their focus on and retention of the most important information from Newsletter #10.

During this lesson, be sure to tell the child about times and places in your life where you have difficulty figuring out what's most important and what happens because of it. This helps let them know that they're not the only person who experiences these problems.

The goal in this lesson is to help the child identify where and when they need to use strategies to help themselves focus on and retain the most important information and ignore non-relevant information.

Area of self-regulation 2: Cognitive			
Area receiving focus 1: Complete and accurate intake of information			
Subskill b: Determine and retain most important and relevant information			
Area of skill development 2: Awareness of Need			
Primary executive functions:		**Secondary executive functions**:	
	Cognitive flexibility		
	Inhibitory control		
	Planning and organization		
	Self-monitoring		
	Working memory		

Comments on executive functions: This activity requires the child to control their attention, monitor their performance and keep information in their working memory. There's also emphasis on planning and organization in that they're required to identify the most important and relevant information and use that information to guide their responses. Cognitive flexibility is needed to shift from topic to topic and setting to setting.

Task structuring:

When focusing on Awareness of Need, structure the task so the child is helped to think of where else they need to determine and remember the most important information and ignore distractions. Examples should be drawn from the child and their family that encompass their life (a) at school,

(b) at home, and (c) in the community. All three settings must be addressed so extension and generalization receive specific focus.

Practice some examples from the child's life and from yours (e.g. look for a pen or marker).

Objective:

The child will be able to indicate at least one example of when it's important to determine and remember the most important and relevant information for each of the three targeted settings with adult support.

Materials:

- Awareness of Need chart (see Resource files - TEMPLATE – *Awareness of Need chart and* ILLUSTRATIONS - *Topics for Awareness of Need chart - Cognitive self-regulation*)

- information from the parent's feedback on Newsletter #11 about times and places where the child needs improved focus on and retention of the most important and relevant information – prepare pictures ahead of time

- books where key objects/characters are hidden (see Resource files - RESOURCES – *Storybooks coordinated with lesson target areas* for suggestions)

Language of spark* *to use in this lesson:*

Key words & phrases:

We, we're ...	Let's ...
You can	Let's think
Where should we start looking?	That's the most important thing.
What can you do to help yourself?	Is that important right now?
What should I do to help myself?	Say it over in your head.
How did you do?	That'll help your brain remember.

Vocabulary & concepts:

Topic – most important thing	Brain
Name (as in the name of something depicted in a drawing)	Important
	Distracted
	Ignore

Introduction:

Explain to the child that you want them to help you think of times when we need to figure out and remember what's most important. Tell them: "We're going to think of things at school, at home, and in other places. Can you think of one thing we do at school/home/other places where we need to figure out and remember what's most important and not get distracted? When it's time to go home, I have to think only about the things I need like my computer, my purse and my car keys. If I get distracted, I might forget something."

Practice:

Be sure to have a list of places and tasks that require the child to determine the most important and relevant information and keep it in mind. School examples include when looking at a book, when looking for your shoes and when listening to other people talk – you have to ignore other things and keep your objective in mind. Home examples can include listening to a story, looking for clothes and following directions. A community example can include wanting to look for a special toy at the store where you can be 'tempted' by so many other things.

Prompting:

If the child becomes distracted or doesn't focus on the most important information, prompt them: "Uh-oh, I think your brain got distracted. What could you do to help yourself?"

Enact an event where you become distracted by some irrelevant information or clue and prompt the child to notice and correct you: "How could I help myself?"

Prompt the child to say directions over to themselves to help their brain remember.

Self-monitoring:

Ask the child, "How can you help yourself remember to figure out and remember what's most important and not get distracted when you're (location or time you and the child added to their Awareness of Need chart)?" Help them think of ways they can remind themselves.

Solidifying:

Help the child review (a) what skills and strategies were learned in the lesson, (b) why it helps to use them and (c) what they noticed when they used them. Some children won't be able to verbalize or indicate some of this information but try to prompt responses from them. Clarify and add information as needed.

Highlighting:

Point out to the child how they figured out and remembered what was most important. Comment positively on their use of any strategy to help themselves, including saying directions over to themselves, being systematic or ignoring distractions.

Additional Comments:

Prompt the child's family to model and comment on their use of labeling things they look at and saying things over in their heads to help them remember. Ask them to use 'self-talk' (thinking out loud) to help the child hear what other people do. For example, they might say, "Okay, now I have to get lunch ready. I need some bread and some cheese and, oh, look at the plant needs some water, I forgot about the poor thing. Oops, the plant's not important right now, I'm trying to make lunch. Now where was I? ......"

If the child gets distracted by unimportant things, have them ask them what they should do to help themselves. Have them use the prompting outlined above.

Make sure they praise them for any self-regulation they exercise, including use of any strategies we have covered to this point.

Ask them for feedback on how well the child does in using strategies.

Lesson C:lir3

Because we want the child to assume more responsibility and control in their Cognitive Self-regulation, we need to reduce our use of direct instruction. At this stage, prompt them with questions like "What could you do to help yourself figure that out?" Don't give them direct instruction. Use indirect prompting and questions whenever possible. Don't feel 'mean' by not helping them – remember, we are helping them become more resourceful and self-reliant.

Working on ignoring is very important to children with ASC, as well as other developmental disabilities, in that they often are overwhelmed by incoming information. It's like every piece of information is given equal weight, regardless of its relevance and importance. In this unit, we have begun work on narrowing that field for the child so they don't feel as bombarded. They're also learning that they can simply not pay attention to some things.

The goal in this lesson is to help the child to become more resilient and advocate for themselves when focusing on and remembering the most important information in a task or activity.

Area of self-regulation 2: Cognitive		
Area receiving focus 1: Complete and accurate intake of information		
Subskill b: Determine and retain most important and relevant information		
Area of skill development 3 & 4: Resilience & Self-advocacy		
Primary executive functions:	**Secondary executive functions:**	
Cognitive flexibility		
Inhibitory control		
Planning and organization		
Self-monitoring		
Working memory		

Comments on executive functions: This activity requires the child to control their attention, monitor their performance and keep information in their working memory. There's also emphasis on planning and organization in that they're expected to work systematically and to identify the most important and relevant information. Cognitive flexibility is important because the child needs to shift their thinking from item to item and determine its importance in each task and to shift from topic to topic and setting to setting.

Task structuring:

Increasingly, provide the child with more complex information. At the Resilience stage, we want to increase their tolerance for material that is likely to distract them. We need them to continue to ignore unimportant information and focus solely on the key ideas and to learn to use strategies to remember them.

When focusing on Self-advocacy, introduce activities and events where there are distracting pieces of information. In this way, the child can learn to be more resilient and change objects, events and locations to help themselves.

Encourage the child to use Turtle Breathing so they can keep themselves calm and focused.

Objectives:

The child will be able to determine and label the most important information in a task or situation at least 80% of the time independently.

The child will be able to resist distractions and non-relevant information at least 50% of the time in daily situations.

Materials:

- worksheets and other activities (e.g. coloring pages) that have a visual component with verbal directions (see Resource files - EXAMPLE - *Verbal direction worksheet for determining the most important information* for an example and RESOURCES - *Internet sites coordinated with lesson activities* and RESOURCES - *Commercially available books and materials for sources*)
- books where key objects/characters are hidden (see Resource files - RESOURCES – *Storybooks coordinated with lesson target areas* for suggestions)
- markers, crayons/colors, sticky notes visual matching tasks with increasing number of distracter items
- recorded sound effects and environmental sounds, music, noises you produce (see Resource files for internet sources of background noise)
- pre-recorded activities with varying types of background noise at different intensities (see Resource files - RESOURCES - *Internet sites coordinated with lesson activities* for sources)
- typical daily activities in a variety of settings that have distracting elements such as other people talking or others doing a variety of activities near them
- study carrel or desk with cardboard screen they can work behind, ear plugs or earphones they can wear to reduce noise, large cardboard 'quiet' box or barrel they can sit in

Language of spark* to use in this lesson:

Key words & phrases:

We, we're ...	Let's ...
You can	Let's think
Where should we start looking?	That's the most important thing.
What can you do to help yourself?	Is that important right now?
What should I do to help myself?	Say it over in your head.
How did you do?	That'll help your brain remember.

Vocabulary & concepts:	
Topic – most important thing	Brain
Distracted	Important
Ignore	Bugging you

Introduction:

Explain to the child that they're so good at figuring out what's important and at working systematically, you're going to let them do it all by themselves. That means if they need help, you'll assist them, but they have such a good brain you know they can do it without you now.

To increase their resilience and ability to remain on task, remind them about ignoring. Tell them, "We can ignore things that aren't important. That can help our brains think better." Model some examples for them: have someone drop an object while you're working, play a recording of sound effects or music, indicate that one of the pictures on your worksheet is bugging you or place a favorite toy on the table. Say, "I can ignore that. It's not important right now. I can tell my brain, don't get distracted brain."

When working on Self-advocacy, tell the child that you know they can figure out what's most important all by themselves. You also know that they can keep their brain from getting distracted. Now you want them to do it all by themselves. Tell them, "If something is bugging you, you can just ignore it. Sometimes, you can go to a place that will make it easier, like the quiet corner/box/barrel, or you can cover your ears with ear plugs or earphones."

Practice:

Introduce more visually complex information and images. For practicing with verbal information, introduce some background noise while you give the direction. Introduce some minor distractions while the child is working. Point out the distraction and ask them what they could do to help themselves. Prompt them to tell their brain to ignore it because it's not important right now. Prompt them to say words to themselves – it's okay if they say them out loud right now. Do some things in their typical daily routines like going to get their shoes: prompt them to say "shoes" or "put on my shoes"' over and over all the way to their shoes. Saying the name or phrase in a sing-song manner may help increase their retention. Saying things over and over, or verbal, rehearsal, not only helps the child remember important information but also to stay focused.

When working on Self-advocacy, give the child opportunities to work on their own so they have chances to maintain their focus, determine what is most important, retain that information and deflect unimportant information and events. Be sure to add distractions so they have a chance to use their ignoring skills.

Prompting:

If the child has difficulty, just say "What could you do to help yourself?" If they're unable to self-correct their behavior, gently remind them of the approach you presented and then let them try.

As the child becomes more automatic and successful, ask, "How did you do?"

Watch the child work and comment whenever they seem to be ignoring a potential distraction. Comment positively on their use of ignoring.

After prompting and reinforcing the child's attempts, start asking them to explain, "Why do you think that's important?" Do this just occasionally so they don't feel they're under interrogation. Accept any reasonable answer, like "We're thinking about only _____ right now" or "That's most important." Having them express their reasoning will help solidify the rationale for looking for and thinking about only what is important.

Self-monitoring:

When the child is working on their own, occasionally ask, "Did you find and remember the most important things?" or "Did you ignore some things to help your brain?"

Solidifying:

Help the child review (a) what skills and strategies were learned in the lesson, (b) why it helps to use them and (c) what they noticed when they used them. Some children won't be able to verbalize or indicate some of this information but try to prompt responses from them. Clarify and add information as needed.

Highlighting:

Point out to the child how they figured out and remembered what was most important. Comment positively on their use of any strategy to help themselves, including Turtle Breathing and self-talk (saying things over to themselves). Continue to highlight and solidify their working systematically. Be sure to highlight the child's focusing on, labeling and remembering objects and events while performing tasks.

Additional Comments:

For some children, it's wise to do a supplemental activity on when and where NOT to ignore things and people. I've rarely found it to be a problem but check to see how the notion of 'ignoring' is working for each child. If they decide to ignore things and people they shouldn't, do a special chart with them about when to pay attention. It's best to phrase it "when to pay attention" rather than "when not to ignore" because very often children on the spectrum pay attention to the last word and we don't want that word to be "ignore". Examples of when they should pay attention are when Mom and/or Dad say it's time to get off the computer, when the teacher says it's time to put things away and when you hear a car coming. Ask the family for suggestions.

Prompt the child's family to model and comment on their use of any of the cognitive strategies. Also, make sure they praise the child for any self-regulation they exercise. If they get distracted by unimportant things or fails to identify the most important information, have them ask them what they should do. Have them use the prompting outlined above.

Ask them for feedback on how well the child does.

Lesson C:le1

> **Send home Newsletter #11.**
>
> Our main goal is to help the child look at a task/situation and determine what may be expected of them. We have worked with them on learning to focus and sustain their attention to the most important information, now we help them use those skills when checking out an activity or situation.
>
> Using signals/clues/models helps the child learn that you can often figure out what to do just by looking. He can figure out if they're supposed to assemble something, circle objects, sit down for supper, enter a group of people, etc. This skill is critical to behavioral, cognitive and Emotional Self-regulation as well as general social functioning.

> **The goal in this lesson** is to help the child figure out what he might be asked to do with a task or activity by looking for signals, clues and models to guide them.

Area of self-regulation 2: Cognitive		
Area receiving focus 1: Complete and accurate intake of information		
Subskill d: Determine task expectations		
Area of skill development 1: Awareness of Ability		
Primary executive functions:	**Secondary executive functions**:	
Cognitive flexibility		
Inhibitory control		
Planning and organization		
Self-monitoring		
Working memory		

Comments on executive functions: This activity requires the child to control their impulses and old habits, monitor their performance and keep information in their working memory while they check out each task. There's increasing emphasis on planning and organization as the child is required to use their prior knowledge and signals/clues/models from the context to help prepare themselves and their performance for each task. Some cognitive flexibility is needed to do this and to perform the tasks.

Task structuring:

Emphasis will be placed on helping the child detect and understand signals and clues and to use models to guide their expectations about what to do. Familiar worksheets and tasks and models are used in this lesson to provide structuring and content. We need them to learn how to scan a task or event, notice just the most important and relevant elements, signals, clues and models and then determine how to proceed.

NOTE: Use of Turtle Breathing before and during tasks should be encouraged.

Objective:

The child will be able to use signals, clues, and models for completing tasks accurately at least 80% of the time with adult support.

Materials:

- familiar worksheets and other hands-on tasks, such as puzzles, shoebox tasks (see the Resource files - RESOURCES - *Internet sites coordinated with lesson activities and* RESOURCES - *Commercially available books and materials*) and tasks with familiar formats
- unfamiliar worksheets/tasks containing similar key elements that suggest how to proceed (see Resource files - RESOURCES - *Internet sites coordinated with lesson activities*)
- worksheets with one item completed or craft activities with a model of the completed task (see Resource files - RESOURCES - *Internet sites coordinated with lesson activities* for suggestions)
- markers, crayons/colors, sticky notes

Language of spark* *to use in this lesson:*

Key words & phrases:

We, we're ...	That's a good way to help your brain remember.
You can	
What do you think we're supposed to do?	You're so clever.
	How did you know what to do?
Oh, it looks like you're not sure.	Let me help you so you know next time.
Did you use signals/clues/a model to figure out what to do?	Can you see some signals or clues that could help us?

Vocabulary & concepts:

Signal – tells us what to do	Model – tell us what to do
Clue – sometimes hiding but tells us what to do	

Introduction:

Signals and clues: "Signals help us know where to go, what to do and what is happening. A stop signal tells us to stop. Your name on your locker tells that the locker belongs to you. We're going to look for signals that tell us what to do. We're also going to look for clues. Just like a detective/police officer. Clues are like signals but they're at little bit sneakier. Sometimes, clues are hiding, and we have to find them."

Guide the child to look for the most important things in their work. Ask them: "What do you think we're going to do here? Can you see some signals or clues that could help us?" If they seem unsure, prompt them with comments like, "I see N-A-M-E and a line. That's a signal telling us what to do. What do you think we're supposed to do?" or "I see three boys but only two chairs. That's a signal telling us to do something – we need to get another chair." Or "I see (on a dot-to-dot activity) some dots and numbers and part of the picture missing. What do you think we're supposed to do here?" or "I see some numbers and a minus sign. What do you think we're supposed to do here?" Point to the important signals and prompt the child to respond as needed.

Models: "Models show us what to do." Show the child a completed (but very simple) craft or toy along with the parts to make it. "See, here's a model. It tells us what to do and where to put the parts." Show the child a worksheet with an example items completed: "Here's a model. This one is done for us and tells us what to do."

Practice:

Signals and clues: Start the child with tasks that are visually-obvious (for example, shoebox tasks). Let them attempt to start on their own. Watch them carefully. Guide and prompt (such as by quietly pointing to a features) if necessary to help them notice clues and signals. Ask the child what the signal or clue was that told them what to do, helping them as needed.

Models: Prompt and praise the child for looking back and forth from their work to the model: Say: "If you check the model and your work, it's a good way to help your brain remember." When they start to show an understanding of the notion of a 'model', provide them with some other materials and ask them how they can figure out what to do.

NOTE: Use of Turtle Breathing before and during looking for signals/clues/models should be encouraged.

Prompting:

If they're starting a task in a way that is intended, "You're so clever. How did you know what to do?" Help them point out key elements that acted as a signal/clue/model for them. For example, there may be a model, printed instructions, a completed example or what you normally do with the objects (like stacking blocks).

If they seem uncertain or is approaching the task in a way that isn't what was intended, comment on it: "Oh, it looks like you're not sure. Let me help you so you know next time." Then point out the main signals/clues/models and remind them of past experiences they're had. Have them complete the task. Provide only prompts and support and not direct instruction for completing the task if at all possible.

Self-monitoring:

After the child has practiced the strategies a few times, let them work on their own a bit. Ask, "Did you use signals/clues/a model to figure out what to do?"

Solidifying:

Help the child review (a) what skills and strategies were learned in the lesson, (b) why it helps to use them and (c) what they noticed when they used them. Some children won't be able to verbalize or indicate some of this information but try to prompt responses from them. Clarify and add information as needed.

Highlighting:

Point out to the child how they figured out what to do from the signals/clues/model. Comment positively on their use of strategies to help themselves. Be sure to highlight the child's looking carefully before performing tasks so they understand how it can assist them. Use of Turtle Breathing before and during looking should be encouraged.

Additional Comments:

This lesson can be a good opportunity to work on signals found in the child's surroundings, like traffic lights, stop signs, wash/restroom signs, etc. You might put together a book of signals with the child, having them find different ones at home, at school and in the community.

Lesson C:Ie2

Before starting this lesson, make sure you received feedback from families on times and places where each child needs to improve regulation of their feet from Newsletter #11.

During this lesson, be sure to tell the child about times and places in your life where you weren't accurate in figuring out what the expectations were and what happens because of it. This helps let them know that they're not the only person who experiences these problems.

The goal in this lesson is to help the child identify when and where they need to look for signals, clues and models to guide their responses.

Area of self-regulation 2: Cognitive		
Area receiving focus 1: Complete and accurate intake of information		
Subskill d: Determine task expectations		
Area of skill development 2: Awareness of Need		
Primary executive functions:	**Secondary executive functions**:	
Cognitive flexibility		
Inhibitory control		
Planning and organization		
Self-monitoring		
Working memory		

Comments on executive functions: This activity requires the child to control their impulses, monitor their performance, and keep information in their working memory while they figure out what to do and while they complete each task. There's increasing emphasis on planning and organization as the child is required to use their prior knowledge and signals/clues/models from the task to help them prepare themselves and their response. Cognitive flexibility is needed especially since different tasks and settings will be looked at.

Task structuring:

When focusing on Awareness of Need, we structure the task so the child is helped to think of where else they need to look for signals, clues and models to tell them what to do. Examples should be drawn from the child (or for the child as need be) that encompass their life (a) at school, (b) at home, and (c) in the community. All three settings must be addressed so extension and generalization receive specific focus.

Objective:

The child will be able to indicate at least one different example of when it's important to look for signals, clues and/or models for each of the three targeted settings with adult support.

Materials:

- Awareness of Need chart (see Resource files - TEMPLATE – *Awareness of Need chart* and ILLUSTRATIONS - *Topics for Awareness of Need chart - Cognitive self-regulation*)
- information from the parent's feedback on Newsletter #11 about times and places where the child needs to look for signals, clues and/or models – prepare pictures ahead of time
- pictures of scenes from school, home, community that contain signals, clues and models (see Resource files - RESOURCES - *Internet sites coordinated with lesson activities*)

Language of spark* *to use in this lesson:*

Key words & phrases:

We, we're ...	How about ....?
What signal/clue/model helped you know what to do?	What does that signal/clue/model tell you to do?

Vocabulary & concepts:

Signal	Model
Clue	

Introduction:

Explain to the child that you want them to help you think of times when we need to look for signals/clues/a model, so you know what to do. Tell them: "We're going to think of things at school, at home, and in other places. Can you think of one thing we do at school/home/other places where we need to look for signals/clues/a model, so we know what to do?"

Practice:

Be sure to have a list of times and places that require looking for signals/clues/models to determine expectations. School examples include a signal for asking permission to go to the bathroom (e.g. one finger up for having to urinate), a visual plan or schedule that signals when something is going to happen, line at the top of a worksheet that signals you need to put your name there and a model of a completed craft project that shows how it should look once you're finished. Home examples can include a table set with silverware and plates which suggests a meal is ready or Mom picks up her keys and heads to the door suggesting that sThey're going somewhere.

Community examples include traffic signals, footprints in the snow or people standing in line for a movie.

Prompting:

Prompt and support the child as needed drawing from information provided by parents. Ask, "How about .....?" (use an example provided by their parents). Act out the scenario if needed to help the child identify the signal/clue/model.

Self-monitoring:

Ask the child, "How can you help yourself remember to look for signals/clues/a model, so you know what to do when you're (location or time you and the child added to their Awareness of Need chart)?" Help them think of ways they can remind themselves.

Solidifying:

Help the child review (a) what skills and strategies were learned in the lesson, (b) why it helps to use them and (c) what they noticed when they used them. Some children won't be able to verbalize or indicate some of this information but try to prompt responses from them. Clarify and add information as needed.

Highlighting:

Point out to the child how they figured out what to do from the signals/clues/model. Comment positively on their use of strategies to help themselves. Be sure to highlight the child's careful looking at a task or situation before starting.

Additional comments:

Prompt the child's family to point out signals, clues and models in everyday life. Also, make sure they praise the child for any self-regulation they exercise, especially Turtle Breathing and talking to themselves about what they need to do (that is, self-talk). Have them use the prompting outlined above.

Ask them for feedback on how well the child does.

Lesson C:le3

Remember to encourage the child to use Turtle Breathing often to make sure they're calm and centered.

The goal in this lesson is to help the child help the child build resilience and develop self-advocacy skills so they can determine the expectations of different task and activities even in more challenging situations.

Area of self-regulation 2: Cognitive		
Area receiving focus 1: Complete and accurate intake of information		
Subskill d: Determine task expectations		
Area of skill development 3 & 4: Resilience & Self-advocacy		
Primary executive functions:	**Secondary executive functions:**	
Cognitive flexibility		
Inhibitory control		
Planning and organization		
Self-monitoring		
Working memory		

Comments on executive functions: This activity requires the child to control their impulses and old habits, monitor their performance and keep information in their working memory while they complete each task. There's increasing emphasis on planning and organization as the child is required to use their prior knowledge and signals, clues and models to help them get ready to complete a task. Cognitive flexibility is needed to perform the tasks as they'll have to use different signals, clues and models for different tasks and settings.

Task structuring:

At the Resilience stage, we want to increase the child's tolerance for novelty and complexity while looking for signals/clues/models. We need them to scan a task or event systematically, notice the most important elements, signals, clues and models and then determine how to proceed.

When focusing on Self-advocacy, we introduce activities and events that aren't completely obvious about the expectations. This may include forgetting to put a line for their name at the top of their worksheet or failing to provide them with directions or a model at all. This is meant to prompt the child to advocate for themselves.

Encourage the child to use Turtle Breathing to keep themselves calm and centered while determining what to do.

Objective:

The child will be able to use signals, clues and models for completing tasks at least 50% of the time independently.

The child will be able to ask for assistance in determining expectations of tasks and activities at least 50% of the time in appropriate situations.

Materials:

- worksheets and hands-on tasks, such as crafts, puzzles, shoebox tasks (see the Resource files - RESOURCES - *Internet sites coordinated with lesson activities*), missing a signal, clue or model such as the puzzle without a picture of what it's supposed to be or a craft that is just the pieces without a finished product

Language of spark* *to use in this lesson:*	
Key words & phrases:	
We, we're …	How did you know what to do?
You're so good at figuring out what to do.	What could you do to help yourself?
	You try your best.
I'm going to let them do it all by yourself.	I'll help you if you use your own brain first."
What signal/clue/model helped you know what to do?	I know you can do good work all by yourself.
You try your best	Sometimes it's hard to figure out what to do.
If you really don't know what to do, you can ask for help.	
How could you figure out what to do?	Your brain and eyes are really working!
Vocabulary & concepts:	
Signal	Model
Clue	

Introduction:

When working on Resilience, explain to the child, "You're so good at figuring out what to do, I'm going to let you do it all by yourself".

When working on Self-advocacy, tell the child: "I know you can do good work all by yourself but sometimes it's hard to figure out what to do. You try your best. If you really don't know what to do, you can ask for help. I'll help you if you use your own brain first."

Practice:

Introduce more tasks that are missing signals, clues and/or models as well as those that have visually complex information or images. Ask them to go ahead on their own. Let them struggle a little bit with the task. Don't jump in to help them too quickly. Give them up to a minute or two to figure out what to do. Remember, you're helping them to build up their ability to cope even in frustrating situations.

Watch them carefully. If they seem to be experiencing too much frustration, help them out with prompts but don't tell them what to do. Help them look for a signal/clue/model and praise them: "You're right, that's a signal/clue/model and that shows us what to do."

When working on Self-advocacy, prompt them by asking what they could do to help themselves. Give them some time to figure out what to do. Then remind them that they can ask you.

Prompting:

Give the child opportunities to try out a task for themselves. Watch them carefully and make sure they're using their systematic approach to finding and using signals, clues and models. Praise their efforts, describing what you see: "I see that you're looking carefully and thinking in your brain. Good work!"

Prompt the child with broad, open-ended questions like "How could you figure out what to do?" Then if they still cannot seem to figure out what to do, give them a more specific prompt like, "How about looking over here for a signal/clue/model?" where you narrow down where they need to search. Don't tell them what to do, use prompting and questions to help them look for signals/clues/models. If they're unable to self-correct their behavior, gently tap your finger on a key signal/clue/model and remind them to use it to help them figure out what to do.

Prompting at the Self-advocacy stage involves asking the child, "What could you do to help yourself?" Elicit information and/or action from them to improve their ability to determine the expectations for a task or situation. Prompt them to ask for help but only when and where necessary.

Self-monitoring:

As the child proceeds with an activity, ask them, "How did you know what to do? (said in a teasing tone to suggest "You sneaky person!") Did you use signals/clues/a model to figure out what to do?" Prompt them to explain how they knew what to do.

Solidifying:

Help the child review (a) what skills and strategies were learned in the lesson, (b) why it helps to use them and (c) what they noticed when they used them. Some children won't be able to verbalize or indicate some of this information but try to prompt responses from them. Clarify and add information as needed.

Highlighting:

Once the child experiences success, prompt them to explain how they figured out what to do. Every so often, use a surprised tone of voice and ask, "Boy, your brain and eyes are really working! How did you know how to do that?" Elicit some rationale from them in a non-threatening and playful way. Don't question them so often that they feel like they're under interrogation!

Point out to the child how they figured out what to do from the signals/clues/model. Comment positively on their use of strategies to help themselves.

Be sure to highlight the child's focusing on and scanning a task or situation before starting to help them understand what to do.

Additional Comments:

Ask the child's parents to prompt them to look for and use signals, clues and models when at home, and in the community. Prompt them to point out signals, clues and models, particularly those that can help guide their behavior. Have them use the prompting outlined above.

Continue to prompt the family to encourage the child to look carefully at a task or situation before trying something to determine the key signals, clues and models. Turtle Breathing should be incorporated whenever possible.

Ask the family to take trips around the community to look for signals, clues and models. Increasingly, point out behavioral models to show what people do in different places, like lining up at fast-food restaurants and stopping at the "Don't Walk" signal.

Lesson C:Nc 1

Send home Newsletter #12.

To this point, the child has learned to focus their attention selectively at the most important information, help themselves remember information by saying it over to themselves, ignore unimportant things and use signals, clues and models. The emphasis in this lesson is to teach the child how to 'construct meaning' from information he hears. It's like taking the pieces of a puzzle and putting them together into a whole scene or object. Children with autism tend to gather pieces of information together as if they were twigs – they're bundled together but they're every which way and the child doesn't make a whole picture out of them. The ability to build a clear and coherent picture out of information is critically important to understanding conversations and stories and for reading comprehension.

The goal in this lesson is to teach the child how to bring pieces of information he hears into a meaningful and logical whole picture.

Area of self-regulation 2: Cognitive			
Area receiving focus 2: Integration of information			
Subskill a: Construct meaning			
Area of skill development 1: Awareness of Ability			
Primary executive functions:		**Secondary executive functions**:	
	Cognitive flexibility		
	Inhibitory control		
	Planning and organization		
	Self-monitoring		
	Working memory		

Comments on executive functions: This activity requires the child to control their impulses, monitor their performance and keep information in their working memory while they work to put the pieces of information together. There's some emphasis on planning and organization as the child needs to manage incoming information and attempt to create a coherent meaning from it. Cognitive flexibility can be challenged because the child, as they assemble the pieces of information, may have to change their initial ideas.

Task structuring:

Emphasis will be placed on helping the child integrate pieces of information into a coherent picture. To do this, tasks are carefully structured so they can 'make pictures' of the information they hear (that is, they can visualize it). Practice material needs to be controlled for (a) 'picture-able' content, (b) the number of sentences, (c) number of 'picture-able' words and (d) the child's familiarity with the content.

The child will be provided with objects to use for acting out the story or they'll be prompted to draw a picture of the words they hear.

Before starting a story, the child is forewarned that they'll be asked four/five questions at the end. The questions will focus be about pictures they make from the words in the story.

Work slowly and carefully on the strategies presented in this lesson. Read the stories slowly, one sentence at a time and give the child lots of time to respond. This is a challenging and difficult area for most children with ASC so work with great patience and understanding.

NOTE: Use of Turtle Breathing before and during tasks should be encouraged to help them stay calm and centered.

Objective:

The child will be able to integrate at least three different but related pieces of information into a logical and reasonable picture at least 80% of the time with adult support.

Materials:

- short descriptive 'stories' three or more sentences in length (see examples in the Resource files - EXAMPLE - *Stories for visualizing information*) and commercially-available materials (see Resource files - RESOURCES - *Commercially available books and materials*)

- questions related to the stories which focus on (a) content ('what' questions about objects, their color, shape, size, quantity, location, action), (b) reasoning ('why' questions), (c) possibilities ('what might happen next') and (d) summary ("what's the story all about?", "What's a good name/title for this story?").

- miniature objects or pictures for each character or object in each story with some extras to act as potential distracters

- colored pencils, erasers and paper for drawing the story that they hear

Language of spark* to use in this lesson:

Key words & phrases:

We, we're …	The drawing is only to help your brain.
We're going to learn how to make pictures in our brains.	Try your best.
We listen to words and make pictures of them.	I'll help you if you use your own brain first.
What's the story all about?	Look how you …
What's a good name/title for this story?	All that's important is that your brain can understand the picture.
Oh, it looks like you're not sure.	Your brain only needs a little bit so it can remember.

Let me help you so you know next time.	Did you make that picture in your brain too?
Did that help your brain?	That's how you can help your brain remember the words in the story.
I'm going to ask you four/five questions about the story when it's done.	

Vocabulary & concepts:	
Name, title	What, who, where, when, why
Remember	Brain

Introduction:

"We're going to learn how to make pictures in our brains. We listen to words and make pictures of them. Right now, we're going to (a) make these objects act out the story OR (b) draw pictures (which ever process you choose for the child). Later, we'll make pictures just in our brains. I'll show you how I can make words into pictures." Read one of the short stories and (a) move the objects around OR (b) draw each piece of information as you read each sentence. Model having to erase something, saying "No, that's not what I want. I can just erase it and start again." Then ask questions about that story, prompting the child to help you.

Practice:

When practicing, do only one story per session because this activity is extremely taxing. If you do more than one story, the experience may become too tiring and negative.

Remind the child that you'll ask them four/five questions at the end. Since The child will be (a) moving and manipulating the objects to coincide with the story OR (b) drawing a picture, the feedback to you is clear. Slowly read only one sentence at a time. Then let them (a) move the objects OR (b) draw. Then read the next sentence. Watch them carefully and intercede when necessary.

A major area difficulty for children with ASC is integrating the pieces of information. They may remember and recall all of the bits but can't easily bring them together. You may find that the child draws individual pieces of information scattered around the page. Review the story and prompt them to put the information together to make "one picture".

Another stumbling block for many children with ASC is determining how much detail is enough. For example, if the story mentions grass, the child may proceed to draw single blades of grass all over the piece of paper. That's a situation where you need to intercede and remind them that they just need a little bit, just enough for their brain to remember there's grass.

Prompting:

If they're approaching the task in an appropriate way, say, "You're so clever. Look how you're making a picture." Help them point out key elements that they pictured, such as color, size, shape or location. For example, you can say, "Look how you made that dog brown just like in the story!"

If the child is worried about their ability to draw different images, tell them the drawing is only to help their brain. It doesn't have to be a beautiful drawing. His brain can understand the picture and that's all that's important.

If the child draws an image in great detail that keeps them from hearing the rest of the story, remind them, "Your brain only needs a little bit so it can remember." Prompt them to move on. If they persist, with the detail, let them experience missing the next pieces of information. That experience may be necessary to prompt them to move on.

If the child is uncertain how to answer a question at the end of the story or seems reticent, prompt them to look at their picture or the objects. Then ask the question again. If they still don't respond accurately, model the response for them.

If they seem uncertain or is approaching the task in a way that isn't going to result in accurate responding, comment on it: "Oh, it looks like you're not sure. Let me help you so you know next time." Then re-read one sentence and prompt them to try again. If they have difficulty, point out the key element(s) and help them respond.

Self-monitoring:

Every two or three sentences, ask the child how they're doing. Ask them, "Did you make that picture in your brain too? Did that help your brain?"

Solidifying:

Help the child review (a) what skills and strategies were learned in the lesson, (b) why it helps to use them and (c) what they noticed when they used them. Some children won't be able to verbalize or indicate some of this information but try to prompt responses from them. Clarify and add information as needed.

Highlighting:

Comment as the child listens to a story about how their drawing or manipulation of the objects is just like in the story. Tell them, "That's how you can help your brain remember the words in the story."

Additional Comments:

Keep in mind that the skills and strategies introduced in this lesson may require a lot of practice to solidify. Also, as information becomes more complex and less easily visualized, they'll have to learn other strategies.

Lesson C:Nc2

Before starting this lesson, make sure you received feedback from families on times and places where each child needs to improve regulation of their feet from Newsletter #12. Also, think of situations where the child has to bring pieces of information together in order to help them remember and understand. For example, when someone gives a multiple step instruction, you have to use strategies to remember it. When listening to or reading a story, you need to develop a picture of the information like placing objects and actions in a setting.

The goal in this lesson is to help the child identify when and where it's important to construct meaning in everyday life.

Area of self-regulation 2: Cognitive		
Area receiving focus 2: Integration of information		
Subskill a: Construct meaning		
Area of skill development 2: Awareness of Need		
Primary executive functions:	**Secondary executive functions**:	
Cognitive flexibility		
Inhibitory control		
Planning and organization		
Self-monitoring		
Working memory		

Comments on executive functions: This activity requires the child to control their impulses, focus their attention, monitor their performance and keep information in their working memory while they work to gather together the pieces. There's some emphasis on planning and organization as the child needs to manage incoming information and attempt to create a coherent meaning from it. Cognitive flexibility can be challenged at this stage because the child, as they assemble the pieces of information, may have to change their initial impression.

Task structuring:

When focusing on Awareness of Need, we structure the task so the child is helped to think of where else they need to pull pieces of information together to create a coherent message. Examples should be drawn from the child (or for the child as need be) that encompass their life (a) at school, (b) at home, and (c) in the community. All three settings must be addressed so extension and generalization receive specific focus.

Objective:

The child will be able to indicate at least one different example of when it's important to make a picture in their brain for each of the three targeted settings with adult support.

Materials:

- Awareness of Need chart (see Resource files - TEMPLATE – *Awareness of Need chart* and ILLUSTRATIONS - *Topics for Awareness of Need charts - Cognitive self-regulation*)
- information from the parent's feedback on Newsletter #12 about times and places where the child needs improved construction of meaning – prepare pictures ahead of time

Language of spark* *to use in this lesson:*

Key words & phrases:

We, we're …	The drawing is only to help your brain.
We listen to words and make pictures of them.	Look how you …
	That's how you can help your brain remember the words.
Oh, it looks like you're not sure.	
Let me help you so you know next time.	How about …?

Vocabulary & concepts:

Remember	Brain

Introduction:

Explain to the child that you want them to help you think of times when we need to make a picture in your brain. Tell them: "We're going to think of things at school, at home, and in other places. Can you think of one thing we do at school/home/other places where we need to make a picture of the words we hear?"

Practice:

Be sure to have a list of places and tasks that require visualizing information. Major ones will include listening to and reading stories, watching a movie or video and understanding directions.

Prompting:

Prompt and support the child as needed drawing from information provided by parents. Ask, "How about …..?" (use an example provided by their parents). Enact scenarios from different contexts in the child's life to provide examples of when it's important to integrate information.

Self-monitoring:

Ask the child, "How can you help yourself remember to make a picture in your brain when you're (location or time you and the child added to their Awareness of Need chart)?" Help them think of ways they can remind themselves.

Solidifying:

Help the child review (a) what skills and strategies were learned in the lesson, (b) why it helps to use them and (c) what they noticed when they used them. Some children won't be able to verbalize or indicate some of this information but try to prompt responses from them. Clarify and add information as needed.

Highlighting:

Point out to the child how they figured out what to do. Comment positively on their use of strategies to help themselves. Tell them, "That's how you can help your brain understand the words in the story."

Additional Comments:

Lesson C:Nc3

We won't do the Self-advocacy phase for the subskill "Construct meaning" until we introduce and practice the strategies for checking whether they understand the information. Once we do that, Self-advocacy is combined in Lesson C:Nm3.

The goal in this lesson is to help the child become better able to use strategies for constructing meaning when larger amounts of information are presented to them.

Area of self-regulation 2: Cognitive		
Area receiving focus 2: Integration of information		
Subskill a: Construct meaning		
Area of skill development 3: Resilience		
Primary executive functions:		**Secondary executive functions**:
	Cognitive flexibility	
	Inhibitory control	
	Planning and organization	
	Self-monitoring	
	Working memory	

Comments on executive functions: This activity requires the child to control their impulses, focus and sustain their attention, monitor their performance and keep information in their working memory while they assemble the pieces. There's some emphasis on planning and organization as the child needs to manage incoming information and attempt to create a coherent meaning from it. Cognitive flexibility can be challenged at this stage because the child, as they assemble the pieces of information, may have to change their initial ideas about what the information was about.

Task structuring:

At the Resilience stage, we want to increase the child's tolerance for increases in the amount of information. The amount of information presented in each story must be tailored to the individual child in terms of the number of sentences they can tolerate in each story. Press their limits to see how much information they can handle. We want to 'stretch' them a little without causing significant frustration. We're getting them ready for Self-Advocating. At this stage, we'll watch the child to make sure we pace the presentation of the information appropriately for them. Later, in the Self-advocacy stage, we'll expect them to request a slower pace.

Objective:

The child will be able to construct meaning from longer stories comprised of more three or four sentences at least 60% of the time independently.

Materials:

- short descriptive 'stories' more than three sentences in length and at a more advanced level (see examples in the Resource files - EXAMPLE - *Stories for visualizing information*) and commercially-available materials (see Resource files - RESOURCES - *Commercially available books and materials*)
- questions related to the stories which focus on (a) content ('what' questions about objects, their color, shape, size, quantity, location, action), (b) reasoning ('why' questions), (c) possibilities ('what might happen next') and (d) summary ("what's the story all about?", "What's a good name/title for this story?").
- miniature objects or pictures for each character or object in each story with some extras to act as potential distracters
- colored pencils, erasers and paper for drawing the story that they hear
- games (see Resource files - RESOURCES - *Commercially available books and materials*)

Language of spark* *to use in this lesson:*

Key words & phrases:

We, we're …	The drawing is only to help your brain.
What's the story all about?	Try your best.
What's a good name/title for this story?	I'll help you if you use your own brain first.
Did that help your brain?	Look how you …
I'm going to ask you four/five questions about the story when it's done.	All that's important is that your brain can understand the picture.
What could you do to help yourself?	Did you make one whole picture in your brain?
That's how you can help your brain understand the words in the story.	

Vocabulary & concepts:

Name, title	What, who, where, when, why
Remember	Brain

Introduction:

Explain to the child that they're so good at making pictures of the words they hear you're going to let them do it all by themselves. That means if they need help, you'll assist them, but they have such a good brain you know they can do it without you now.

Practice:

Introduce longer stories and/or those with more detailed images. Read one sentence at a time and let them draw a picture of the information before you present the next sentence.

Play games that require accumulation of information (see Resource files for suggestions)

Prompting:

Prompt them with questions like "What could you do to help yourself?" Don't give them direct instruction. Use indirect prompting and questions if at all possible.

If the child is n't proceeding with a task in an effective manner, just say "It looks like you're having some trouble. What can you do to help yourself?" If they're unable to self-correct their behavior, remind them to make a picture of the words.

As the child becomes more automatic, ask, "Did you make one whole picture in your brain?"

Self-monitoring:

After two or three sentences, ask the child how they're doing. Ask them, "Did you make that picture in your brain too? Did that help your brain?"

Solidifying:

Help the child review (a) what skills and strategies were learned in the lesson, (b) why it helps to use them and (c) what they noticed when they used them. Some children won't be able to verbalize or indicate some of this information but try to prompt responses from them. Clarify and add information as needed.

Highlighting:

Comment as the child listens to a story about how their drawing is just like in the story. Tell them, "That's how you can help your brain understand the words in the story."

Additional Comments:

Lesson C:Nm1

Send home Newsletter #13.

This is a crucial step in developing cognitive self-regulation skills. We have worked to this point with the child to help them use strategies to selectively focus their attention on and remember the most important information. We've also worked with them in learning how to develop a clear and complete picture of information he hears. Now, we are moving on to help them look at that information and decide if they understand it. We start in simple ways (such as not being able to hear the information at all) and then work toward more complex information and situations.

The goal in this lesson is to help the child learn to identify when they don't understand something presented to them.

Area of self-regulation 2: Cognitive			
Area receiving focus 2: Integration of information			
Subskill a: Monitor comprehension			
Area of skill development 1: Awareness of Ability			
Primary executive functions:		*Secondary executive functions*:	
	Cognitive flexibility		
	Inhibitory control		
	Planning and organization		
	Self-monitoring		
	Working memory		

Comments on executive functions: This activity requires the child to control their impulses, focus their attention, keep information in their working memory while they work to construct meaning and then check to make sure they understand it. There's emphasis on planning and organization as the child needs to manage incoming information and attempt to create and check the coherence. Cognitive flexibility can be challenged at this stage because the child, as they construct meaning and checks their understanding, may have to change their ideas about the meaning of the information.

Task structuring:

When focusing on comprehension monitoring, we introduce stories and direction that are either unclear or missing important information. To do this, stories/directions are presented with key information obscured (such as being masked by noise) so they can't hear it. The child is prompted to request repetition (asking you say the sentence again) or clarification (this is more specific information like "Did you say the dog was black?") of the information to help their understanding.

Objective:

The child will be able to indicate failure to understand verbal information by requesting clarification or repetition with at least 80% accuracy.

Materials:

- directions with one key piece of information obscured per sentence (see Resource files – EXAMPLE - *Listening with pieces of information obscured* for examples and RESOURCES - *Commercially available books and materials for resources* for materials) – for the activities in this lesson, it's best to pre-record the material so you're free to prompt the child and also you can provide 'proof' to the child that they really were unable to proceed with the information they were given.
- short stories like those used in the previous lessons on construction of meaning (see Resource files - EXAMPLE - *Stories for visualizing information* for examples and RESOURCES - *Commercially available books and materials* for resources)
- optional, colored pencils, erasers and paper for following the directions as needed

Language of spark* *to use in this lesson:*

Key words & phrases:

We, we're ...	Say that again, please.
If you can't hear all of the words, you need to stop me and ask me to say it again.	(Can you) say that again, please?
	Do you know what to do?
Did you really need to have that repeated?	Do you know ...?
Make a picture in your brain.	Let's listen again and see if we can figure out what to do.
Make sure to tell your brain to listen carefully.	Did you make sure you knew what to do?

Vocabulary & concepts:

Making a picture in your brain	Know
	Listen(ing)

Introduction:

Tell the child: "This time, we're going to do some tricky stories/directions. Some of the stories/directions don't have all the information we need. If you're not sure what to do, you need to stop me and ask me to say it again. You can say, "(Can you) say that again, please". For children who aren't yet using the "Can you" sentence form, just prompt them to say, "Say that again, please." It's often helpful to say it in a sing-song manner because the melody will help the child produce the whole phrase or sentence.

Practice:

Present a direction with a key word or phrase obscured. This can be done by producing noise (like coughing, sneezing, sounding a noisemaker) instead of saying the word(s). Let the child proceed as far as they can. If they stop, ask them, "Do you know what to do?" If they seem unsure, remind them, "If you're not sure, you can ask me to say it again. You can say, "Can you say that again, please?""

If they try to follow the direction or act on the information even without the key word(s), stop them and question, "Do you know what to do?" If necessary, ask them more specific information about what they heard, for example, "Do you know what color to make that dog?" or "Do you know where to put the circle?" If the child is unconvinced that there was something wrong with the story/direction, restate/replay it and ask them to try again.

If they start requesting repetition or clarification more often than he really need to, stop them and ask, "Did you really need to have that repeated? What did it say?" See if they can repeat the information. If not, prompt them, "Let's listen again really carefully this time and see if we can figure out what to do."

Progressively, have the child practice listening to stories and following directions by "making a picture in your brain" rather than using drawings or other props. It may, however, be necessary for them to continue sketching if auditory processing is particularly challenging for them.

Prompting:

Prompt the child with "What could you do to help yourself?" Elicit appropriate requests for repetition or clarification to improve their ability to understand the story/direction completely.

Praise their efforts, describing what you see: "I see that you're looking carefully and listening carefully and thinking in your brain. I couldn't trick you. Good listening!"

Self-monitoring:

After the child becomes more consistent in the accuracy of their requests and their watching you, ask, "Did you make sure you knew what to do? Make sure to tell your brain to listen carefully."

Solidifying:

Help the child review (a) what skills and strategies were learned in the lesson, (b) why it helps to use them and (c) what they noticed when they used them. Some children won't be able to verbalize or indicate some of this information but try to prompt responses from them. Clarify and add information as needed.

Highlighting:

Point out to the child how they listened carefully and helped make sure they knew what to do.

Additional Comments:

For a few children, it's important to have 'reliable' information about what part of stories or directions were obscured or missing – they may dispute it! That's why pre-recording was suggested. Having the information pre-recorded allows you to review it with the child to 'prove' that they really couldn't hear and understand it.

Don't remove the use of sketching to support comprehension if it's important to the child. This may be a skill that will provide support to them throughout their life.

Lesson C:Nm2

Before starting this lesson, make sure you received feedback from families on times and places where each child needs to improve regulation of their feet from Newsletter #13.

The goal in this lesson is to help the child identify when and where in their daily life they need to make sure he understand information he hears.

Area of self-regulation 2: Cognitive
Area receiving focus 2: Integration of information
Subskill b: Monitor comprehension
Area of skill development 2: Awareness of Need

Primary executive functions:		**Secondary executive functions**:	
	Cognitive flexibility		
	Inhibitory control		
	Planning and organization		
	Self-monitoring		
	Working memory		

Comments on executive functions: This activity requires the child to control their impulses, focus their attention, monitor their performance and keep information in their working memory while they work to ensure they understand it. There's some emphasis on planning and organization as the child needs to manage incoming information and attempt to create and check their understanding. Cognitive flexibility can be challenged at this stage because the child, as they check their understanding, may have to change their initial impression.

Task structuring:

When focusing on Awareness of Need, we structure the tasks so the child is helped to think of where else they'd need to request repetition or clarification, so they understand everything. Examples should encompass their life (a) at school, (b) at home, and (c) in the community. All three settings must be addressed so extension and generalization are sufficiently broad.

Objective:

The child will be able to indicate at least one different example of when it's important to make sure they know what to do for each of the three targeted settings with adult support.

Materials:

- Awareness of Need chart (see Resource files - TEMPLATE – *Awareness of Need chart* and ILLUSTRATIONS - *Topics for Awareness of Need charts - Cognitive self-regulation*)
- information from the parent's feedback on Newsletter #13 about times and places where the child needs improved comprehension monitoring – prepare pictures ahead of time
- storybooks on what happens when someone forgets to listen carefully (see Resource files - RESOURCES – *Storybooks coordinated with lesson target areas*)

Language of spark* *to use in this lesson:*

Key words & phrases:

We, we're …	Say that again, please.
Can you think of one thing we do at school/home/other places where we need to be careful about knowing what to do?	How can you help yourself remember to use your good listening?

Vocabulary & concepts:

Making a picture in your brain	Know
Listen(ing)	Remember

Introduction:

Explain to the child that you want them to help you think of times when we need to know what to do. Sometimes, there's a noise so we can't hear everything. Sometimes people speak too quietly for us to hear. Sometimes we forget to listen carefully when someone is talking. Sometimes we just can't remember what the person said." Tell them: "We're going to think of times at school, at home, and in other places when it's really important to know what to do. Can you think of one thing we do at school/home/other places where we need to be careful about knowing what to do?"

Practice:

Be sure to have a list of places and times that require careful attention and comprehension of information.

For a break and also to provide further examples, present stories that show what might happen when you don't hear information accurately.

Prompting:

Enact an event where you don't hear something the child says correctly/completely and proceed with partial information. Prompt the child to notice and correct you.

Self-monitoring:

Ask the child, "How can you help yourself remember to use your good listening when you're (location or time you and the child added to their Awareness of Need chart)?" Help them think of ways they can remind themselves.

Solidifying:

Help the child review (a) what skills and strategies were learned in the lesson, (b) why it helps to use them and (c) what they noticed when they used them. Some children won't be able to verbalize or indicate some of this information but try to prompt responses from them. Clarify and add information as needed.

Highlighting:

Point out to the child when they listen carefully and helps make sure they knew what to do.

Additional Comments:

Continue watching for the child to ask for repetition or clarification more often than they need or less often than they need. This may be an indication of failure to generalize but also fatigue. Be sure to give them fairly short practice sessions with breaks from listening.

Lesson C:Nm3

To this point, we've taught the child how to cope with listening in noise, how to ignore unimportant things, how to construct meaning from information he hears and how to check to make sure they understand that information. Now, we are going to bring this all together to help them increase their ability to cope with everyday distractions and to advocate for themselves. We are increasing the information load, adding distractions and not providing the child with any support material (they need to advocate for themselves and ask for it if they need it).

Don't feel mean by not helping the child right away. Remember, we're helping them become more resourceful and self-reliant.

The goal in this lesson is to help the child be better able to cope in more challenging situations and advocate for themselves if they're having

Area of self-regulation 2: Cognitive

Area receiving focus 2: Integration of information

Subskills a & b: Construct meaning & Monitor comprehension

Area of skill development 3 & 4: Resilience & Self-advocacy

Primary executive functions:		Secondary executive functions:	
	Cognitive flexibility		
	Inhibitory control		
	Planning and organization		
	Self-monitoring		
	Working memory		

Comments on executive functions: This activity requires the child to control their impulses, monitor their performance and keep information in their working memory while they work to ensure they understand it. There's some emphasis on planning and organization as the child needs to manage incoming information, attempt to create and check the coherence as well as determine what to do to help themselves (self-advocate). Cognitive flexibility can be challenged at this stage because the child, as they check their understanding, may have to change their initial impression and they have to determine how to self-advocate.

Task structuring:

At the Resilience stage, we want to increase the child's tolerance for dealing with incomplete information in more challenging settings. Situations and activities must be expanded to help them learn to deal with more variables simultaneously. For the story activities, we will increase the amount of information presented to gently 'press' the child's limits.

When focusing on Self-advocacy, introduce activities and events that prompt the child to use the skills and strategies taught and practiced in these lessons on their own. We want to challenge them and present situations and tasks that will give them opportunities to practice their self-advocacy skills.

Objective:

The child will request repetition or clarification of information and/or help when they don't fully understand with at least 60% accuracy when working independently.

Materials:

- directions with one key piece of information obscured per sentence (see Resource files – EXAMPLE - *Listening with pieces of information obscured* for examples and RESOURCES - *Commercially available books and materials for resources* for materials) – use pre-recorded material so the child can work on their own

- descriptive 'stories' more than three sentences in length and at a more advanced level (see Resource files - EXAMPLE - *Stories for visualizing information* for examples and RESOURCES - *Commercially available books and materials* for resources)

- questions related to the stories

- background noises and other potential distractions or disturbances; add recorded environmental sounds or turn up a radio or music in the background (see Resource files - RESOURCES - *Internet sites coordinated with lesson activities* for sources)

- distractions or interruptions, such as other people entering the situation and having conversations

Language of spark* *to use in this lesson:*

Key words & phrases:

We, we're …	Say that again, please.
If you really have a hard time listening and understanding, you know how to ask people to say things again.	(Can you) say that again, please?
	Sometimes, it's too noisy to listen well.
	Sometimes, you might get distracted.
It's your turn to help yourself.	Sometimes you might have a hard time remembering all of the story.
I will help you as much as I can.	If that happens, you could go to a quieter place or you could ask everyone to be quieter.
What can you do to help yourself?	
Did you make a picture in your brain?	You made sure you knew what to do.
Did you check to make sure you understand everything?	Good thinking!

215

Did you ignore things that aren't important?"	
Vocabulary & concepts:	
Making a picture in your brain Listen(ing) Ignore Think(ing)	Know Remember All by yourself

Introduction:

Following verbal directions: Explain to the child that they're so good at figuring out what to do if they don't understand something, you're going to let them do it all by themselves. Explain that sometimes noise and sounds make it hard to listen, but they can ignore them. "If you really have a hard time listening and understanding, you know how to ask people to say things again."

"Sometimes, it's too noisy to listen well. Sometimes, you might get distracted. If that happens, you could go to a quieter place or you could ask everyone to be quieter. It's your turn to help yourself. I'll help you as much as I can."

Show them how to turn the recorded directions off and on so they can start and stop them when they're ready.

Listening to stories: "We're going to do some stories together. I'll read the story and you make a picture in Sometimes noise and sounds make it hard to listen but you can ignore them. Sometimes you might have a hard time remembering all of the story. If you really have a hard time listening and understanding, you know how to ask people to say things again. You also know how to ask for things that might help you."

Practice:

Following verbal directions: Let the child listen to the directions and respond to them on their own. Play some background noise or introduce other distractions, like having other people come and talk to you.

Listening to stories: Start reading a story to the child without your putting out pencils, paper, objects, etc. Read the story slowly but don't stop at the end of each sentence as we did before. Once you finish the story, ask the child the questions. Play some background noise or other distracting feature.

Prompting:

For both activities, if you notice that the child is experiencing frustration, stress or general confusion, ask them, "Are you okay? What can you do to help yourself?" Turtle Breathing should be the first thing they try.

Prompt them to think of things on their own but, as needed, remind them of things they can do. For example, they can ask to have things repeated. Remind them also they can go to a quieter place or ask other people to be quieter.

Self-monitoring:

After the child requests clarification or repetition or some other form of assistance that indicates they're trying to make sure they understand, praise them, "You made sure you knew what to do. Good thinking!"

After the child listened to a story or set of directions, ask questions like, "Did you make a picture in your brain? Did you check to make sure you understand everything? Did you ignore things that aren't important?"

Solidifying:

Help the child review (a) what skills and strategies were learned in the lesson, (b) why it helps to use them and (c) what they noticed when they used them. Some children won't be able to verbalize or indicate some of this information but try to prompt responses from them. Clarify and add information as needed.

Highlighting:

Praise their efforts, describing what you see: "I see that you're looking carefully and thinking in your brain AND you're ignoring noises. Good thinking!"

Point out to the child when they listen carefully, asks for help, materials or changes that assist them in making sure they know what to do.

Point out to them when they attempt to make the listening situation better for themselves in any way.

Additional Comments:

Continue to be very careful that the child doesn't over-use the requests for repetition and clarification. Some children will start using them instead of listening carefully.

Don't remove the use of sketching to support comprehension if it's important to the child. This time, however, they need to ask for the materials needed for sketching – you 'forgot' to put them out.

Prompt the child's family to model requests for repetition and clarification and point it out to the child – "that way I can make sure I understand everything." Also, make sure they praise them talking to themselves – it's a good way to help them remember strategies and 'think in their brain'.

Prompt parents to model self-advocacy to improve their ability to listen, such as turning the radio or music down. Make sure they point it out to the child so their self-advocacy skills can be solidified, reinforced and expanded.

Ask the parents for feedback on how well the child does.

Lesson C:Ept1

Send home Newsletter #14 when you start this lesson. Include a copy of the list of major features for describing objects, list of additional features for describing scenes and the list of major components for relating events.

We have focused to this point on helping the child understand what the most important information is, how to take in accurate and complete information and how to make sure he put the pieces together and understood it. We're now switching focus to helping the child regulate their output of information to make sure it's understandable to other people. We do that by teaching them what information is needed for describing objects, scenes and events.

Our main goal in this area is to help the child determine what's most important and relevant to tell you, to plan their response and then provide precise information. There's an important distinction that the child must learn between too little and too much information. By using a barrier and identical activities, we set up a scenario where a fair amount of detail is needed. In this situation, their failure to provide sufficient information becomes concretely obvious because your activities won't match. They may provide more detail than needed and start bogging down. It may take some time to help them understand what necessary <u>and</u> sufficient information is. Take the time now but keep it fun.

NOTE: Be careful not to be too helpful with the child. Be very strict with yourself and only follow exactly what the child says. Don't fill in the blanks and do what you think they want you to do. The instructions must be clear and complete and understandable to people who don't know the child or anything about them. Make it playful but be strict. Don't feel 'mean'. We are trying to help the child

---

The goal in this lesson is to help the child plan and provide information important to helping other people understand their thoughts and ideas when he describes objects, scenes and sequences of events.

Area of self-regulation 2: Cognitive
Area receiving focus 3: Expression of knowledge
Subskill a: Plan and tailor
Area of skill development 1: Awareness of Ability

Primary executive functions:		*Secondary executive functions:*	
	Cognitive flexibility		
	Inhibitory control		
	Planning and organization		
	Self-monitoring		
	Working memory		

Comments on executive functions: This activity requires the child to control their impulses and old ways of doing things, monitor their performance and keep information in their working memory while they work to put together their ideas. There's a great deal of emphasis on planning and organization as the child needs to think ahead about how to form a complete and coherent message. Cognitive flexibility is challenged at this stage because the child, as they assemble the pieces of information and tries out different explanations, may have to change their approach.

Task structuring:

In the Awareness phase, we want to draw the child's attention to how to plan precise and understandable expression of their ideas and how to begin tailoring them to the listener. To start, we use really simple pictures and tasks that have only a few objects and features in them. We structure tasks so the child is provided clear and concrete feedback about the clarity of their message (by using barrier tasks). Then we introduce describing scenes which include actions, feelings, time, etc. Finally, we help the child describe events.

Before starting all barrier activities, be review the duplicate pictures carefully with the child to establish that both your and their activities are identical.

NOTE: Use of Turtle Breathing before and during tasks should be encouraged.

Objective:

The child will be able to provide precise and understandable information about objects, scenes and sequences of events when performing structured tasks at least 80% of the time with adult support.

Materials:

- list of major features to include in descriptions – number, size, shape, color, location (see Resource files - ILLUSTRATIONS - *Major and additional features for describing objects and events*)
- duplicate coloring pages or cut-and-paste activities with simple objects, animals or people (see Resource files - RESOURCES - *Internet sites coordinated with lesson activities*)
- list of other features to include when describing scenes – object, person, animal, action, feelings/mood, time, comparison (see Resource files - ILLUSTRATIONS - *Major and additional features for describing objects and events*)

- duplicate pictures scenes, cut-outs to make a scene, cut-outs to make a creature (see Resource files - RESOURCES - *Internet sites coordinated with lesson activities*)
- list of story features to include when describing a sequence of events – time, person/animal, place, events, ending (see Resource files - ILLUSTRATIONS - *Major and additional features for describing objects and events*)
- sequence pictures (duplicate set, one with pictures separated and the other shown in a sequence), wordless storybooks, etc. (see Resource files - RESOURCES - *Internet sites coordinated with lesson activities and* RESOURCES – *Storybooks coordinated with lesson target areas*)
- crayons/colors, colored markers or colored pencils, glue or paste
- barrier to block the child's view of your (duplicate) activity – can be a folder, binder or easel placed between you and the child that is tall enough and wide enough to make sure they can't see your work

Language of spark* *to use in this lesson:*

Key words & phrases:

We, we're ...	How about ....?
You and I both have the same coloring/gluing.	Say it over in my brain.
	Ask if I'm not sure.
You've got to tell me what to color/glue.	I won't be able to see what you're doing because we have this barrier in front of us.
Those other things aren't important right now.	
What can you do to help yourself?	I didn't have to say anything about the (feature) of (object) because (feature) was most important.
What did you do to help yourself?	
If there's only one in a picture, you only need to tell its name.	Let's use our finder fingers to check to see if they're the same/identical.
If there's more than one, you just have to tell the things that make them different.	Can you say that again please?
	Did you tell me all of the important parts so I could understand what to do?

Vocabulary & concepts:

Teacher	Same, identical
Quantity	Location
Size	Shape
Color	Important/not important
Compare	Brain
Order	Name

Introduction:

Describing objects: "We're going to do some coloring/gluing but this time, you're going to be the teacher. You and I both have the same coloring/gluing and you've got to tell me what to color/glue. The only trouble is, I won't be able to see what you're doing because we have this barrier in front of us. You've got to use your words to tell me what to do. I need to know what things to color/glue. Here's a list of important things you might need to tell me so my picture will look the same as yours. Sometimes, I'll need to know where to put things. Sometimes, you'll have to tell me how many things, the size, the shape and the color. Let's give it a try. I'll be the teacher first so you can find out what it's like." Before starting, be sure to show the child that both coloring/gluing activities are the same for you and the child. Put the list of major features out so both you and the child can see it.

Give them one direction at a time, pointing to each major feature as you mention it. For example, as you say, "Color the big dog brown", point to size and then color on the list. Remind them to say the direction over in their brain and be sure to ask you to say it again if they're not sure. Let the child respond to your direction and you do what you asked them to do. After the first few directions, point out to the child, "I didn't have to say anything about the number of dogs because size was most important. I didn't have to talk about the shape of the dog or where it was because there's only one big dog. Those other things aren't important right now."

After each direction, remove the barrier so you can compare the two drawings. Say, "Let's compare our pictures and see if they're the same/identical." Use your finder fingers to examine both pictures and name each feature to see if they're the same.

If the pictures are the same, comment on the child's good listening, replace the barrier and give them another direction. Then recheck the two pictures to see if they're the same and so on, one direction at a time during this introduction phase.

If the two pictures aren't the same, comment, "Oh, oh, maybe I didn't tell you the most important things. Do you remember what I said?" If the child can't recall what you said, tell it to them again and ask, "What can you do to help yourself?" Prompt them to remind themselves to "say it over in my brain" and "ask if I'm not sure" (model, "Can you say that again please?").

Do a few more directions, including all major features by the time you're done. Let the child make mistakes. That helps them learn.

Describing scenes: "We're going to do some coloring/gluing but this time, we're going to do a whole scene, like at a park or school. You and I both have the same coloring/gluing and you've got to tell me what to do. We'll have the barrier again, so I won't be able to see what you're doing. You've got to use your words to tell me what to do. I need to know what things to color/glue. We're going to use the same list of important things we used last time but we're also going to add some things. Sometimes, I'll need to know which person or animal or thing to look for, what they're doing, how they're feeling and what time it's. Sometimes, it helps if you're not sure what to name something, you can compare it to other things, like "It looks like a duck but has fur" or "It's the same color as chocolate ice cream" or "It's the same shape as a leaf". Let's give it a try. I'll be the teacher first so you can find out what it's like." Before starting, be sure to show the child that both coloring/gluing activities are the same for you and the child. Put the list of major features and the list of other features out so both you and the child can see them.

Give them one direction at a time, pointing to each major or other feature as you mention it. For example, as you say, "Find the happy man who's walking on the sidewalk and color their shirt blue", point to feelings, person, action, location and then color on the lists. Let the child respond to your direction and you do what you asked them to do. Remind them to say the direction over in their brain and be sure to ask you to say it again if they're not sure. Check with them to make sure your pictures are identical. Point out to the child, "I had to tell where the man was because there are lots of men in this picture. I had to tell you the man was happy because there are two men on the sidewalk and only one looks happy – see, they're smiling."

After each direction, remove the barrier so you can compare the two scenes. Say, "Let's compare our pictures and see if they're the same/identical." Use your finder fingers to examine both pictures and name each feature to see if they're the same.

If the pictures are the same, comment on the child's good listening, replace the barrier and give them another direction. Then recheck the two pictures to see if they're the same and so on, one direction at a time during this introduction phase.

If the two pictures aren't the same, comment, "Oh, oh, maybe I didn't tell you the most important things. Do you remember what I said?" If the child can't recall what you said, tell it to them again and ask, "What can you do to help yourself?" Prompt them to remind themselves to "say it over in my brain" and "ask if I'm not sure" (model, "Can you say that again please?").

Do a few more directions, including all major and other features as appropriate. Let the child make mistakes. That will help their learning as well as their use of rehearsal (saying the direction over in their brain) and asking for repetition of directions when needed.

Describing a sequence of events: "We're going to tell some stories. Here's a list of the important things to tell. We have to tell when the story happens – you know, like once upon a time or one day. Then we have to tell who the main person in the story is. Then we tell where they live. Next we have to tell what happens. To start, we're just going to tell 1/2/3 things (depending on the child) that happen in the story and then how they feel in the end. How does just about every story end? … and they lived happily ever after … that's how they feel. Let's give it a try. Here is a story shown in some pictures. I've got the same pictures but mine aren't put together like yours. You've got to tell me the story, so I know what order to put them in. We'll put up the barrier again, so I don't peek." Put the list of story features out so both you and the child can see them.

Have the child tell the story and you place each picture in front of you in the order they say. Let them tell the whole story. Request repetition or clarification when needed and comment on why you needed to ask (for example, "I wasn't sure …" or "I didn't say it over in my brain."). Then compare the picture sequences to see if they're the same.

Practice:

Describing objects: Before starting all tasks, be sure to show the child that both coloring/gluing activities are the same for you and the child. Then put the barrier between you.

Prompt the child to look carefully at their picture and use their finder finger to check everything. Then prompt them to figure out where to start.

Let the child know that it's their turn to be the 'teacher'. Prompt them to think about what they'd like to color/glue first. Remind them to be the teacher and tell you what to do. Show them the list of major features and keep it in front of them for reference. Let them attempt one instruction. Take away the barrier and compare your pictures to see if they're the same (be sure to use your finder finger and name each feature on the two activities).

If the child's activity and yours look the same (that is, their instructions were clear and you understood them), praise them for thinking carefully and using their words so well. Continue with the task, checking after every instruction to make sure you understood.

If the child's activity and yours look different, check very carefully with the child what might have been missed in their instructions – check it against the list of major features. Sometimes, children will dispute your listening skills and indicate that they told you what to do but you didn't listen. Don't argue with them. Just tell them you'll listen more carefully next time and ask them if you need help. Review the major features they need to tell you before trying again.

Make occasional mistakes so they get a chance to correct you and prompt you to "say it over in your brain" and "ask to say it again if you're not sure".

If the child describes very detailed information that's more than you need in this situation (for example, using every one of the major features when only a few were necessary), name each feature and ask them if it's important to tell you the feature. Explain the logic, "If there's only one in a picture, you only need to tell its name. If there's more than one, you just have to tell the things that make them different."

Describing scenes: Before starting all tasks, be sure to show the child that both coloring/gluing activities are the same for you and the child. Then put the barrier between you.

Prompt the child to look carefully at their picture and use their finder finger to check everything. Then prompt them to figure out where to start.

Let the child know that it's their turn to be the 'teacher'. Prompt them to think about what they'd like to color/glue first. Remind them to be the teacher and tell you what to do. Show them the lists of major and other features and keep them in front of them for reference. Let them attempt one instruction. Take away the barrier and compare your pictures to see if they're the same (be sure to use your finder finger and name each feature on the two activities).

If the child's activity and yours look the same (that is, their instructions were clear and you understood them), praise them for thinking carefully and using their words so well. Continue with the task, checking after every instruction to make sure you understood.

If the child's activity and yours look different, check very carefully with the child what might have been missed in their instructions – check it against the list of major features. Sometimes, children will dispute your listening skills and indicate that they told you what to do but you didn't listen. Don't argue with them. Just tell them you'll listen more carefully next time and ask them if you need help. Review the major or other features they need to tell you before trying again.

Make occasional mistakes so they get a chance to correct you and prompt you to "say it over in your brain" and "ask to say it again if you're not sure".

If the child describes very detailed information that's more than you need in this situation (for example, using every one of the major features when only a few were necessary), name each feature and ask them if it's important to tell you the feature. Explain the logic, "If there's only one in a picture, you only need to tell its name. If there's more than one, you just have to tell the things that make them different."

Describing a sequence of events: Proceed on with other picture sequences using the barrier. Add wordless storybooks.

NOTE: If the child is including all important pieces of information and is able to construct reasonable stories with the wordless books, move on to telling stories about things that have happened to them. You can try things like what they did last weekend or telling about a time when they hurt themselves. You may have to model this for them first. In the beginning, keep the stories simple with just a few main events.

If the child includes all story features on the list even if it's not the best story, praise them for thinking carefully and using their words so well. This is a building process where more detail is added over time.

If the child doesn't include all features in their story, stop them and check with them child what they missed. Have them start the story again at that point and proceed on.

Make occasional mistakes so they get a chance to correct you and prompt you to "say it over in your brain" and "ask to say it again if you're not sure".

Prompting:

Use the list of major features to prompt the child to include more or less information.

Pretend not to understand unless their description is sufficiently precise. Request repetition or clarification as needed.

Praise the child for precise but not overly-detailed information.

Self-monitoring:

After the child completes a few directions or a story, ask, "Did you tell me all of the important parts so I could understand?"

Prompt them to explain their thinking and planning ("What did you do to help yourself?" – that is, how they used the feature lists and made a picture in their brain).

Solidifying:

Help the child review (a) what skills and strategies were learned in the lesson, (b) why it helps to use them and (c) what they noticed when they used them. Some children won't be able to verbalize or indicate some of this information but try to prompt responses from them. Clarify and add information as needed.

Highlighting:

Point out to the child how they used clear words and told you exactly what to do/what happened. Highlight how your picture or some aspect of it looks identical. Tell them what a good job they did.

Additional Comments:

Lesson C:Ept2

> **Before starting this lesson**, make sure you received feedback from families on times and places where each child needs to improve regulation of their feet from Newsletter #14.

> **The goal in this lesson** is to help the child identify when and where they need to use the strategies introduced and practiced in the previous lesson in order to express their ideas and thoughts clearly and in a manner that's understandable to other people.

Area of self-regulation 2: Cognitive			
Area receiving focus 3: Expression of knowledge			
Subskill a: Plan and tailor			
Area of skill development 2: Awareness of Need			
Primary executive functions:		**Secondary executive functions**:	
	Cognitive flexibility		
	Inhibitory control		
	Planning and organization		
	Self-monitoring		
	Working memory		

Comments on executive functions: This activity requires the child to control their impulses and old ways of expressing themselves, monitor their performance and keep information in their working memory while they work to put together their responses. There's a great deal of emphasis on planning and organization as the child needs to think ahead about how to form complete and coherent messages. Cognitive flexibility is challenged at this stage because the child, as they assemble the pieces of information and tries out different explanations, may have to change their approach.

Task structuring:

When focusing on Awareness of Need, we structure the task so the child is helped to think of where else they need to use precise and complete directions, descriptions and explanations. Examples should be drawn from the child (or for the child as need be) that encompass their life (a) at school,

(b) at home, and (c) in the community. All three settings must be addressed so extension and generalization receive specific focus.

Objective:

The child will be able to indicate at least two different examples of when it's important to use precise words for each of the three targeted settings with adult support.

Materials:

- Awareness of Need chart (see Resource files - TEMPLATE – *Awareness of Need chart* and ILLUSTRATIONS - *Topics for Awareness of Need charts - Cognitive self-regulation*)
- information from the parent's feedback on Newsletter #14 about times and places where the child needs to communicate more clearly – prepare pictures ahead of time

Language of spark* *to use in this lesson:*

Key words & phrases:

We, we're ...	How about ....?
Can you think of one thing we do at school/home/other places where we need to tell people really clearly what to do/what we're thinking?	How can you help yourself remember to use your good talking when you're ...

Vocabulary & concepts:	
Good talking	

Introduction:

Explain to the child that you want them to help you think of times when we need to think about and explain things really clearly to other people. Tell them: "We're going to think of when we need to use our good talking at school, at home, and in other places. Can you think of one thing we do at school/home/other places where we need to tell people really clearly what to do/what we're thinking?"

Practice:

Be sure to have a good list of places and tasks that require them to use precise language. Examples can include giving instructions about how to perform a task or how to turn on a computer or TV.

Prompting:

Add some humor to your discussion by describing how forgetting to tell someone a specific feature (like number, size, shape, color or location) might cause confusion and problems at school, home, and in the community. For example, you might say, "Push the button" without telling which one, red for off or green for on. It's always helpful to add incidents from your own life about when you forgot to provide all of the needed information and someone became confused or did something you didn't intend.

Self-monitoring:

Ask the child, "How can you help yourself remember to use your good talking when you're (location or time you and the child added to their Awareness of Need chart)?" Help them think of ways they can remind themselves.

Solidifying:

Help the child review (a) what skills and strategies were learned in the lesson, (b) why it helps to use them and (c) what they noticed when they used them. Some children won't be able to verbalize or indicate some of this information but try to prompt responses from them. Clarify and add information as needed.

Highlighting:

Point out to the child how they thought about what to say and used careful directions.

Point out when the child as the listener requests repetition and clarification of information when they're uncertain.

Additional Comments:

Prompt the child to engage peers, siblings and other family members in barrier games. This can provide effective feedback for the child. Other children tend to be fairly "brutally honest" and are more likely to make comments that are direct and to the point if the messages aren't clear.

Lesson C:Ept3

This is the last lesson in the Cognitive Self-regulation unit.

Copy and complete the **Certificate of Completion** (see Resources files – *Certificate of completion - Cognitive self-regulation unit*) and have it ready to give to the child at the end of this lesson.

The goal in this lesson is to help the child continue to use clear and understandable descriptions of their thinking and ideas even when in less than optimal settings, with their advocating for themselves as needed.

Area of self-regulation 2: Cognitive		
Area receiving focus 3: Expression of knowledge		
Subskill a: Plan and tailor		
Area of skill development 3 & 4: Resilience & Self-advocacy		
Primary executive functions:	**Secondary executive functions**:	
Cognitive flexibility		
Inhibitory control		
Planning and organization		
Self-monitoring		
Working memory		

Comments on executive functions: This activity requires the child to control their impulses, monitor their performance and keep information in their working memory while they work to assemble the necessary ideas. There's a great deal of emphasis on planning and organization as the child needs to think ahead about how to form a complete and coherent message. Cognitive flexibility is challenged at this stage because the child, as they assemble the pieces of information and tries out different explanations, may have to change their approach as they monitor the accuracy of their listener.

Task structuring:

At the Resilience stage, we want to increase the child's tolerance for dealing with varying listener needs by adjusting the detail they use. We'll introduce varied types of information, including descriptions of objects, description of scenes and relating events as well as different listeners.

When focusing on Self-advocacy, we introduce activities and events that aren't complete and precise, and the child has to adjust themselves or the task on their own. Tasks will be structured so the child has opportunities to be 'teacher' and student with a variety of other people. These experiences will help them advocate for themselves.

NOTE: Use of Turtle Breathing before and during tasks should be encouraged.

Objectives:

The child will independently adjust the amount of detail they provide when giving directions and describing objects and events to others at least 50% of the time by checking their accuracy of understanding.

The child will be able to indicate to others that they don't fully understand their message at least 80% of the time independently.

The child will be able to independently modify their expression of thoughts and ideas based on listener feedback at least 60% of the time.

Materials:

- list of major features to include in descriptions – number, size, shape, color, location (see Resource files)
- duplicate coloring pages or cut-and-paste activities with simple objects, animals or people (see Resource files)
- list of other features to include when describing scenes – object, person, animal, action, feelings/mood, time, comparison (see Resource files)
- duplicate pictures scenes, cut-outs to make a scene, cut-outs to make a creature (see Resource files)
- list of story features to include when describing a sequence of events – time, person/animal, place, events, ending (see Resource files)
- sequence pictures (duplicate set, one with pictures separated and the other shown in a sequence), wordless storybooks, etc. (see Resource files)
- crayons, colored markers or colored pencils, glue or paste
- barrier to block the child's view of your (duplicate) activity – can be a folder, binder or easel placed between you and the child that is tall enough and wide enough to make sure they can't see your work
- games (see Resource files)

Language of spark* *to use in this lesson:*

Key words & phrases:

We, we're ...	If somebody doesn't understand, they might ask you to say it again.
I know you can do good talking and listening all by yourself.	You know how to do that.
Remember, we need to make a good plan in our brains first and then use all the things you know to talk about like the things on these lists.	You know that if you don't understand something, you can ask the other person to help.
We're going to practice with you as the teacher sometimes and sometimes with other people as the teacher.	If you really don't know what to do, you can ask for help. I will help you, but you have to use your own brain first.
	What could you do to help yourself?

	Did you tell all of the important parts so (person) could understand what to do?
Vocabulary & concepts:	
Brain Plan Understand	Remember Teacher

Introduction:

After practicing describing objects, scenes and events (as in Lesson C:Ept1), explain to the child that now they get to teach other people. Invite peers, other adults, parents and siblings to learn from the 'teacher' about what to do.

Tell the child: "I know you can do good talking and listening all by yourself. Remember, we need to make a good plan in our brains first and then use all the things you know to talk about like the things on these lists. If somebody doesn't understand, they might ask you to say it again. You know how to do that. You know that if you don't understand something, you can ask the other person to help. We're going to practice with you as the teacher sometimes and sometimes with other people as the teacher. If you really don't know what to do, you can ask for help. I will help you, but you have to use your own brain first."

Invite peers, other adults, parents and siblings to learn from the 'teacher' about what to do. Also give them opportunities to act as the teacher so the child can deal different approaches used by different people.

Practice:

Play barrier games or other games that require clear and complete expression of thoughts and ideas (see Resource files for suggestions)

Remind them to be the teacher and tell you/the other person what to do. Let them attempt one instruction. Let them take away the barrier and compare the pictures to see if they're the same being sure they use their finder finger and names each feature.

If the child's activity and your/the other person's look the same (that is, their instructions were clear and you understood them), let them praise you/the other person for thinking carefully and listening so well. Continue with the task, checking every instruction or two to make sure you/the other person understood.

If the child's activity and yours look different, prompt them to check very carefully what might have been missed in their instructions – check it against the list of major features. Sometimes, children will dispute your listening skills and indicate that they told you what to do but you didn't listen. Don't argue with them. Just tell them you'll listen more carefully next time and ask questions if you're not sure. Then review the major features they need to tell you.

If the child describes very detailed information that's more than you need in this situation (for example, using every one of the major features when only a few were necessary), name each feature and ask them if it's important to tell you the feature. Explain the logic, "If there's only one in a picture, you only need to tell its name. If there's more than one, you just have to tell the things that make them different."

Prompting:

Use the list of major features, other features and/or features of events to prompt the child to include more information.

Make sure that everyone proceeds with an instruction from the child only if their description is sufficiently precise. Do not fill in the blanks. Request repetition or clarification as needed.

Praise the child for precise but not overly-detailed instructions.

Coach the child as needed when they're 'teaching' other people. Use nonverbal means as much as possible. Tap your finger on a feature on the lists of features and components if they forgot to include it. For example, if they forgot to tell the time of an event, tap your finger on that box on the *List of major components for relating events*.

Prompting should involve asking, "What could you do to help yourself?" Elicit information and/or action from them to improve descriptions whenever possible. Keep the option of asking for help as a last resort. We want them to adjust their own behaviors first.

Self-monitoring:

After the child completes a few directions or descriptions, ask, "Did you tell all of the important parts so (person) could understand what to do?" Prompt them to explain the thinking and planning they did.

Solidifying:

Help the child review (a) what skills and strategies were learned in the lesson, (b) why it helps to use them and (c) what they noticed when they used them. Some children won't be able to verbalize or indicate some of this information but try to prompt responses from them. Clarify and add information as needed.

Highlighting:

Point out to the child how they used clear words and explained exactly what to do or listened carefully and asked for repetition/clarification when needed. Tell them what a good teacher/listener they're.

Additional Comments:

By inviting family members into practices where the child is the 'teacher', they have an opportunity to learn about how they're prompted to give precise and complete information. They can be encouraged to use those techniques in daily settings.

Another benefit of using family members is that the child gets to experience what it's like to control the behavior of others in positive ways. They also learn that they must use their precise language with their family as well as other children and their teacher or therapist.

CHAPTER 8 - IMPROVING EMOTIONAL SELF-REGULATION WITH spark*

Within the Behavioral Self-regulation unit, we helped the child develop control of their body, breathing and voice. In the Cognitive Self-regulation unit, work was done to improve the child's ability to focus and sustain attention and to detect and interpret relevant and important information. They also learned to construct meaning from that information and to monitor and repair their understanding if necessary. Then the child was taught strategies to help them express their thoughts and ideas clearly.

All of these skills and strategies can now be brought together to improve the child's Emotional Self-regulation and form the foundation for social competence and peer acceptance.

What self-regulation skills are important in the emotional realm?

The ability to identify emotions and events that cause them is an important foundation skill. Preschool children are more likely to be viewed as 'socially competent' if they can accurately identify emotional expressions and recognize events that elicit particular emotional reactions[269]. This early ability seems also to have longer term implications. Preschoolers who could recognize and label emotions were rated as having better social behavior and adjustment four years later[270].

Self-regulating behavior and emotions and using inhibitory control are also important. Children considered to be socially competent are better at regulating their emotions and behavior when excited or upset[271] and at controlling their impulses when they have to wait for a reward[272]. Children who can cope with emotional ups and downs, maintain their own emotional equilibrium, and recover from setbacks and disappointments are more likely to be liked by their peers[273].

Cooperation, sharing, and helping others are other important skills in Emotional Self-regulation. Peers are more likely to accept other children who share with and help others[274]. The ability to cooperate and control disruptive behavior is also central to peer acceptance[275].

What is Emotional Self-regulation?

The Emotional Self-regulation unit encompasses a number of skills and strategies that form a basis for developing social skills. Among those skills and strategies are recognizing and identifying emotions and regulating behavior and reactions to emotional ups and downs.

We don't work in any way to deny, dismiss, or stifle the child's emotions. Instead, they learn to more accurately detect, understand, and express emotions with a sense of control and optimism.

The lessons in this unit are based on the belief that children with ASC don't lack an understanding of or caring for other people. Their appreciation of social interactions may be incomplete or faulty, but they generally are motivated to interact and engage with other people.

A great many children with autism are aware of their social difficulties and their impact on others. The difficulties they experience are often due to their imprecise and inaccurate intake of relevant information. If they don't develop a complete and appropriate depiction of the social interaction and situation, children with ASC are more likely to react or respond in ways that seem inappropriate.

Organization of spark* Emotional Self-regulation unit

There are three main areas of focus for Emotional Self-regulation. They include detecting social clues, interpreting social clues, and forming a response. The subskills in **spark*** lessons were selected based on their importance to forming a foundation for social skill and social competence as discussed in the information above.

The goals of this unit are to provide the child with clear structures and logic for more accurately identifying social clues, ways to interpret them, and then some ways for responding. The goal isn't to teach social skills but to help the child use their now slowed and more focused brain and body to employ all of the various strategies practiced in the previous units. We have worked on identifying the most important and relevant information, on identifying signals, clues, and models, etc. Now is the opportunity to put that knowledge and those skills into the social realm.

The areas of focus and subskills are shown on the next page in Figure 16.

EMOTIONAL SELF-REGULATION		
Areas of focus		
Detection of social clues	Interpretation of social clues	Formation of response

Subskills

a. Gestures

b. Facial expressions

c. Person & setting

Areas of skill development

1. Awareness in Others and in Self

2. Awareness of Need

3. Resilience

4. Self-advocacy

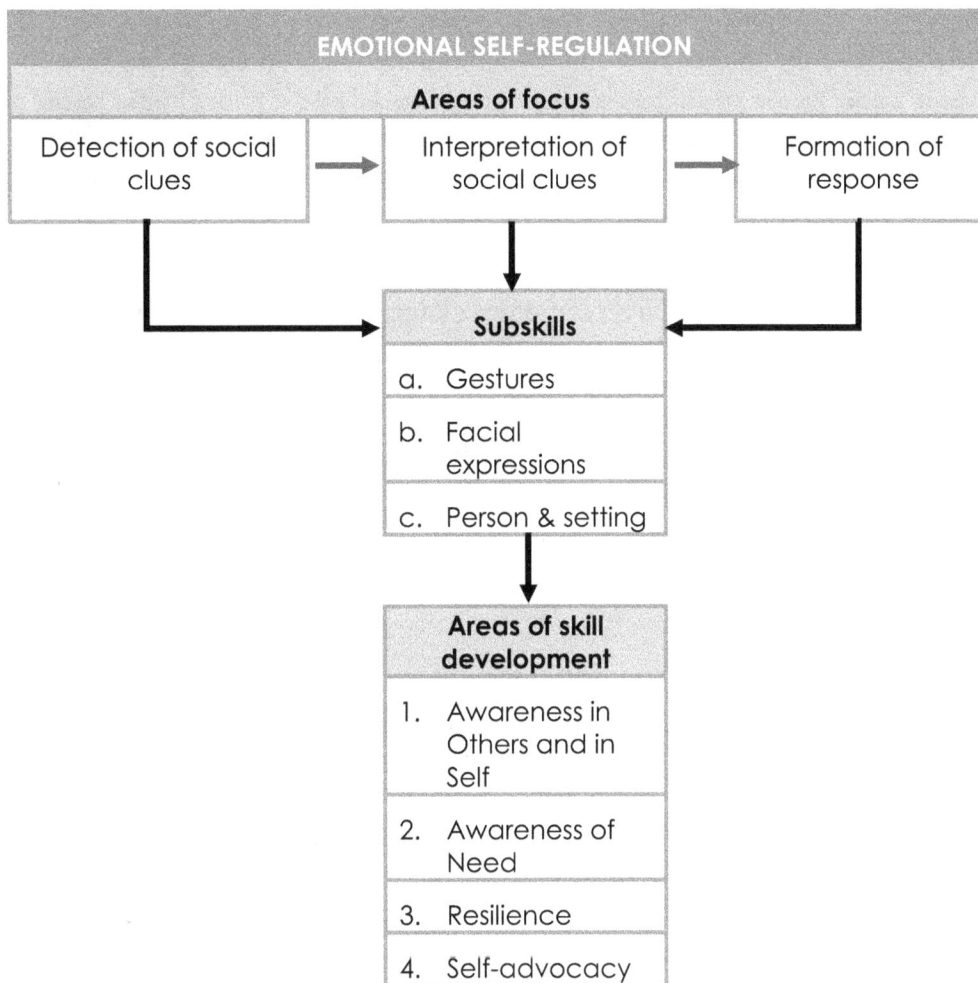

Figure 15. Diagram of the areas of focus, subskills and areas of skill development included in the Emotional Self-regulation unit

Areas of focus

Detection of social clues

We know that people with ASC have difficulty making and maintaining eye contact with others. They also tend to look less than typically-developing peers at the mouth and body of others and more at objects in a social setting[276]. When working with children with autism, it's always wise not to assume they notice or identify information. That's what we focus on in Detection of social clues. We work with the child to make sure they notice the most important and relevant information in each subskills area. The lessons narrow down the number of critical pieces of information so the child has a clearer idea about what aspects of the social clues they should pay attention to.

Interpretation of social clues

Once the child has learned which things to notice, they're helped to interpret what they might mean. The meanings used in **spark*** are simple and basic so the child can experience some initial certainty in the social world. They aren't meant to be exhaustive. Instead, they're intended to help the child construct meaning from the information they gathered during the detection phase.

Formation of response

This process helps the child do some basic problem solving. They've learned to gather key information and interpret it. Now they learn some fundamental ways to respond.

Subskills

Only a select set of gestures and facial expressions are included. They're intended to start the child on the journey of detecting, interpreting, and using non-verbal communication. The skills included help the child begin to figure them out and use them in understanding and expressing themselves.

Gestures

One of the earliest indicators of autism is difficulty understanding the nonverbal and gestural behaviors of other people[277]. Children with autism also exhibit deficits in their spontaneous use of communicative gestures[278], They use fewer gestures, especially those involving joint attention or expressing emotions. They usually don't have difficulty with gestures that serve needs[279], like taking someone's hand and leading them to the refrigerator for a drink.

Gestures include body actions and nonverbal signals that communicate different ideas. The gestures included in this unit let the child to remain at a distance from others since physical contact can be uncomfortable for many children with ASC. All of the gestures are shown in Table 3 on the next page with their communicative intents and primary social functions. They all encourage engagement with others in different ways.

Before starting gestures lessons, it's critical that you speak to the child's parents to determine if the use of the selected gestures is acceptable within their culture and their family. For example, some cultures view pointing as rude so it's important to find some acceptable substitution. With some aboriginal cultures, pointing is indicated with pursed lips and the head turning toward the object of interest. A 'thumbs up' gesture, in some Indian cultures, is used to indicate that something was poorly done rather than well-done.

	Gesture	Communicative intent	Primary Social Function
1.	Pointing*	"look" **NOTE:** Substitute another gesture if necessary	engagement
2.	shaking head	"no"	disapproval, denial
3.	nodding head	"yes"	approval, agreement
4.	wave	"hello" or "come closer" "goodbye" or "stay away"	engagement disengagement
5.	thumbs up	"good job", "good work", "nice" **NOTE:** Substitute another gesture if necessary	approval

Table 3. Gestures included in **spark*** Emotional Self-regulation, the emotional states expressed and main facial characteristics.

Facial expressions

It's well-known that people with autism have difficulty recognizing and identifying emotions in themselves[280] and others[281,282]. Facial expressions communicate a lot about our emotional state. If you don't understand what they mean, your ability to navigate the social world will be impacted.

There are seven universal facial expressions[283], including anger, fear, disgust, contempt, surprise, sadness/distress and enjoyment. Facial expressions included in **spark*** Emotional Self-regulation are shown in Table 4 below.

Emotion	Emotional state expressed	Main facial characteristics		
		eyebrows	eyes	mouth
Happy	pleasure, comfort, amusement, enjoyment, friendliness	raised	open slightly	corners up
Sad	displeasure, loss, discomfort, pain, helplessness	lowered	slightly closed	corners turned down slightly
Afraid	concern, dread, worry, danger, threat	raised	open wide	open
Angry	hostility, annoyance, opposition, irritation, resentment	lowered	slightly closed	corners turned down

Table 4. Emotions included in **spark*** Emotional Self-regulation, the emotional states expressed, and main facial characteristics.

We focus on eyebrows, eyes, and mouth to make detection and information gathering simpler. Eyebrows are included because nearly all facial expressions involve either brow raising or lowering[284]. Brow lowering is used mainly in negative emotions, like sadness or anger. Brow-raising usually expresses surprise or interest. Eyes opening and closing add to the information needed to figure out the emotion expressed. The shape of the mouth also provides helpful information. The corners of the mouth tend to be turned up with positive emotions and down with negative emotions.

Person and setting

This area addresses teaching the children to identify basic differences in forms of communication that help maintain the relationship between them and other people. This involves politeness only to the extent that we're concerned with the cultural appropriateness of the child's behavior. For example, children are more likely to grab or push peers and siblings but not parents or teachers. They learn that they can yell at siblings or friends but should be more reticent about raising your voice with adults. When the child is with adults other than their parents, they learn to be more careful not to order them to do things or be impolite. The different people considered in this section will be peers, siblings, parents, and other adults. The dimensions are age differences (adult versus child) and familiarity to the child. The person and setting subskills are practiced so the child begins to understand these as important variables.

Special note on teaching politeness: Interestingly, typically developing children are less 'polite' than you might think. A study of politeness in two to five-year old children[285] found that only three of the 22 children observed spontaneously said "hi" and "goodbye" and only 7% said "thank you" on their own in an experiment. Parents had to prompt the children to elicit politeness from them. Keep these low figures in mind when working with children on developing situationally-appropriate language. We don't want to prompt children to be oddly polite for their culture or their peer group.

Special note about eye contact. Notice that eye contact isn't addressed directly in **spark***. The reason for this is that eye contact is encouraged within appropriate and meaningful contexts only and not as a separate, isolated entity. We'll introduce the notion of looking in the direction of the speaker to help the child understand information. This includes place deixis (pronounced: dike-sis) which is an expression that requires you to check the setting to understand the location of something. For example, if you say, "Put the spoon there", the child will have to look where the speaker is looking or pointing to understand the location. Also, directions, like "Do this", make the child have to look at the speaker to understand what to do. Person deixis will also be incorporated into comments and directions. Person deixis requires the child to look where the speaker is looking or pointing in order to understand who they're talking about. For example, for the command "Give the spoon to them", the child has to look where the speaker is looking or pointing to know which person they're referring to.

Areas of skill development

Within each area of focus, we'll work toward the child's assuming more control and responsibility for self-regulation. The progression includes three areas of skill development: Awareness in Others and in Self, Awareness of Need, and Resilience.

1.   **Awareness in Others and in Self.** Initial work is done on helping the child become aware of each social clue and its basic meaning in others and then they'll identify it in themselves.

2.   **Awareness of Need.** After the social clues are identified and practiced, focus is given to application and generalization to major settings in the child's life. They're supported in recognizing places and times when the social clues would be helpful to them.

3.   **Resilience.** The child is helped to solidify their use and understanding of the clues so they're more resilient and less readily affected by things that could cause disruptions and distractions. In the Resilience stage, we help them gain confidence in their ability to detect, interpret, regulate, and modulate emotions in everyday situations. We also want to help 'toughen' them so they can deal with more disruptions and changes to prepare them for real world situations.

Turtle Breathing is used to help the child focus their attention on their breathing as a way to calm and center themselves. They'll also be helped to use other strategies to calm themselves and change their state of mind if needed.

Strategies taught in building resilience focus on helping children become less immediately reactive to events and situations. They emphasize looking at the situation and using strategies to keep yourself calm for the moment. The include being able to deal with emotions by keeping them away, putting them away, or thinking of something pleasant. These strategies are used just to buy time so the child can either get help or think calmly about the situation. They aren't meant to stifle emotions.

4.   **Self-advocacy**. The child is prompted to apply the knowledge and skills they're developed to help themselves make use of each clue in daily settings. They're encouraged to ask for help when needed and to arrange their environment so it's easier for them to function. This may mean that they choose to leave a situation or task and/or to use their Turtle Breathing or another strategy.

spark* **Emotional Self-regulation lesson content**

The lessons that follow are formatted to help you work systematically through each subskill. Each figure that follows provides an example of the information shown in every lesson.

With all instructions in the lessons, care has been taken to provide clarity while still allowing for flexibility and creativity in the individual practitioner. Lessons are laid out and sequenced so the child is progressively placed in a position where they can assume increasing control over their behavior, thinking, and emotions.

Executive functions

Each lesson shows which of the five main executive functions is a primary focus and which ones are secondary. Brief explanations are provided about the rationale for designating some functions as primary and others as secondary (see the example below).

Lesson identifying information: area of self-regulation, area of focus, subskills & area of skill development

Area of self-regulation 3: Emotional

Area of focus 1-3: Detection, interpretation and formation of social clues

Subskill 1: Gestures

Area of skill development 1: Awareness in Others and in Self

Primary executive functions:		*Secondary executive functions*:	
	Inhibitory control		Cognitive flexibility
	Planning and organization		
	Self-monitoring		
	Working memory		

Executive functions receiving primary and secondary focus, plus comments

Comments on executive functions: This activity requires the child to control their impulses and attention and monitor their performance. There's also emphasis on planning and organization and working memory since they must retain information and think ahead to their responses. There isn't a large emphasis on cognitive flexibility since the child is taught specific gestures and is responsible only for detecting, interpreting and using that small set.

Task structuring:

Suggestions for organizing activities & things to watch out for

In these initial stages, gestures will be exaggerated so the child is readily able to discern them. Each gesture is introduced individually with its meaning. In the Cognitive Self-regulation lesson C:le1, we introduced the idea of signals and how they help us figure things out. In these lessons about understanding and using social gestures, emphasis should be placed on how gestures are signals as well.

Throughout this unit, more executive functions are included in **spark*** units. Self-monitoring is stressed consistently as is inhibitory control. Planning and organization and working memory are needed to succeed with each activity. Cognitive flexibility will enter incrementally into all activities, particularly when the emphasis is placed on determining when and where to use each subskill. See the example on the next page.

Task structuring:

In the Task structuring: section of each lesson, there's advice about how to arrange and organize the activity. Suggestions are provided for optimizing learning. See the excerpt on the previous page for an example. It's important to arrange tasks so sufficient control and calmness is maintained when needed. That means the child can do stimulating and exciting activities but must then learn to return to a calmer state afterward.

Objectives:

Objectives are written as individual child goals with a description of the target behavior and accuracy or frequency expected. The level of accuracy of frequency is typically 80%. Due to the nature of children with ASC and with life in general, achieving success on four out of five tries should be considered quite solid learning. For activities that require extension into daily life, the accuracy levels are reduced to reflect the reality of the challenges they'll likely encounter.

Materials:

Concerted effort has been made to either include materials in the Resource files or require only a few other items to implement each lesson. Suggestions and examples of materials are provided but feel free to use other resources.

Suggestions are also made for storybooks that can complement the lessons. Care has been taken to ensure that most of the books don't suggest or model undesirable behavior. Children on the autism spectrum often pick up on these negative models and start using the behaviors.

The main options presented won't involve the child's use of technology, but meaningful technology should be incorporated whenever possible. It's critical that technology increases child participation and interest and doesn't take time away from interacting with the child.

Language of spark*

For each lesson, key words and phrases for promoting the cognitive and social-emotional goals of each interaction are highlighted to help you remember to use them. In addition, important vocabulary and concepts you will be using are listed. An example is shown below.

Area of self-regulation 3: Emotional
Area of focus 1-3: Detection, interpretation and formation of social clues
Subskill 1: Gestures
Area of skill development 1: Awareness in Others and in Self

Objective: level of accuracy or frequency of use needed for child to move to next lesson

Objectives:

The child will be able to imitate the five key gestures from the adult model and produce them with verbal prompting with at least 80% accuracy...

Materials:

Materials suggested for the lesson, indicating those available in the Resources files

- illustrations of gestures with printed meaning on each (see Resource files - ILLUSTRATIONS - *Key gestures*)
- for pointing practice, it's helpful to have something interesting to look at/for like an interesting object or a person entering the room

Language of spark* *to use in this lesson:*

Key words & phrases:

Language of spark* key words and phrases to use in the lesson

We, we're ... Say 'Look over there/here' with your body. Say 'no/yes' with your body. Say 'hello/goodbye with your body. Say 'good job/nice, I like that' with your body.	We're going to learn how to talk with our bodies! We can use our bodies to say lots of things even without any words! They're signals that help us know what to do.

Vocabulary & concepts:

Language of spark* vocabulary and concepts to use in the lesson

Signal

Introduction

The Introduction section of each activity is a script of the instructions and explanations to be provided to the child. The introduction is used to engage each child in the lesson and its objectives. An example is shown on the next page.

With all instructions, care has been taken to use the Language of **spark*** and provide clarity. Allowance is made also for each person using **spark*** to have some flexibility and to be creative but it's critical that you keep in mind that the words have been carefully crafted.

Practice

This section suggests ways you can engage the child to practice the skills and strategies. The Practice section is a chance to help the child explore the skills and strategies presented in the lesson. An example of practice information is presented on the next page.

Metacognition, or thinking about our thinking and behavior, is emphasized throughout the Emotional Self-regulation unit as it was in the other units. The child is helped to develop metacognitive strategies that will help them monitor and optimize their thinking and responding. In the beginning, we prompt them to 'think out loud' using self-talk. This will give you a chance to monitor what they're thinking and saying to themselves. It's also an opportunity to help shape and prompt what they say. Over time, they can be helped to internalize the self-talk and 'just say it in your brain'.

Area of self-regulation 3: Emotional

Area of focus 1-3: Detection, interpretation and formation of social clues

Subskill 1: Gestures

Area of skill development 1: Awareness in Others and in Self

Introduction:

"We're going to learn how to talk with our bodies! We can use our bodies to say lots of things even without any words! They're signals that help us know what to do. I'm going to show you some things and you try them for yourself. Watch and listen carefully."

Pointing: Show the child 'pointing' at a distance with your index finger and arm outstretched. Tell them, "That says, 'Look over <u>there</u>.' You try it, say 'Look over there' with your body." Let them try it out.

Now, show them pointing close up. Say, "If I point right here (close to yourself), my body is saying 'Look <u>here</u>'. You try it, say 'Look here' with your body." ....

Script used to Introduce each lesson

Practice:

In practice, use verbal prompts first and see if the child remembers the gesture that goes with each comment or directive. Ask them, "How could you show me the signal for 'look over there'?" If they don't recall the gesture, show them the illustration and let them try. If they have difficulty making the gesture, model it for them and then practice again......

Suggestions for practicing skills & strategies presented in the lesson

Prompting

This section provides verbal and nonverbal prompts that should be used to establish, solidify, and extend skills learned within the lesson. Children are helped to understand learning is a process. With time and repeated practice, things will get easier and more accurate. Right now, don't expect perfection. You'll have to tolerate 'less-than-perfect' work until your brain and your body have more experience. An example of prompting is shown on the next page.

> ***Area of self-regulation 3***: Emotional
>
> ***Area of focus 1-3***: Detection, interpretation and formation of social clues
>
> ***Subskill 1:*** Gestures
>
> ***Area of skill development 1***: Awareness in Others and in Self

Ways to prompt the child to practice

> ***Prompting:***
>
> In appropriate situations, you can prompt the child to gesture. For example, if they like something, say, "You can show that with your body. Why don't you give it a try?"

Always prompt them to think for themselves by asking, "What can you do to help yourself?" By asking rather than telling, the child is encouraged to think for themselves and not rely on adults around them to direct them.

Give the child positive messages about their ability to reason and problem-solve. Simply telling the child, "You have a good brain" will typically keep them trying.

Self-monitoring

Because our goal is to help the child assume control over their own emotions, we need to teach them to evaluate their own performance from an early stage. That way they can determine the accuracy and adequacy of their own thinking and behavior. Children with ASC also can be quite perfectionistic about their application of skills, so the system of self-monitoring helps them watch and celebrate their progress.

Solidifying

To help solidify learning from each lesson, children are helped to reflect on what they learned. They're prompted to review (a) what they learned, (b) why it's important and (c) what they noticed when they used the skills and strategies in the lesson. Some children won't be able to verbalize this information. But every effort should be made to help them reflect on the lesson, whether they verbalize it, indicate it nonverbally, or you state it for them. See the section on the next page.

Highlighting

Suggestions are made in this section about how to highlight the child's use of their self-regulation skills in day-to-day life and how to help them solidify them in daily situations. Within each session, the child is also helped to reflect on what they learned, what it means and what they might have noticed when they used the skills and strategies. An example of lesson plan suggestions is shown below.

Area of self-regulation 3: Emotional

Area of focus 1-3: Detection, interpretation and formation of social clues

Subskill 1: Gestures

Area of skill development 1: Awareness in Others and in Self

Self-monitoring:

When the child uses gestures of any sort, ask, "Did you say something with your body? I think you made a signal. Can you think what it told me?"

Solidifying:

Help the child review (a) what skills and strategies were learned in the lesson, (b) why it helps to use them and (c) what they noticed when they used them. Some children won't be able to verbalize or indicate some of this information but try to prompt responses from them....

Highlighting:

When other people use gestures of any sort, point them out to them. Point out how their bodies helped to signal things. Ask, "What do you think they were saying with their body?"

When the child uses gestures of any sort, point it out to them....

> Ways to promote self-monitorina
> Prompting the child to reflect on their

> Ways to highlight child's use of skills

Additional comments

Any features, skills and strategies that are critically important will be highlighted in this section on each lesson, such as suggestions for extension and generalization.

spark* **Observational assessments**

In the observational assessment, an excerpt is shown on the next page, evaluation is done by sampling the child's ability to spontaneously use the Emotional Self-regulation subskills. The complete form is in the Resource files (FORM - Observational assessment - Emotional self-regulation file).

In the observational assessment, watch the child in daily settings and look for their use of the subskills. This can be challenging because opportunities to use all of the skills may not arise. Watch them during a variety of activities, particularly ones that involve interaction with other people.

Then place a check mark (✔) in the box that corresponds to the frequency of use of each subskill: Never, Sometimes (more than 0% but not more than 75% of the time) or Most of the time (more than 75% of the time).

Spark* *Observational assessment – Emotional Self-regulation*						
Areas of focus and subskills	**Exhibits independently in everyday settings:**					
	Never		Sometimes		Most of the time	
	Under-stands	Uses	Under-stands	Uses	Under-stands	Uses
Gestures						
pointing for engagement						
shaking head to deny or disapprove						
nodding head to agree or approve						

Documenting progress through spark* lesson objectives

On the form (in the Resource files - FORM - Achievement of lesson objectives - Emotional self-regulation) is each major area of focus, task variation, and area of skill development included in the program, along with the objective. The date on which the lesson was started is noted in the second column from the right. Then, after a period of time that's appropriate to the child and/or program, the child's progress is noted. Progress toward the objective is marked as: A – objective achieved; D – skill developing but the child demonstrates it below the criterion level; or N - no discernible progress

spark* *Achievement of Lesson Objectives- Emotional Self-regulation*						
Areas of focus	**Objective** The child will be able to	**Areas of skill development**	**Date started**	**Evaluation Date(s)**		
Detection, interpret-ation and formation of gestures	imitate the five key gestures from the adult model and produce them with verbal prompting with at least 80% accuracy	Awareness in Others and in Self				
	to look where the speaker is pointing or looking or look directly at the speaker to ensure they understand directions involving person or place deixis at least 50% of the time	Awareness in Others and in Self				

spark* **Emotional Self-regulation Lesson Plan Users Guide**

On the next page is a table showing the **spark*** Emotional Self-regulation **Scope and Sequence**.

Column	Information included
#1	Lesson Codes: E – Emotional Self-regulation plan DIF – Detecting, interpreting and forming a response g – Gestures e – Emotions ps– Person and setting When you see the letter **N**, it means that a **Newsletter** is sent home at the beginning of this lesson.
#2	Pages - page numbers for that lesson
#3	Area of focus
#7	Social clue
#8, 9, 10	Areas of skill development – indicated with a check mark (✔)
Newsletters should be sent home at the start of these lessons:	
Lesson	**Newsletter #**

E:DIFg1	15
E:DIFe1	16
E:DIFe2	17
E:DIFps1	18

Rhymes, songs, storybooks and illustrations appropriate for each lesson included the Resource files are referenced in the Materials section of each lesson plan.

Every effort has been made to limit each lesson to two pages, but three pages were required for more complex lessons. This was done so you can photocopy the pages for quick reference when working with a child.

Just a reminder:

Each component in the **spark*** Emotional Self-regulation unit takes small but important steps. Each step builds on the next. To form a solid foundation, please don't skip any lesson.

spark* **Emotional Self-regulation Scope and Sequence**

Lesson	Pages	Area of Focus	Social clue	Areas of skill development			
				Awareness in other & self	Awareness of Need	Resilience	Self-advocacy
E:DIFg1 **N**	249-253	Detection, interpretation, formation	gesture	✔			
E:DIFg2	254-256	Detection, interpretation, formation	gesture		✔		
E:DIFg3	257-260	Detection, interpretation, formation	gesture			✔	✔
E:DIFe1 **N**	261-264	Detection, interpretation, formation	emotion	✔			
E:DIFe2 **N**	265-267	Detection, interpretation, formation	emotion		✔		
E:DIFe3	268-273	Detection, interpretation, formation	emotion			✔	✔
E:DIFps1 **N**	274-277	Detection, interprctation, formation	person/setting	✔			
E:DIFps2	278-281	Detection, interpretation, formation	person/setting		✔		
E:DIFps3	282-285	Detection, interpretation, formation	person/setting			✔	✔

Emotional Self-regulation Lessons

Each component in the Emotional Self-regulation unit takes small but important steps. Every step builds on the next, forming a solid foundation of self-regulation. Don't skip any of the lessons. Each lesson may take minutes, hours or days or weeks to establish solidly dependent on the child and the situation. Each subskill will need to receive consistent focus and support in daily life. Remember, we're developing skills that will serve the child throughout their life, not just today.

Review the lesson carefully before starting. You might want to copy the scripts, so you have the words close at hand when working with each child. Use the exact terms, definitions and reasons presented in the lesson.

Follow the lessons exactly in terms of how information is presented, vocabulary used, and definitions presented.

NOTE: Turtle Breathing should be used on a consistent basis to help both the child and adult calm and center themselves. Model Turtle Breathing before activities and during them, especially when extra effort is required. Prompt the child to use their Turtle Breathing by asking, "What could you do to help yourself calm your body and your brain?" If they don't respond by doing their Turtle Breathing, prompt them more directly with, "Let's do our Turtle Breathing to help calm our brains and our bodies."

SPECIAL NOTE ABOUT EYE CONTACT: In this unit, we work with each child to understand that looking and watching other people can help us understand what's going on. We **DO NOT** require children to make eye contact. They are encouraged, through meaningful activities, to look in the direction of the other people. Eye contact can cause processing and sensory overloads for people with autism[286,287].

Lesson E:DIFg1

Send home Newsletter #15 plus the illustrations of key gestures.

In the next lessons, we initially present a small set of commonly-used signals for the child to learn, practice, and identify. Our goal isn't to teach them every social gesture ('signal'). We want to prompt them to look for gestures as helping to make meaning and emphasize what you're saying. Practice material includes sets of standard signals used in charades and areas of interest to the child (for example, sports or trains). Again, our goal is to help them detect and understand that gestures have purpose and meaning.

Be careful not to down-play the use of words too much. The child needs to know that they can use their words at the same time they gesture. The gestures just help other people understand better.

When working on person and place deixis, don't require the child to watch at all times. Most children with ASC overload if they have to pay attention constantly to both visual and verbal information. Our goal is for the child to look at the speaker in situations where it's necessary and appropriate for communication. Right now, we want them to look at the speaker <u>only</u> when we use person or place deixis.

Make practice playful and fun. Be sure to use a mirror large enough for the child to see themselves when making gestures.

Be sure to prompt the child to use Turtle Breathing before and during tasks to help them be calm and centered. Model the use of Turtle Breathing, reminding them that it helps your brain and your body work better.

The goal in this lesson is to help the child understand that gestures have meaning and they can help you understand what someone is trying to communicate as well as help you communicate your ideas.

Area of self-regulation 3: Emotional		
Area of focus 1-3: Detection, interpretation and formation of social clues		
Subskill 1: Gestures		
Area of skill development 1: Awareness in Others and in Self		
Primary executive functions:	*Secondary executive functions*:	
Inhibitory control		
Planning and organization		
Self-monitoring		
Working memory		
Cognitive flexibility		

Comments on executive functions: This activity requires the child to control their impulses and attention and monitor their performance. There's also emphasis on planning and organization and working memory since they have to retain information and think ahead to their responses. There is increasing emphasis on cognitive flexibility since the child is being exposed to a wider variety of gestures which also draws in eye contact.

Task structuring:

In the initial stages, gestures will be exaggerated so the child's more likely to notice. Each gesture is introduced individually with its meaning. In the Cognitive Self-regulation lesson C:le1, we introduced the idea of signals and how they help us figure things out. In these lessons about understanding and using social gestures, emphasis is placed on how gestures are signals as well. Using a large mirror allows the child to see how their body looks when they're making different gestures. This is important feedback for most children.

When working on person and place deixis, make the sessions feel like an opportunity to play 'tricks' on the child. Making practice playful and fun will more likely stimulate their interest in making sure they don't let you fool them.

Objectives:

The child will be able to imitate the five key gestures from the adult model, produce them with verbal prompting and respond appropriately to the adult's use of the gestures with at least 80% accuracy.

The child will be able to look where the speaker is pointing or looking or look directly at the speaker to ensure they understand directions involving person or place deixis at least 50% of the time.

Materials:

- illustrations of gestures with printed meaning on each (see Resource files - ILLUSTRATIONS - *Key gestures*
- large mirror
- for pointing practice, have something interesting to look at/for like an interesting object or a person entering the room
- verbal directions that involve person or location deixis, that is, words and phrases in a sentence that need contextual information to understand them (see the Resource files - MATERIAL - *Directions containing place or person deixis*)

Language of spark* *to use in this lesson:*	
Key words & phrases:	
We, we're ... Say 'Look over there/here' with your body. Say 'no/yes' with your body. Say 'hello/goodbye with your body. Say 'good job/nice, I like that' with your body. How could you show me the signal for '_____'? Can you show how to say ___ with your body? I think you made a signal. What do you think they were saying with their body? Wow, I tricked you this time. You forgot to look. How about I try it again? I guess you forgot.	We're going to learn how to talk with our bodies! We can use our bodies to say lots of things even without any words! They're signals that help us know what to do. Look what my body is saying – it made a signal for '_____'. You can show that with your body. Why don't you give it a try? Did you say something with your body? What did that signal mean? Wow, you really know how to look when someone's talking. I didn't trick you at all. What are you going to do next time, so I don't trick you?
Vocabulary & concepts:	
Signal Understand Listen(ing)	Trick Look(ing) Forget

Introduction:

Basic gestures: "We're going to learn how to talk with our bodies! We can use our bodies to say lots of things, even without any words! They're signals that help us know what to do. I'm going to show you some things and you try them for yourself. Watch and listen carefully."

Pointing: Show the child 'pointing' at a distance with your index finger and arm outstretched. Tell them, "That says, 'Look over there.' You try it, say 'Look over there' with your body." Let them try it out using a large mirror so they can see themselves.

Now, show them pointing close up. Say, "If I point right here (close to yourself), my body is saying 'Look here'. You try it, say 'Look here' with your body."

Shaking head "no": Say, "Now we're going to use our bodies to say 'no'. Say something like "Am I a baby?" and then shake your head 'no' in an exaggerated way without saying anything. Point out how you could say 'no' with your body and not say any words. Have the child try head shaking using a large mirror so they can see themselves. Then ask a question that you know they'll respond to with 'no'.

Nodding head "yes": Say, "Now we're going to use our bodies to say 'yes'". Ask yourself something, like "am I a ___?" and then nod your head 'yes' in an animated way without saying anything. Point out how you could say 'yes' with your body and not say any words. Have the child try head nodding using a large mirror so they can see themselves. Then ask a question that you know they'll respond to with 'yes'.

Waving: Say, "Now we're going to use our bodies to say 'hello'. This is a funny one because it can also say "good-bye". Say 'hello' and wave. Then say "good-bye" and then wave. See, they look the same. Let's try saying 'hello'." Prompt the child to try waving using a large mirror so they can see themselves. Say. "Now let's try saying "good-bye." Have the child wave again.

Thumbs up: Say, "Now we're going to use our bodies to say, "good job" or "nice, I like that". Here's what it looks like. You try it but don't use any words." Prompt them to try the gesture using a large mirror so they can see themselves. Then say, "Look, your body is saying "good job" or "nice, I like that" without any words.

Person and place deixis: For directions involving deixis, introduce them by saying, "Sometimes we have to look <u>and</u> listen to understand things. When I say, do this (clap your hands), you have to look at me to know what to do. Sometimes we have to look where I am looking and sometimes where I am pointing. You know about looking where my finger is pointing because we already practiced that. Sometimes, I will just look with my eyes so you'll have to see if you can find out where I am looking."

Practice:

Basic gestures: In practice, use verbal prompts first and see if the child remembers the gesture that goes with each comment or directive. Ask them, "How could you show me the signal for 'look over there'?" If they don't recall the gesture, show them the illustration and let them try. Be sure to use a mirror so they can see themselves make each gesture. If they have difficulty making the gesture, model it for them and then practice again.

At other times, make one of the gestures yourself and don't speak at the same time so the child has to rely on the gestural information only. See if the child notices. If they don't, draw their attention to it: "Look what my body is saying – it made a signal for 'look at this'". If they notice the gesture, ask them what your body is telling them.

Person and place deixis: For directions involving deixis, practice each type including looking at you (not necessarily make eye contact, just in your direction) to understand what action to make ("Do this") or looking at a person or location to see where you're pointing or looking ("Look there/at them"). Make the gestures large and obvious for a while until the child becomes more consistent in looking to determine what to do. Ensure that practicing is playful, like you're trying to play tricks on the child so if they don't look you 'got him'!

Prompting:

Basic gestures: In appropriate situations, prompt the child to use one of the gestures. For example, if they like something, say, "You can show that with your body. Why don't you give it a try?" Give them as little prompting as possible, like using the statement above. If they don't seem to understand what you mean, point out what the child seemed to be experiencing (that is, they like something, they agree with something) and ask, "Can you show how to say ___ with your body?" If they still have difficulty, then model the gesture for them and have them imitate it while you describe what the gesture means.

Person and place deixis: Use requests, questions and comments involving person and/or place deixis. When the child responds appropriately by looking, comment, "Wow, you really know how to look when someone's talking. I didn't trick you at all."

If the child doesn't look, say, "Wow, I tricked you this time. You forgot to look. How about I try it again?" Show the child again and prompt them to look to find out what you're talking about. Praise them for looking.

Self-monitoring:

Basic gestures: When the child uses gestures of any sort, ask, "Did you say something with your body? I think you made a signal. What did that signal mean?" The mirror may be helpful so the child can see themselves.

Person and place deixis: After you use person or place deixis, ask the child, "Did you understand what I was saying?" If they had looked and were able to respond, elicit a "yes" or nod from them and comment, "You bet. You did a really good job of looking and listening." If the child had failed to look, elicit a "no" or head shake. Then comment, "I guess you forgot. What are you going to do next time, so I don't trick you?"

Solidifying:

Help the child review (a) what skills and strategies were learned in the lesson, (b) why it helps to use them and (c) what they noticed when they used them. Some children won't be able to verbalize or indicate some of this information but try to prompt responses from them. Clarify and add information as needed.

Highlighting:

Basic gestures: When other people use gestures of any sort, point them out to them. Point out how their bodies helped to signal things. Ask, "What do you think they were saying with their body?"

When the child uses gestures of any sort, point it out to them. Point out how their body helped to make signals of things that they were thinking. Ask, "What was your body saying?"

Person and place deixis: When you or anyone else uses person or place deixis, point them out to them. Point out how their bodies helped to signal things. Ask, "What do you think they were saying with their body?"

Additional Comments:

Share the gestures with the family and ask them to Inject the gestures into everyday life such as, when they do a really good job of something, give them a thumbs-up. Then say, "You know what that signal means, right? It means that you did really good work."

Prompt the family to use gestures around the child so they have opportunities to detect and interpret others' gestures.

Lesson E:DIFg2

Be sure to have information from the parents about times and places where gestures would help the child communicate as well as understand what others are saying.

When working on person and place deixis, don't make the child watch at all times. Most children with ASC overload if they have to pay attention constantly to both visual and verbal information. Our goal is for the child to look at(in the general direction of) the speaker in situations where it's necessary and appropriate for communication. Right now, we want them to look at the speaker <u>only</u> when we use person or place deixis.

The goal in this lesson is to help the child figure out where and when they need to look for gestures and 'signals' to help them understand and to use them to help others.

Area of self-regulation 3: Emotional		
Area of focus 1-3: Detection, interpretation and formation of social clues		
Area of skill development 2: Awareness of Need		
Social clue 1: Gestures		
Primary executive functions:	**Secondary executive functions:**	
Cognitive flexibility		
Inhibitory control		
Planning and organization		
Self-monitoring		
Working memory		

Comments on executive functions: This activity requires the child to control their impulses and attention and monitor their thinking and responses. There's also emphasis on planning and organization and working memory since they have to retain information and think ahead to their responses. There's emphasis on cognitive flexibility since the child is expected to think about application of the gestures in other settings.

Task structuring:

When focusing on Awareness of Need, we structure the task so the child is helped to think of where else they'd need to look for and use gestures as signals. Examples should be drawn from the child (or for the child as need be) that encompass their life (a) at school, (b) at home, and (c) in the community. All three settings must be addressed so extension and generalization receive specific focus.

Objective:

The child will be able to indicate at least one different example of when it's important to use gestures for each of the three targeted settings with adult support.

Materials:

- Awareness of Need chart (see the Resource files - TEMPLATE – *Awareness of Need chart* and *ILLUSTRATIONS - Topics for Awareness of Need charts - Emotional self-regulation*)
- illustrations of gestures with printed meaning on each (see Resource files - ILLUSTRATIONS - *Key gestures*)
- information from the parent's feedback on Newsletter #15 about times and places where gestures would help the child communicate – prepare pictures ahead of time

Language of spark* *to use in this lesson:*

Key words & phrases:

Where do you need to use your body to make signals? Your signal helped me understand that you ____. How can you help yourself remember to look when someone is talking?"	Let's think about when we have to look carefully so we can understand what other people are saying. How can you help yourself remember to use signals?

Vocabulary & concepts:

Signal	Understand

Introduction:

Explain to the child that you want them to help you think of times when we need to use our bodies to say things. Tell them: "If we use our bodies <u>with</u> our words, other people will understand better. If we look carefully when someone's talking, they might use signals that help us understand. Sometimes, we don't even need to say words, just use our body to make signals. Right now, we're going to think of things at school, at home, and in other places. Can you think of one thing we do at school/home/other places where we need to use our bodies to tell people things or watch other people's bodies?"

Practice:

"Where do you need to use our bodies to make signals? Let's put a picture on the chart for you." Examples: when someone is far away from you or when in a noisy place.

After they're able to provide at least one example, say, "Let's think about when we have to look carefully so we can understand what other people are saying." Examples can be drawn from the list of sentences containing person and place deixis from the Resource files.

Prompting:

If the child has difficulty coming up with ideas, suggest some from the family information and from your experience with them.

During these activities, be sure to catch the child using gestures. Praise them more often than reminding them. Comment whenever you see them gesturing in any meaningful way, not just the ones targeted. Give an interpretation to each gesture (for example, "Your signal helped me understand that you liked that.") and how it helped you understand what they were thinking and saying.

Self-monitoring:

Ask the child, "How can you help yourself remember to use signals?" and "How can you help yourself remember to look when someone is talking?" Help them think of ways they can remind themselves as necessary.

Solidifying:

Help the child review (a) what skills and strategies were learned in the lesson, (b) why it helps to use them and (c) what they noticed when they used them. Some children won't be able to verbalize or indicate some of this information but try to prompt responses from them. Clarify and add information as needed.

Highlighting:

Point out to the child how they used their body to signal what they were thinking.

Also, be sure to highlight gestures that you and other people use.

Additional Comments:

Ask the child's family for feedback on how well the child does in using and interpreting gestures. Also, make sure they praise the child for any gestures they use and/or watch.

Lesson E:DIFg3

In this lesson, we provide the child with some dramatic experiences with gestures to help them focus more attention on them and learn that they have meaning. We also need to make sure we give them practice using words with appropriate gestures to nonverbal and verbal systems join together to enhance and punctuate communication.

The goal in this lesson is to help the child be better able to understand and use gestures in more challenging situations and advocate for themselves if they're having difficulty.

Area of self-regulation 3: Emotional		
Area of focus 1-3: Detection, interpretation and formation of social clues		
Area of skill development 3 & 4: Resilience & Self-advocacy		
Social clue 1: Gestures		
Primary executive functions:	*Secondary executive functions:*	
Cognitive flexibility		
Inhibitory control		
Planning and organization		
Self-monitoring		
Working memory		

Comments on executive functions: This activity requires the child to control their impulses and attention and monitor their behavior and thinking. There's also emphasis on planning and organization and working memory since they have to retain information and think ahead to their responses. There's even more emphasis on cognitive flexibility since the child is expected to apply gestures in other settings and use gesturing to simulate actions with objects.

Task structuring:

At the Resilience stage, we want to increase the child's ability to cope with gestures. We need them to learn how to detect them and use them in daily settings. We focus on Self-advocacy throughout these activities, expecting the child to ask for help or clarification is they're unsure of the meaning or use of different gestures.

Objective:

The child will be able to detect, interpret, and use gestures with at least 50% accuracy to communicate ideas.

The child will ask for help or for clarification if unsure of the meaning of a gesture at least 50% of the time when they fail to respond.

Materials:

- game of simple charades (see Resource files - MATERIAL - *Cards for a game of simplified charades* and MATERIAL - *Standard signals in charades*) – use with a game-board or card-format to give the charade cards a game-like atmosphere

- if the child is interested in sports, use sports referee signals while playing a game or play with vehicles and use train hand signals (see Resource files - RESOURCES - *Internet sites coordinated with lesson activities*) – introduce signal systems from other areas that interest the child just so long as they represent a standard set of signals.

Language of spark* *to use in this lesson:*

Key words & phrases:

What am I showing you with my body?	You can describe things with your body. You can make an action and pretend to do something.

Vocabulary & concepts:

Signal	Describe
Clues	Pretend

Introduction:

Use of gestures to provide clues about objects and actions: Introduce the child to the idea of charades: "You can describe things with your body. You can make an action and pretend to do something. These are clues. Like, you can go like this (pretend to hammer, drink without the real objects). What am I showing you with my body?"

Use of other signal systems: Say, "I know you really like ___. Let's pretend to be (referee, train man, etc.). We can use signals to tell other people what we're thinking." Show the child how referees or train men signal and what they mean.

Practice:

Use of gestures to provide clues about objects and actions: Do a few of the action suggestions to make certain that the child understands charades. Give them a card to act out to ensure they get the idea and act out an action for them to make sure they interpret your actions appropriately. Then play a game of charades, including other people if possible.

This activity will help work on self-advocacy skills. Explain to the child that you and them (and anyone else who is around) are going to use only your bodies to signal, no words, for five to 10 minutes (extend or shorten the time as appropriate). Say, "We have to use our bodies to signal to other people what we're thinking and/or what we want. It might get a little frustrating but it's lots of fun too. Remember what we learned before about what we do if we don't understand? We ask for help. We can signal that we don't understand like this (put your hands up and shrug your shoulders)." Use gestures only for the allotted time while doing a simple activity. Make 'body signals' time fun and funny, showing your own exasperation with using gestures only. Don't break the silence but don't cause undue frustration in anyone.

Use of other signal systems: Set up a game where the selected signal system will have meaning. Take turns being the referee or train man and use gestures to signal to each other. You can use words in this activity to accompany gestures and to question or comment on the gestures used by the other person.

Prompting:

When the child uses gestures or any sort, praise them. Comment whenever you see them using meaningful gestures, not just the ones targeted. Give an interpretation to each gesture and how it helped you (or another person) understand what the child was thinking.

During the periods of silence ('body signal' times), you'll have to show your praise through the "thumbs up" gesture so you don't break the no-talking rule.

Your responses to the charades, referee and train man signals will provide feedback and should act as praise to the child. If they need more feedback, be sure to give it to them.

Self-monitoring:

After 'body signals' time, ask the child how they liked using only their body to tell other people things. You can express your own frustrations if it will be helpful.

After the child has used a gesture, ask, "Did you show me what you were thinking with your body?" Remind them, "We need to use our words too so other people will understand us better. If we use words AND body signals, other people will really know what we're saying."

Ask the child, "How can you help yourself remember to use body signals?" Help them think of ways they can remind themselves as necessary.

Solidifying:

Help the child review (a) what skills and strategies were learned in the lesson, (b) why it helps to use them and (c) what they noticed when they used them. Some children won't be able to verbalize or indicate some of this information but try to prompt responses from them. Clarify and add information as needed.

Highlighting:

Point out to the child how they used gestures and 'body signals' to tell what they were thinking. Highlight for them how 'body signals' help but it doesn't replace words for telling people things. They just help.

Be sure to highlight gestures that you and other people use.

Additional Comments:

Keep these activities as playful and positive as possible. They can be challenging so know when to stop and try again later.

Make up a copy of the charade game cards to play in other settings. If appropriate, the game can be played at home with family members. If they forget to use or misinterprets gestures, ask them to remind them of what they mean.

Make sure they praise the child for any self-regulation they exercise, especially Turtle Breathing and self-talk.

Ask the family for feedback on how well the child does.

Lesson E:DIFe1

Send home Newsletter #16 plus the illustrations of key features of the targeted emotions.

Facial expressions are presented by teaching the child to look only at their eyebrows, eyes, and mouth or those of the other person. We only work on a small set of features and a limited set of four facial expressions. Our goal is to teach the child where to look and how to put those pieces of information together to figure out what the emotion is. The clues act like a formula where you can say, "if there's ___ and ___ and ___, then the person must be feeling ___."

We want the child to learn a consistent system of analysis, not every emotion. The child has already worked on constructing meaning in the Cognitive Self-regulation unit so combining the information from three facial features should pose no significant problems for them.

In this lesson, we also help the child understand why showing and detecting emotions might be useful.

The goal in this lesson is to help the child use major facial features in detecting different emotions in themselves and others.

Area of self-regulation 3: Emotional			
Area of focus 1-3: Detection, interpretation and formation of social clues			
Area of skill development 1: Awareness in Others and in Self			
Social clue 2: Emotions			
Primary executive functions:		**Secondary executive functions:**	
	Cognitive flexibility		
	Inhibitory control		
	Planning and organization		
	Self-monitoring		
	Working memory		

Comments on executive functions: This activity requires the child to control their impulses, focus their attention and monitor their thinking and behavior.

There's also emphasis on planning and organization and working memory since they have to remember information and think ahead to their responses. There is some emphasis on cognitive flexibility since the child is taught to focus on multiple pieces of information and construct meaning from them.

Task structuring:

A highly analytical approach will be used for detecting, interpreting, and expressing emotion. Each of the four key emotions will be analyzed with the child, examining (from the top to the bottom of the face – being systematic!) eyebrows, eyes, and mouth. The clues provided by eyebrows, eyes and mouth tie in with the concept of 'clues' introduced in the Cognitive Self-regulation unit, Lesson C:le1. Simple determinations will be made: eyebrows will be raised or lowered, eyes will be wide open, open a little, or slightly closed, and the mouth will be open or the corners turned up or down. These features will be associated with the name for the emotion and the emotional state expressed by it.

In these initial stages, emotions will be exaggerated so the child is readily able to discern them. Each emotion is introduced with the meaning.

Objective:

The child will be able to imitate the four key facial expressions from the adult model, produce them with verbal prompting and respond appropriately to the adult's use of the facial expressions with at least 80% accuracy.

Materials:

- photos of emotions with emotion name printed on each – select these from magazines or other sources (you can use photos of the child and their family if they're available) to represent children and adults the child could relate to – avoid using clipart and line drawings because tend to be exaggerated and don't necessarily depict authentic emotions
- chart for representing key facial features for each of the four emotions (see the Resource files - TEMPLATE - *Chart for representing key emotions*)
- mirror

Language of spark* to use in this lesson:

Key words & phrases:

We're going to learn how to find the clues that tell how somebody feels.	Start at the top and find clues in their eyebrows, their eyes and their mouth to figure how they feel
What feeling could that be?	How could you show that you're ___?
If we show other people how we feel, they can help us.	If we see how other people feel, we can help them.

Vocabulary & concepts:

Eyebrows Mouth Feelings	Eyes Clues

Introduction:

"We're going to learn how to find the clues that tell how somebody feels. We look at their face. Start at the top and find clues in their eyebrows, their eyes and their mouth to figure how they feel. I'm going to show you some faces, and we'll try to figure out the clues that tell how the people feel. If we show other people how we feel, they can help us and if we see how other people feel, we can help them."

Happy: "When you're happy, the clue is your eyebrows go up. Let's try that. The next clues are: your eyes are open and your mouth goes up at the corners. Let's try that. Wow, now you look happy." Point to each box on the chart corresponding with the 'happy' clues.

Sad: "When you're sad, one clue is: your eyebrows go down. Let's try that. The other clues are: your eyes are a little bit closed and your mouth goes down at the corners. Let's try that. Wow, now you look sad." Point to each box on the chart corresponding with the 'sad'.

Afraid: "When you're afraid, one clue is: your eyebrows go up. Let's try that. The other clues are: your eyes are big and wide open and your mouth is open. Let's try that. Wow, now you look afraid." Point to each box on the chart corresponding with the 'afraid' features.

Angry: "When you're angry, one clue is: your eyebrows go down. Let's try that. The other clues are: your eyes are closed a little bit and your mouth turns down at the corners. Let's try that. Wow, now you look angry." Point to each box on the chart for 'angry' features.

Practice:

Practice analyzing the three facial features on each face shown in the pictures. Help the child work systematically from the eyebrows, to the eyes and to the mouth matching the characteristics with each main feature in the chart. Sort the pictures and ALWAYS examine each key facial feature and then arrive at a conclusion about what the emotion is. Do it like a logic statement: eyebrows are ___, eyes are ___ and mouth is ___ so they must feel ___." Let the child do more and more of this analysis on their own. After completing each analysis, practice making the emotion with them, looking in the mirror to match the key facial features.

Remove the chart of key facial features and work through some analyses with the child. Let them do some on their own. If they have difficulty, prompt them to recall the clues that go with each emotion. If they have problems recalling all of them, ask them to make the expression themselves. Then ask them, "What feeling could that be?" If continues to have difficulty figuring out the emotion, show them the chart and match each key facial feature to their own face and that of the person in the picture. Review the key facial features with them, having the child describe each.

Prompting:

In appropriate situations, you can prompt the child to use different facial expressions. For example, if they like something, prompt them to give smile.

Self-monitoring:

When the child uses facial expressions of any sort, ask, "Did your face show how you feel? Your face looks ___. Is that how you feel?"

Solidifying:

Help the child review (a) what skills and strategies were learned in the lesson, (b) why it helps to use them and (c) what they noticed when they used them. Some children won't be able to verbalize or indicate some of this information but try to prompt responses from them. Clarify and add information as needed.

Highlighting:

When other people use the key facial expressions, point them out. Point out how their faces gave clues to show how they feel.

When the child uses any of the key facial expressions, point it out to them. Point out how their face helped to tell how they were feeling.

Additional Comments:

Many children with ASC have apraxia, or difficulty commanding their muscles to act the way they want, so may have problems forming the different facial expressions. Use a mirror and prompt the child to move one facial feature at a time so the final state is achieved. You may have to physically assist them in forming the different expressions.

Prompt other people to use the key facial expressions around the child so they have the opportunity to detect others' expressions. Also have them point out the child's facial expression.

Lesson E:DIFe2

Be sure to have information from the parents about what things at home, school and in the community make the child and other family members feel happy, sad, afraid and angry.

This lesson gives an opportunity for the child to connect emotions with events and situations.

The goal in this lesson is to help the child identify when and where they experience the key emotions.

Area of self-regulation 3: Emotional			
Area of focus 1-3: Detection, interpretation and formation of social clues			
Area of skill development 2: Awareness of Need			
Social clue 2: Emotions			
Primary executive functions:		**Secondary executive functions:**	
	Cognitive flexibility		
	Inhibitory control		
	Planning and organization		
	Self-monitoring		
	Working memory		

Comments on executive functions: This activity requires the child to control their impulses, focus their attention, and monitor their thinking and behavior. There's also emphasis on planning and organization and working memory since they have to retain information and think ahead to their responses. There's more emphasis on cognitive flexibility since the child is expected to think about application of the emotions in other settings.

Task structuring:

When focusing on Awareness of Need, we structure the task so the child is helped to think of where they or others might experience the different emotions. Examples should be drawn from the child (or for the child as need be) that encompass their life (a) at school, (b) at home, and (c) in the community. All three settings must be addressed so extension and generalization receive specific focus.

Objective:

The child will be able to indicate at least one different example of when they or others might experience each of the key emotions for each of the three targeted settings with adult support.

Materials:

- Awareness of Need chart (see the Resource files - TEMPLATE – *Awareness of Need chart* and *ILLUSTRATIONS - Topics for Awareness of Need charts - Emotional self-regulation*)
- Chart with main clues for detecting emotions (see the Resource files - TEMPLATE - Chart for representing key emotions)
- information from the parent's feedback on Newsletter #16 about times and places that have recently made the child and/or family members feel happy/sad/afraid/angry – prepare pictures ahead of time

Language of spark* to use in this lesson:

Key words & phrases:

Can you think of ....? How can you help yourself remember how these feelings look?"	We're going to ....

Vocabulary & concepts:

Feel, feelings	

Introduction:

Explain to the child that you want them to help you think of times when we feel different ways. Tell them: "We're going to think of things at school, at home, and in other places that make us feel happy or sad or afraid or angry. Can you think of one thing at school/home/other places where we might feel ___? When I play with my dog, I feel happy. How about you?

Explain to the child that you and they're going to think of times and places when they feel different ways.

Practice:

Elicit examples from each of the three different settings. "When might you feel happy/sad/afraid/angry at home/school/in the community? Let's put a picture on the chart for you. How about when _____?" Add more pictures, getting at least one idea for each key emotion in each main location.

Prompting:

If the child has difficulty coming up with ideas, prompt them with experiences from the storybooks. Also suggest some ideas from the information their parents have provided.

Self-monitoring:

Ask the child, "How can you help yourself remember how these feelings look?" and "How can you help yourself remember to look at someone's eyebrows, eyes and mouth to figure it out?" Help them think of ways they can remind themselves as necessary.

Solidifying:

Help the child review (a) what skills and strategies were learned in the lesson, (b) why it helps to use them and (c) what they noticed when they used them. Some children won't be able to verbalize or indicate some of this information but try to prompt responses from them. Clarify and add information as needed.

Highlighting:

Point out to the person may be feeling that way (for example, they didn't like someone taking their bike).

Additional Comments:

Prompt the child's family to add pictures to the Awareness of Need chart about situations that make the child feel happy, sad, afraid and angry. Make sure they don't use any information that will cause the child to become upset by the information. Ask them to let you know about any information they add.

Lesson E:DIFe3

Send home Newsletter #17.

Turtle Breathing will be used more fully in this unit. The child will be helped to focus on and direct their attention to their breathing. They'll then be prompted to think about their positive thoughts and to breathe in the positive ideas, inflating them like a balloon and breathing out the negative ones.

The two processes of Turtle Breathing and mental imaging ("making a picture in your brain") introduced in the Cognitive Self-regulation unit will be joined to increase the child's resilience and self-advocacy. We'll incorporate Turtle Breathing as a means of refocusing attention and calming the mind and body. Then we work on reviewing what is happening and how the child or the other person feels. The next step is to determine what to do in response.

NOTE: It's critically important that, if the child feels sad, angry or afraid, he always tell their parents first before attempting to resolve some of the issues.

The goal in this lesson is to increase the child's ability to cope with emotions and their associated feelings, learning how to detect the emotions in themselves and others and how to respond to their feelings in productive and socially-appropriate ways.

Area of self-regulation 3: Emotional

Area of focus 1-3: Detection, interpretation and formation of social clues

Area of skill development 3 & 4: Resilience & Self-advocacy

Social clue 2: Emotions

Primary executive functions:		**Secondary executive functions:**	
	Cognitive flexibility		
	Inhibitory control		
	Planning and organization		
	Self-monitoring		
	Working memory		

Comments on executive functions: This activity requires the child to control their impulses and monitor their thinking and behavior. There's also emphasis on planning and organization and working memory since they have to retain information and think ahead to their responses. There's increased emphasis on cognitive flexibility since the child is expected to learn and apply coping strategies when they detect emotions in themselves and others.

Task structuring:

Start with emotions in others and use storybooks to give them a context. Storybooks provide a 'safe' place to start where the characters are fictitious, and the events are removed from the child. They permit us to identify and discuss emotions and situations with more objectivity with less risk of upsetting the child. Then we re-enact scenes from the stories to give the child an opportunity to practice and deal with the emotion within the safe and known storybook context.

For sad, afraid and angry, the child will be introduced to some basic tools to help to help them deal with them. The main ways of changing emotional state will be using Turtle Breathing along with the Thinking-Planning sequence which involves helping them identify what is happening, how the character is feeling, why they're feeling that way and what they can do to help themselves change their emotional state. Ways of helping the character may include (a) taking on the opposite state of mind with a 'Shield' to protect them (that is, happy instead of sad, brave instead of afraid and happy instead of angry), (b) completely removing the thoughts associated with it by using the Brain Box or (c) thinking their Happy Thoughts and pushing the other thoughts away. The approach taken will depend on how the emotions are dealt with in the storybook selected.

For happy, the child can use some basic tools to help extend it. The main ways of extending the emotional state will be to use the Thinking-Planning sequence where they identify what is happening, checks how the character is feeling, why they're feeling that way and what they can do to help themselves remember that emotional state.

As the first step toward helping the child deal with emotions in themselves, they'll help re-enact stories presented previously. This will give them an opportunity to pretend they're experiencing the emotion and possibly to think of different ways to changing or extending the feelings experienced.

The final stage in working on Resilience and Self-advocacy will be to re-enact emotional situations from the child's everyday life. These will involve play-acting scenarios provided by the child's parents where the child experienced the four basic emotions.

Objective:

The child will be able to detect and interpret key emotions in others and use strategies appropriate to extending or controlling the feelings at least 50% of the time.

The child will be able to detect and interpret key emotions in themselves and use strategies appropriate to extending or controlling the feelings at least 50% of the time.

Materials:

- storybooks that incorporate different emotions (see suggestions in the Resource files - RESOURCES – *Storybooks coordinated with lesson target areas*; use storybook databases noted in the Resource files - RESOURCES - *Internet sites coordinated with lesson activities* to locate others) with special emphasis on similar experiences the child has had.

- visual support for Breathe-Think-Plan sequence to use with other people or characters (see the Resource files - TEMPLATE - *Breathe-Think-Plan*) and with the child's emotions (see the Resource files - TEMPLATE - *Breathe-Think-Plan*) - laminate these so child's responses can be entered on the chart in print and/or pictures
- paper, markers or clipart for the Breathe-Think-Plan chart
- "Brain Box" (any receptacle with a lid) for putting feelings in so they won't 'bug' the child
- Information from the child's family about at least four different situations that happened recently that caused the child to react in each way - happy, sad, afraid and angry
- Sheet of cardstock for their Happy Thoughts (see Resource files - TEMPLATE - *Happy Thoughts bubble*)
- Sheet of cardstock for making a Shield (see Resource files - TEMPLATE - *Shield*)
- Chart with main clues for detecting emotions (see Resource files - TEMPLATE - Chart for representing key emotions)

Language of spark* **to use in this lesson:**	
Key words & phrases:	
We can control our brains, our bodies and our feelings by doing some important things.	Breathe in and out using our Turtle Breathing and feeling how our breath feels and sounds coming in and out.
How is the person feeling?	That helps our brain and our body be calm so we can think better.
We can figure that out by checking the clues on their face.	Why do we think they feel that way?
If they feel ____, what could they do?	If you can't figure it out, you can ask, "Why's they feeling ____?"
Let's look at her/their face.	What could you do to help yourself?
How do you think they feel?	First, they/you should tell their parents so they can help them/you.
Let's take that feeling out of ___ brain.	If they/you feel ___, what could they/you do?
Now it won't bug ___.	What can you do next time?
I think you've got a good idea.	
How did you know that?	
Vocabulary & concepts:	
Feel, feeling(s)	Clue(s)
Plan (that's when we figure out what to do)	Happy Thoughts
	Brain Box
Shield	Protect
	Take it out of your brain
Introduction:	

Emotions in others. Explain to the child, "We can control our brains, our bodies and our feelings by doing some important things. We're going to do three things:

1. *Breathe*: Breathe in and out using our Turtle Breathing and feeling how our breath feels and sounds coming in and out. (show the picture stimulus for the breathing-Breathe-Think-Plan picture sequence with only the Turtle Breathing picture showing) That helps our brain and our body be calm so we can think better.

2. *Think*: (Show the child the Thinking-Planning chart and point to each box) We have to think:

   i.   How is the person feeling? We can figure that out by checking the clues on their face. Does they look happy, sad, angry or afraid?

   ii. Why do we think they feel that way? If you can't figure it out, you can ask, "Why're they feeling happy/sad/angry/afraid?

2. *Plan: (*Show the child the last box on the Thinking-Planning chart) That's when we figure out what to do.

   "If they feel happy‚ what could they do? They could make a picture in their brain about that Happy Thought. Then they could think about it at other times to make them feel happy. They can use their Happy Thoughts."

   "If the person feels sad/afraid/angry, what could they do? First, they should tell their parents so they can help them. Then, they could protect themselves with this Shield so it doesn't bug them anymore OR they could take it out of their brain and put it in the Brain Box. They could also use their Happy Thoughts so their brain can think only about things that make them happy. Which one would you like to use, the Shield or the Brain Box or the Happy Thoughts?"

   The Shield is really strong, and things just bounce off of it. It can help protect you.

   The Brain Box is a special box where we can put things that bug our brains. Sometimes, things bug us, and it makes it hard to think. We can just take it out of our brains and put it in the box. It's safe in the box and we can take it out again if we want to. I'm going to give it a try. Let's take that feeling out of (character's) brain. Now it won't bug them.

   The Happy Thoughts bubble can let them fill their brain will things that make them happy.

Emotions in the child themselves. Explain to the child, "We can control our own brains, bodies and feelings by doing the same three things:

1. *Breathe*:

2. *Think*:

   i.   How am I feeling? We can figure that out by checking the clues. Do I look happy, sad, angry or afraid?

   ii. Why do I feel that way?" Ask yourself, "Why am I feeling happy/sad/angry/afraid?"

3. *Plan: (*Show the child the last box on the Thinking-Planning chart) That's when we figure out what to do. Do I use my Happy Thoughts bubble, my Shield or my Brain Box?

Practice:

Emotions in others. Explain to the child, "We're going to look at some stories where people are feeling different ways. That'll help us think of different things that can help each person."

Read a storybook that contains one or more of the key emotions.

Use the book's storyline and pictures to help identify the different emotions. When you encounter one of the key emotions, say, "Let's look at her/their face. How do you think they feel?"

When the child labels the emotion, say, "I think you've got a good idea. How did you know that?" You're now eliciting the clues that led them to make the conclusion.

If the child has difficulties identifying the emotion, take out the key facial features chart and prompt them to use it to decide how the person feels.

Then, use the story context to help them figure out why the character may be feeling the emotion; ask, "Why do you think they feel ___? Let's look and think really carefully." This is an opportunity to use their 'finder finger' and examine the scene in the storybook and to recall events. Help them construct information to decide what may to causing the person to feel as they're.

Ask the child why the character is feeling that way. Then ask them to help the character use the Breathe-Think-Plan process. Let them lead the way, providing support and prompts only as needed.

Emotions in themselves. Help the child re-enact storybook scenes that caused emotion in the character. Use the three-step Breathe-Think-Plan to arrive at a resolution. Make sure the child expresses the character's emotion and then uses self-talk to help themselves go through the process of Breathe-Think-Plan. Incorporate the Brain Box, Shield and Happy Thoughts where appropriate.

Review with the child the situations indicated by the parents to arouse the different emotions in them. Help them use the Breathe-Think-Plan process, incorporating the Brain Box, Shield and Happy Thoughts where appropriate.

"If you feel happy, what could you do? You can think about things that make you happy. Let's make a Happy Thoughts bubble for you to help you remember." Help the child make their own Happy Thoughts thought bubble, gluing pictures or photos of objects, people and/or events that make them feel happy.

"If you feel sad/afraid/angry, what could you do? First, you should tell your parents so they can help you. Then, you could use your Shield to protect you and make things bounce right off of it OR you could take it out of your brain and put it in the Brain Box. You could also think about your Happy Thoughts." Help the child decorate their Shield and/or their Brain Box to personalize it and make it their own and to put pictures of things that make them happy on their Happy Thoughts bubble.

Prompting:

When the child sees other people express emotions, especially sadness, fear and anger, prompt them to think through the three-step Breathe-Think-Plan process to determine what the person could do.

When the child is beginning to react emotionally to something, intercede before they escalates. Prompt them with, "What could you do to help yourself?" and tap your finger on the Breathe-Think-Plan chart and have the

Shield, Happy Thoughts, and Brain Box available. If the child responds and doesn't continue to escalate in their emotion, praise them for such good thinking. If they continue to escalate, prompt them just to use their Turtle Breathing. Don't discuss the steps until they're calmed back down. At that time, discuss the situation with them and ask them "What can you do next time?"

Self-monitoring:

Ask the child, "How can you help yourself remember to breathe-think-plan?" and "How can you help yourself to use your Shield, Happy Thoughts and Brain Box? Help them think of ways they can remind themselves as necessary.

Solidifying:

Help the child review (a) what skills and strategies were learned in the lesson, (b) why it helps to use them and (c) what they noticed when they used them. Some children won't be able to verbalize or indicate some of this information but try to prompt responses from them. Clarify and add information as needed.

Highlighting:

Whenever the child uses their Turtle Breathing, self-talk and any aspect of the Breathe-Think-Plan process, mention it and praise them. Describe what they did and how it can help them.

Additional Comments:

Make up a copy of the Breathe-Think-Plan chart and the Shield, Happy Thoughts and Brain Box for home, and other important settings. Prompt the child's family to model their own use of the process in daily situations and to ask the child what they could do to help themselves. If they forget to use the Breathe-Think-Plan process and the Shield, Happy Thoughts or Brain Box, have them use the prompting outlined above but only if their emotions have not already escalated. If the child's emotions have already escalated, remind them not to talk too much but their best approach may be to model and suggest Turtle Breathing.

Ask them for feedback on whether the child used any aspect of the process in daily settings.

Lesson E:DIFps1

Before this lesson, ask the child's family for photos of parents, siblings, anyone else who may live at their house as well as extended family members, school mates, bus drivers, teachers, etc. with whom they have frequent contact. Also, be sure to collect information about how they wish the child to behave with different people and in different settings.

Send home Newsletter #18.

We now put together many of the skills and strategies the child has learned to this point. They're learned about time and place during the Awareness of Need activities. In the next three lessons, they'll learn to put these together and form more general rules.

The concept of a stranger is difficult for all children to understand and I didn't want to induce any fear in our children. The idea of familiarity and whether I 'know' a person isn't concrete enough. Children might see the same person on a street corner day after day and consider them a friend. I decided a solid first step is to distinguish between people who live in my house and people who don't.

The goal in this lesson is to help the child learn to adjust how he behaves based on different situations and people present.

Area of self-regulation 3: Emotional		
Area of focus 1-3: Detection, interpretation and formation of social clues		
Area of skill development 1: Awareness in Others and in Self		
Social clue 3: Person/Setting		
Primary executive functions:	**Secondary executive functions:**	
Cognitive flexibility		
Inhibitory control		
Planning and organization		
Self-monitoring		
Working memory		

Comments on executive functions: This activity requires the child to control their impulses and monitor their behavior and thinking. There's also emphasis on planning and organization and working memory since they have to retain information and think ahead to their responses. There is emphasis on cognitive flexibility since the child has to switch between the different person/setting parameters and learn to respond accordingly.

Task structuring:

These tasks will be structured such that the child can quite readily discern key clues, including age and familiarity of the person. People will be sorted into those who are familiar ("live in my house") and strangers/unfamiliar ("don't live in my house") and whether they're grownups/adults or children. You may have to make some adjustments for families where the parents live apart. The distinctions of 'live in my house' and 'don't live in my house' are sufficiently concrete to make sense to most children. They, along with age of the person, are important in teaching the child to determine how they should regulate themselves.

Objective:

The child will be able to detect and interpret major person and setting clues with at least 80% accuracy.

Materials:

- Photos of parents, siblings and extended family members with whom the child has frequent contact and pictures of people selected from magazines whom the child will have no way of knowing – have both group photos and head-shots
- Chart for sorting people on the Person 2 X 2 table (see the Resource files - TEMPLATE - *Person 2 X 2 table*)

Language of spark* *to use in this lesson:*

Key words & phrases:

We're going to use clues and models to help us figure out what to do every day.	Should we .....?
	How about we do this?
	Do you think they'd like that?
We know how to use clues and models already.	Would you like that?"
This time we're going to use them to figure out what to do with other people.	I think they'd like that a lot better because .....
	I really don't think that's a good idea because ...
How can you help yourself remember when to control your voice and body?	We need to use ....

Vocabulary & concepts:

Clues	

Introduction:

"We're going to use clues to help us figure out what to do every day. We know how to use clues already. This time we're going to use them to figure out what to do when we're around other people."

Practice:

"Let's look at some pictures of people you know and see if we can figure out whether they're children or adults. Then we'll find out if they live at your house or not. Let's try those things first". Sort the people into each of the four categories: adults who live at my house, adults who don't live at my house, children who live at my house and children who don't live at my house.

Once the pictures are sorted and placed on the chart in the appropriate squares, say, "Now we have to figure out what voice we should use and how we should control our bodies and our brains with each group." Review each box, starting with adults who live at their house; ask, "Should we use a loud voice, quiet voice or in between with these people? Should your body be slow, fast or in between?" Glue the appropriate pictures for voice loudness and body speed in the quarter circle in that square. Then move on to the other squares on the Person 2 X 2 table and ask the same question.

Prompting:

If the child identifies the correct voice and body speed for a person (that is, it agrees with information obtained from their parents), tell them, "Wow, you know everything! That's exactly what your mom/dad said too."

If they suggest a different voice loudness and/or body speed than their parents indicated, ask, "Do you think that's a good idea? Show me how you use your body and your voice when you're with ___." Have them act out how they'd move their body and use their voice. Ask, "Do you think (the identified person or people) would like that?" Help them change their mind by making other suggestions, including extreme ones: ask "How about we do this?" (use different voice loudness and/or body speed). Ask, "Do you think they'd like that? Would you like that?" If you induce them to change their mind, show your agreement, "Yes, I think they'd like that a lot better because ..... (give a simple explanation)." If they don't change their mind, tell them, "I really don't think that's a good idea because ... (give a simple explanation). We need to use .... (describe appropriate voice and body speed)."

Self-monitoring:

Ask the child, "How can you help yourself remember when to use the right voice and body speed with different people?" Help them think of ways they can remind themselves as necessary.

Solidifying:

Help the child review (a) what skills and strategies were learned in the lesson, (b) why it helps to use them and (c) what they noticed when they used them. Some children won't be able to verbalize or indicate some of this information but try to prompt responses from them. Clarify and add information as needed.

Highlighting:

Praise the child whenever identifies how to adjust their behavior based on person age and familiarity. Ask them what clues they used. You can also highlight the things you noticed, pointing them out on the chart and saying, "I saw that you were ___, just like on the chart."

Additional Comments:

Share the chart with the family so they know what the child is learning and what the expectations can start to be. Ask them to prompt the child to remember to figure out the clues in different situations and how their voice and body are supposed to be.

Ask them to prompt and highlight using the same procedures as outlined above.

NOTE: Be sure that everyone doesn't just focus on calm, quiet behavior. The child needs to understand that sometimes it's okay to be active and noisy.

When other people adjust their behavior, based on person, have them point it out to the child saying, "Did you see what they did with their body and their voice? How did they know what to do?"

Have them prompt the child to use their Turtle Breathing while they figure out what to do in different situations and also if they're becoming dysregulated, overly-excited, etc.

Lesson E:DIFps2

In this lesson, we're going to 'fine-tune' behavioral, cognitive and Emotional Self-regulation in relation to people and/or settings (a) at school, (b) at home, and (c) in the community. All three settings must be addressed so extension and generalization receive specific focus.

Be sure to get Information from the family about important settings/situations in the (a) home, such as mealtime, bedtime and play and (b) the community some of which are challenging for the child and what their expectations are in terms of the child's activity level, voice volume, the amount of emotional expression, how well they need to listen and comply with the wishes of others.

The goal in this lesson is to help the child become put together more information about the type of self-regulation they need with different people in different settings by looking for clues and models within each situation.

Area of self-regulation 3: Emotional

Area of focus 1-3: Detection, interpretation and formation of social clues

Area of skill development 2: Awareness of Need

Social clue 3: Person/Setting

Primary executive functions:		Secondary executive functions:	
	Cognitive flexibility		
	Inhibitory control		
	Planning and organization		
	Self-monitoring		
	Working memory		

Comments on executive functions: This activity requires the child to control their impulses and attention and monitor their performance. There's also emphasis on planning and organization and working memory since they have to remember information and think ahead to their behavior and thinking. There's more emphasis on cognitive flexibility since the child is expected to think about application of the person/setting clues in a variety of settings.

Task structuring:

When focusing on Awareness of Need, we structure the task so the child is helped to detect the major clues in daily situations, interpret those clues in terms of behavior and then respond appropriately. Scenes will be presented in pictures and photos only so the child has a chance to stand back from the situation and be coached before using their strategies and skills in real life.

Objective:

The child will be able to detect and interpret clues and models in more challenging situations and determine appropriate responses to least three different examples with adult support.

Materials:

- Pictured scenes and photographs of different settings familiar to the child such as mealtime, grocery store, bedtime, group play, doctor's office, playground, school/preschool, etc. If these aren't readily available, get a list of these places and their addresses and capture images of them from Google.

- Information from the family about situations which usually are challenging for the child in terms of behavior, thinking and emotions

- Information on developing social stories (see the Resource files - RESOURCES - *Internet sites coordinated with lesson activities*)

Language of spark* *to use in this lesson:*	
Key words & phrases:	
We're	Let's ....
Should	What are some clues?
You're right	Is there a model?
How can you help yourself remember to look for clues and models, so you know what to do?"	
Vocabulary & concepts:	
Clue	Model

Introduction:

"Now, let's look at pictures of different places and figure out whether our body and our brain can/should be slow and quiet, in between or fast and noisy."

Explain to the child that you want them to help you figure out the clues and models that can help them know what to do in different places. Select one photo/picture at a time and determine the main clues or models (for example, everyone is seated at the dinner table), what that suggests to the child (they should be seated too) and how they should respond (sit down).

Practice:

Introduce a picture of a home setting (such as mealtime) and ask the child, "Should our bodies and brains be slow and quiet, in between or fast and noisy?" Then ask, "What are some clues we can use to help ourselves know what to do? Is there a model?" Help them focus on the clues (those are the age and familiarity features figured out in the previous lesson) and name them: "You're right there are adults and children who live at your house so what does that tell us?" This is when we introduce setting differences: "We use our in-between voice and body when we're with adults who live at our house. We can use a louder voice and fast body with children who live at our house, but this is at dinner time. What do you think we should do? Is there a model for us to follow?" Help them consider what other people are doing in the picture: "What's everyone doing in this picture?" As needed have them use their 'finder finger' and look to see if the people are standing or sitting or running around and if they're yelling or whispering or using their normal voice. Summarize the information: "You're right, they're all sitting down and using their normal voices. That's our model. Now we know what to do."

Add more pictures including ones from home, school and in the community. Help determine how they should regulate themselves based on the clues and models using the same approach as outlined in the previous paragraph.

Prompting:

Prompt them to use self-talk to guide their thinking. For example, "everybody is sitting down so I need to sit down."

Prompt the child to use their Turtle Breathing while looking at a situation and figuring out what to do.

Self-monitoring:

Ask the child, "How can you help yourself remember to look for clues and models, so you know what to do?" You can prompt them to use self-talk (to the tune of *Here We Go Round the Mulberry Bush*, like, "I need to look for clues and models, clues and models, clues and models ......"

Solidifying:

Help the child review (a) what skills and strategies were learned in the lesson, (b) why it helps to use them and (c) what they noticed when they used them. Some children won't be able to verbalize or indicate some of this information but try to prompt responses from them. Clarify and add information as needed.

Highlighting:

Praise them as much as possible for appropriate responding even if just certain aspects of their responses are accurate. Be sure to highlight any self-regulation they used, especially Turtle Breathing and self-talk.

Develop social stories with the child, using the information gleaned from practice with them. Include information about major clues and models, interpretation of them and appropriate responding.

Additional Comments:

Share copies of social stories with the child's family and ask them to review the stories before the child enters the identified situations. Have them prompt them to use self-talk to remind themselves of what to do and Turtle Breathing to remain calm.

Prompt them to model their own self-talk, identifying main clues and models for self-regulation, what they mean and how they will respond.

Ask them for feedback on how well the child does.

Lesson E:DIFps3

Before starting, get information from the child's family about activities at home, school and in the community that have a 'negotiable' element. That is, activities where they can have some choice about where, when, and how it's done. For example, can he negotiate when to stop playing on the computer, in what order to do an activity, where they can eat their snack, where he sits in the car, the order in which errands are done, etc.

Copy, complete and give out the Certificate of Completion at the end of this lesson (see Resources files - MATERIAL - *Certificate of completion - Emotional self-regulation unit*).

The goal in this lesson is to help the child cope more readily in daily situations, stay calm, and advocate for themselves by attempting to negotiate change.

Area of self-regulation 3: Emotional
Area of focus 1-3: Detection, interpretation and formation of social clues
Area of skill development 3 & 4: Resilience & Self-advocacy
Social clue 3: Person/Setting

Primary executive functions:		**Secondary executive functions:**	
	Cognitive flexibility		
	Inhibitory control		
	Planning and organization		
	Self-monitoring		
	Working memory		

Comments on executive functions: This activity requires the child to control their impulses and monitor their behavior, thinking and emotions. There's also emphasis on planning and organization and working memory since they have to retain information and think ahead to their responses. There's a lot of emphasis on cognitive flexibility since the child is expected to think about application of the person/setting clues in other situations.

Task structuring:

At the Resilience and Self-advocacy stage, we want to increase the child's ability to cope with temptations to become dysregulated. We need them to learn how to use their Turtle Breathing and self-talk as well as their Happy Thoughts bubble, Shield and Brain Box to keep themselves regulated.

Objectives:

The child will be able to regulate their behavior, thinking and emotions appropriately during activities at least 60% of the time.

The child will be able to calmly suggest changes to ongoing activities that will help them remain regulated at least 60% of the time.

Materials:

- storybooks that focus on dysregulated characters (see Resource files - RESOURCES – *Storybooks coordinated with lesson target areas*)
- group games that are especially exciting and stimulating (see Resource files - RESOURCES - *Internet sites coordinated with lesson activities* and MATERIAL – *Games for practicing self-regulation*)
- information from the family about negotiable activities and the amount of leeway possible
- *Stop Think Control* song for regaining self-regulation (see Resource files - MATERIAL - *Songs to help regain self-regulation*)

Language of spark* *to use in this lesson:*

Key words & phrases:

We, we're …	How about ….?
You know ….	Be calm, it's okay, maybe next time.
Sometimes, we might want to change what we're doing.	We have to figure out how to make sure our brain and body don't get too excited

Vocabulary & concepts:

Clue	Model
Excited	

Introduction:

Problem-solving with storybooks: Explain to the child, "You know how to make their body and brain work really well. You know how to figure out what to do and then tell their body and brain what to do. We're going to read some stories. See if you can help the people in the stories. They really need your help.

Dealing with exciting group games: Say, "Now we're going to play some games. First, we have to watch to figure out what to do in the game. Then we have to figure out how to make sure our brain and body don't get too excited." Let them make some suggestions then add, "I've got a good song that really helps a lot of kids keep from getting too excited. Let's give it a try." Sing the *Stop, Think, Control* song with actions and get the child to join in. Say, "How about, if you look like you're getting too excited, I could tap my control spot (from the song – located on your wrist where a watch might be worn) to remind you to calm yourself down. Would that be a good idea?"

Self-advocacy: Say, "Sometimes, we might want to change what we're doing. If we want to change something, we take a Turtle Breath and then say, "How about _____?" and suggest something else to do. If you don't want to play with airplanes, you could say, "How about we play with cars?" If you don't want to stop playing on the computer, you could say, "How about five more minutes?" Sometimes, the other person doesn't want to change. We just have to take a Turtle Breath and tell ourselves to "Be calm, it's okay, maybe next time".

Practice:

Problem-solving with storybooks: Read storybooks about dysregulated characters, prompting the child to identify problem responses or behaviors, what the characters should do and why. Help them identify a range of possibilities, including when that behavior might be appropriate.

What do we do if they don't want to?

Dealing with group games: Once the child has (a) figured out from clues and models how to play the game and (b) planned what they can do to help themselves from getting too excited, let them join in. Stand back as much as possible to let them cope and self-advocate as much as possible.

Self-advocacy: Model use of "How about ..." initially to negotiate small and fairly inconsequential changes. For example, you may suggest changing the order of two activities. Wait for the child's response and accept whatever they say. If they don't wish to change, model telling themselves "Be calm, it's okay, maybe next time." If they agree to the change, prompt them to make one. Introduce "How about ..." suggestions in other situations, such as while playing.

Prompting:

If you find the child becoming overly-excited or upset, start singing the Stop-Think song for regaining self-regulation and/or use self-talk. As needed, stop them and prompt them to take a Turtle Breath before resuming. You may have to stop the activity for a while until they regain equilibrium. Remind them of what they can do to help themselves.

Prompt the child to use their Happy Thoughts, Brain Box or Shield if they're feeling stressed.

Self-monitoring:

After the child has used Turtle Breathing, self-talk and any other appropriate strategy to maintain self-regulation, ask, "Did you tell your body and your brain what to do?" Praise them for any efforts they made to maintain or regain self-regulation.

Solidifying:

Help the child review (a) what skills and strategies were learned in the lesson, (b) why it helps to use them and (c) what they noticed when they used them. Some children won't be able to verbalize or indicate some of this information but try to prompt responses from them. Clarify and add information as needed.

Highlighting:

Point out to the child how they used their Turtle Breathing, self-talk and any other appropriate strategy to maintain self-regulation.

Be sure to highlight self-regulation that you and other people use.

Additional Comments:

Prompt the child's family to highlight and praise their use of them in daily situations. Ask them for feedback on how well the child does.

CHAPTER 9 - SELF-REGULATION IN CONTEXT

Self-regulation allows a child to take control of their executive functions. They can then plan, modify, and direct their attention, behavior, thinking and emotions so they're healthy and appropriate to their age, their family, and to the context. They can organize activities, tasks, their thinking, and behaviors so learning and dealing with the world are easier. Undesired behavior, thoughts, and emotions can be inhibited in situationally-appropriate ways. New ways of acting, thinking, and responding can replace old habits. The child learns ways to help themselves identify and remember important and relevant information and make sense of it. They also discover that they can monitor, reflect on, and adjust their thinking, feelings, and actions. This helps them identify key features in a situation and think about their options before deciding how to respond or react. Through this process, they learn how to be more flexible in their thinking and responding to events and people around them.

By developing these self-regulation skills, children learn to behave intentionally and thoughtfully. These skills are important for any child but are especially relevant for children who experience uneven development. This includes children with ASC as well as children with other developmental concerns, like Fetal Alcohol Spectrum Disorder, Fragile X and Attention Deficit Hyperactivity Disorder.

Self-regulation in the spark* context

The goal of *The Autistic Child's Guide* is to inspire people to embrace Behavioral, Cognitive, and Emotional Self-regulation as important foundation skills for children with ASC. The skills and strategies presented in **spark*** aren't exhaustive but represent a solid foundation on which more advanced skills can be built.

spark* is a **systematic, incremental approach** for teaching self-awareness and self-regulation of three different areas: behavior, cognitive processes, and emotions. As you saw in the lessons outlined in each of the three units, it provides a well-planned process for incrementally developing self-regulation. The skills and strategies learned to deal with Behavioral Self-regulation serve as a base for both cognitive and emotional self-regulation.

spark* is a **unique evidence-based model** for teaching self-regulation. It has clinical efficacy, being developed and tested over many years in clinical settings. It was tried and tested on individual children and with groups of children with ASC. More recently, controlled pilot studies have been completed with spark* to examine its impact with school-aged children on the autism spectrum.

spark* is informed by current neurology and **addresses five major executive functions** underlying each self-regulation activity. It focuses on increasing each child's conscious control of these key executive functions: inhibitory control, planning and organization, working memory, self-monitoring and cognitive flexibility.

spark* is **suitable for children from two years of age through 8 years**. It works progressively from imitation of easy actions so even young child and/or those who are considered 'lower functioning' can be engaged in learning self-regulation. spark* then continues through to self-direction/control of behavior, thinking and emotions.

An important and unique feature of spark* is specific emphasis on **teaching the children to become more resilient and to advocate for themselves**. These skills and strategies will help them cope and learn more readily in everyday settings. Use of self-advocacy marks the emergence of the truly participating and reciprocating person. We help the children be less passive and more active and engaged in their lives.

A critical element in the work to help the children become more resilient is teaching them **self-calming strategies**. The calming and centering we teach children within spark* can have profound effects when practiced consistently. The children learn, first of all, what the sensation of 'calm' feels like. Children on the autism spectrum typically have little idea how their brains and bodies may feel when they're not tense and on high alert. By introducing simple breathing and focusing on the air coming in and out of their body, each child gets an opportunity to let their mind and body be still. This is an important first step to detecting when and where they feel stress and anxiety; they need the contrast to discern what 'not stressed' feels like. Slow and calm breathing is that simple mechanism. A parent whose child participated in spark* reported how, when her child was escalating into a meltdown, they were able to stop the progression of behavior by starting their Turtle Breathing (introduced in the Behavioral Self-regulation unit). This is an exciting and encouraging account, especially because Turtle Breathing was able to calm them even after they had already started to escalate.

Autonomy, **systematic withdrawal of adult direction** and the child's ability to think and make decisions on their own are important early focuses in spark*. Typically, when working with children with autism, the main approaches involve 'doing for' the child and 'doing to' them. When 'doing for' a child, we change key features in their environment in the hope that these will make learning and living easier. For example, we may use visual schedules and streamline their daily environment to make it clearer to the child what is expected. This certainly isn't a bad thing, but we want them ultimately to be able to organize themselves as well as cope with uncertainty. When we 'do to' our children, we tell them what to do and how to do things and expect them to learn from that experience. There are times and places where this is important and has a great deal of impact. In both approaches, there's a time for this to be reduced and for the child to take more control and responsibility for their actions and thinking. In spark*, adult direction and adult organization and planning of learning activities are consistently removed and reduced in order for the child to take control.

Generalization of self-regulation skills is explicitly taught through the Awareness of Need, Resilience and Self-advocacy activities. During those phases, a major focus is placed on extending skills and strategies into day-to-day settings. Each child is helped to identify where and when to use these skills and strategies and how to use them even in the presence of distractions, temptations, and disruptions. This helps generalization as well as flexibility and resilience.

A great deal of emphasis in spark* is placed on **improving each child's self-awareness and self-monitoring**. The child becomes more aware of their ability to control their body, their attention, their thinking and their emotional responses. Then they're helped to become alert to what they can do and within what contexts. At that point, they can more easily take responsibility for their behavior and thinking. When children with autism are taught to become conscious in these ways, they not only use and generalize the skills and strategies, they remind others about what's appropriate. A therapist who uses spark* told me about a young boy they had been working with who reminded their mother, when entering their church, that they needed to use their quiet voice. We can be pretty sure our teaching strategies have been effective when we get this type of response from children, especially those on the spectrum. We can also be fairly certain that the child will generalize this learning to new settings, not just the ones we've used in teaching.

spark* uses a **positive and enjoyable approach** to teaching and learning. Music, rhythm, storybooks, games and many other activities are used to introduce and practice skills and strategies. The Language of spark* also focuses on the positive. Through the carefully-selected words and phrases, we help to activate each child's thinking. At the same time, we're providing them with a sense of competence, control and participation. There's clear emphasis on building the child's sense of self-efficacy, or belief in themselves as a learner.

Earlier[288] it was suggested that people with ASC fail to achieve higher levels of education, employment and independence because of (a) problems planning and organizing their lives, (b) difficulty dealing with social and sensory demands of day-to-day life and (c) poor self-advocacy skills. The skills and strategies in spark* start children on the road to developing these skills. They learn to manage and direct their bodies, thinking and emotions more reliably and appropriately. The seeds of self-advocacy as well as self-reliance and autonomy are planted from an early stage.

Development of self-regulation typically occurs over at least the first two decades of life, but we have repeatedly witnessed how spark* helps our children make significant gains. We see them move from being driven by many biological needs to increased voluntary control of their behavior, thoughts and emotions. We find them becoming less reliant on manipulating concrete objects to imagining and visualizing. We also observe less dependence on adult direction and more confidence in their own perceptions. spark* forms a solid foundation for continuing advancement of learning and autonomy.

Skills & strategies in the context of spark*

The spark* journey in promoting development of self-regulation begins with Behavioral Self-regulation of simple hand movements, a type of action that's readily established and practiced. Self-regulation of these actions is carefully and slowly advanced by systematically altering movement variations and reducing adult involvement and modeling. Once all of the Behavioral Self-regulation skills are established and extended into everyday life, they serve as a base for developing Cognitive Self-regulation. Improved behavioral and cognitive self-regulation also figure importantly in the child's development of emotional self-regulation. With the child able to consciously control their body and take in clear and complete information, they're ready to improve their ability to systematically review events going on around them and determine the most relevant information. They're then in a better position to detect and interpret social clues and respond to them calmly and appropriately.

Continuity in areas of skill development

The progression within each area of focus is repeated throughout spark*. First, the lesson focuses on the child's **Awareness of ability**. We introduce and then practice carefully-planned activities to make sure that they know what we're asking and can do it on their own. The more important feature of this step is **self-awareness**. During this process, they find they're able to move, think, see, hear and feel and they can control how they do these things. They also learn that they can control how those things impact them and that they can manage them.

Second, the child is helped to learn when and where they can use their self-regulation skills and strategies – **Awareness of Need**. This stage induces more self-awareness as well as **self-reflection and flexibility**. They become aware of situational differences and is helped to think about or reflect on what they mean. As you likely noted in the lessons, the child was asked over and over "How did do?" which is intended to prompt them to self-monitor and reflect on what they did.

Resilience is the next process that each child is helped to learn. In playful ways they become aware that they can cope in different situations with disruptions and temptations. They find that they can be more flexible and can cope with uncertainty. This is a part of real life that all of us have to develop, including children on the autism spectrum. It may initially be quite fragile in our children, but it will improve over time.

Self-advocacy helps the child learn that they can fend for themselves in day-to-day life. We cannot be totally responsible for the child's ability to cope. At some point, they need to take more responsibility for themselves and that's what self-advocacy is about.

Continuity in areas of focus

Areas of focus for spark* were specifically selected to ensure that the skills and strategies can be used in a wide range of situations. This means that the same skills and strategies are more readily extended and transferred from unit to unit in spark* and from setting to setting. Figure 17 on the next page shows the continuity of major skills and strategies introduced and extended over the spark* lessons and units.

Control of the child's body presented in the Behavioral Self-regulation unit provides a more stable base for refining their attention and developing conscious control of their executive functions. As these develop, they can more on to such skills as determining the most important and relevant information in a task or situation – a skill that have both cognitive and social implications.

Turtle Breathing, introduced in the Behavioral Self-regulation unit, is revisited again and again as we focus on Cognitive and then Emotional Self-regulation. Turtle Breathing becomes an important mechanism in everyday life for the child to calm and center themselves.

Imitation skills are important to learning self-regulation. The child learns to become less dependent on adults to tell them or show them what to do.

They begin to look to peers and not be frozen in their tracks if an adult isn't directing them.

Figure 16. Example of continuity of skills and strategies across **spark*** units and their implications.

Area of focus	Behavioral Self-regulation	Cognitive Self-regulation	Emotional Self-regulation	Implications
Control of body				• More stable base for learning & developing conscious control of executive functions • More consistent sustained attention
Turtle Breathing				• Strategy for self-calming & centering • Develop sense of 'calm' & reduced anxiety • More stable base for learning • Improved focused attention
Imitation of others				• Reduced dependence on adults for direction • Increased focus on peers as models
Construction of meaning & comprehension monitoring				• improved accuracy in detecting &interpreting social clues • better understanding during conversations • increased ability to learn in group settings
Use of models, signals and clues				• increased awareness of objects & people • improved detection & interpretation of social clues • increased use of others as a model for social expectations

During the Cognitive and Emotional Self-regulation units, the child is helped to look for and use **models, signals and clues** to guide their responses. They become increasingly aware that others are a resource for determining and evaluating their own behavior and performance.

Construction of meaning and comprehension monitoring are further examples of skills presented in **spark*** that have long-term implications to the child's ability to cope and learn in daily settings. His increased ability to build on and check the meaning of information they hear and sees significantly improves their ability to learn in natural settings and to enjoy social interactions. They can more readily interpret social clues and follow and contribute to conversations. Learning in group settings, where children with ASC are often quite 'lost', will also be enhanced by these skills and strategies.

spark* **in a research context**

A number of therapists who use **spark*** have provided feedback to us. They reported that, after several months of using **spark*** with children, considerable amounts of generalization of skills and strategies reported by families and others involved with the children. Other major trends include:

- **Increased copying of other people**, looking to others as models.

- **More participation in group activities**, following other people's lead.

- **Playing more with other children**, even sharing preferred toys.

- **Increased eye contact** and watching other person when talking, asking questions and making comments.

- **Better understanding and use of natural gestures** to supplement communication.

These changes encompass using models, attending to other people and events, eye contact and use of gestures. The curious and fascinating thing is that these children had only worked on the Behavioral Self-regulation unit. None of the trends observed were focused on within that unit. Another interesting observation made by a speech-language was a large increase in mean length of utterance, the measure used to describe both length and complexity of sentence use. They found this with a number of the children and, as yet, isn't easily explainable on the basis of self-regulation (they hadn't yet worked on the Expression of Knowledge section of the Cognitive Self-regulation unit). It seems that the work on executive functions, specifically attention, planning and organization and working memory, is at the center of all of the changes noted in both social and communication skills.

spark* has also been the subject of research studies[289,290]. These studies included of groups of six to eight children with autism, between seven to 12 years of age, who participated in **spark***. As an intervention program, **spark*** was found to be acceptable to the children and their families; that is, no one dropped out of the study. The findings from three measures indicate statistically significant changes in the following areas after just ten sessions with **spark***:

- **Behavioral Self-regulation** (as measured on the *Behavior Rating Inventory of Executive Function*) – the children showed increased ability to maintain control of their behavior and emotional responses. This included appropriately inhibiting thoughts and actions and being more flexible in the way they approached situations.

- **Behavioral rigidity** (as measured on the *Autism Spectrum Rating Scale*) – the children showed greater tolerance for change to their routines and activities in everyday situations.

- **Affect recognition** (as measured on the *NEPSY-II*) – the children showed increased ability to recognize different emotional expressions, like happy, sad, anger, etc., as depicted in photos of people's faces.

- **Inhibition** (as measured on the *NEPSY-II*) – the children were able to control automatic responses and switch more readily between different ways of responding.

This last area was an interesting phenomenon since the Emotional Self-regulation unit wasn't even started with these children. It's likely that work on self-regulation with specific emphasis on executive functions impacts a larger realm – this is the hope when focusing on executive functions. When a child is helped to focus their attention, increase their inhibitory control and improve their planning and organization and working memory, their ability to discern important information in the world around them develops.

There were some interesting trends found in the data from the *Autism Spectrum Rating Scale*. They didn't reach statistical significance but were strong positive indicators. The trends included improved peer socialization (for example, playing more with others, developing and maintaining relationships with other children), less unusual behavior (for example, insisting on doing things the same ways, over-reacting to sensory input) and decreased stereotypy (for example, focusing on one subject, lining up objects).

These trends support some of the anecdotal information from therapists as well as the other research data. It appears that, when children participate in **spark***, they show improvement not only in executive functions but also in broader social and linguistic realms. This supports the contention that executive functions and self-regulation are foundation skills to other major areas of development.

Self-regulation in the everyday context

Self-regulated behavior is subtle: when it occurs, you often don't notice. An example of a typical scenario will illustrate this point. Recently, I was promoting the notion of 'ignoring' with some preschoolers. The flip-side and unstated alternative was "You don't have to clobber X; you can just ignore them." I noticed that the boy's younger sister was dolloping play foam onto their head. I watched carefully, ready to intercede as need be. The little boy continued with their play and didn't even look at their little sister. They soon moved on to another activity. I commented, "Ben, you really did a good job there with your sister when they were trying to bug you." They replied calmly, "I was ignoring her." That's self-regulation. You have to notice what is missing – Ben didn't yell or hit their sister.

When children start to exercise self-regulation, you may find yourself feeling a sense of relief. You may experience more peace and quiet. You may begin to 'put down your guard' and feel you don't have to be so hyper-alert. You may reach the end of your day and wonder, "Why aren't I exhausted?" Ask yourself: "What was so much better today than yesterday?" Review with your child all the times during the day when both you and they exercised self-regulation. Celebrate the successes.

Stay alert to the child's use of self-regulation so you can highlight it and increase the likelihood that it will happen again. Some behaviors to watch for are included in Table 5 on the next page. The behaviors in the first column show that the child has an awareness of the usefulness and application of self-regulation. The second column describes examples of resilient behavior and positive attempts to cope. The third column provides instances of self-advocating by the child to maintain their position and equilibrium.

When you notice the child using self-regulation skills and strategies, highlight them. Praise them and let them know how they helped themselves use their good thinking.

Support the child's growing autonomy

Every child wants autonomy to some degree. They want to have a sense of choice and freedom[291]. With the development of autonomy, they develop more self-determination and perseverance, along with a greater sense of achievement[292]. But, why would we give autonomy to a young child? Isn't it just like being overly-indulgent? No, autonomy in the **spark*** model refers to the child's developing a sense of their own effectiveness as a learner and moving from being regulated by other people to becoming self-regulated. It doesn't mean that the child is free to do whatever they want. The child has to behave according to cultural and societal values and standards, just like everyone else, but they can control the rudder on their own ship and learn to navigate on their own. They develop a sense of personal causation but, with it, we want to make sure they learn a sense of personal responsibility.

To support each child's growing autonomy, give them choices[293] about what to do, how and/or when or by giving a reason when choice is limited. Choice is a powerful validation of the importance of the child's input. It can be very simple: you decide which tasks, but the child determines the order for completing them or you offer milk and juice and the child selects one.

Table 5.
Examples of self-regulated behavior showing awareness, resilience and self-advocacy.

Behaviors that suggest self-regulation		
Awareness of self-regulation	Resilience in using skills & strategies	Self-advocacy in helping themselves self-regulate
• Initiating activities on their own • Planning their own tasks, activities and goals • Self-monitoring their progress on tasks • Making reasoned choices and decisions • Cooperating with siblings and peers • Learning from what other people are doing • Attributing their achievements and failures to factors they can control such as effort	• Controlling their attention • Resisting distractions • Persisting in the face of difficulties, distractions or disruptions • Enjoying solving problems • Remaining calm when dealing with change, challenges and disappointments • Bouncing back more readily after disappointments	• Trying new tasks with few hesitations • Finding things they need to accomplish something without adult help • Sharing and taking turns independently • Asking for help when needed • Negotiating when and how to do things

Adult involvement needs to be carefully balanced. You always focus on long-term goals for that child and keep your expectations high. At the same time, give them sincerity, warmth and respect[294].

To exercise self-regulation, we need to ensure the child CAN. That is, they're Calm, Alert and Nourished. If they're tired, not feeling well or hungry, don't press for self-regulated behavior from them.

The emotional climate used around the child is also very important to their learning. When you interact with them, be calm, positive, optimistic and confident. Take a few Turtle Breaths before interacting with the child; it'll make a significant difference in how they respond to you.

To encourage family involvement, **spark*** includes a series of 18 newsletters to help parents understand the areas of focus and how they can promote the development of self-regulation at home, and in the community. In order to make content and activities relevant to each family, parents are asked to provide information on key areas of concern and need for self-regulation in their child.

Words we use shape and are reflective of our relationship with the child. Listen to yourself talk to them. What are they learning about learning? Is learning joyful and enjoyable to them? Is it joyful and enjoyable for you? Your words should act to help the child be more motivated and to learn more about themselves. Everything you say must be sincere and honest but make sure you tell them about what they do well. We can all flourish with a little encouragement and the knowledge that others believe in our abilities. The Language of **spark*** lets the child know that you're there to support them but they need to do as much as possible on their own and, next time, you'll ask a little more.

Self-regulation can be taught even to very young children. Some of the things that parents and teachers do naturally can enhance self-regulation skills. For example, action songs and rhymes are excellent media for practicing control of actions and thinking. Storybooks can provide 'safe' settings for experiencing a variety of emotions. As shown in **spark***, expensive equipment and specially-designed computer games aren't necessary to foster the improvements in self-regulation skills.

Some ways to foster self-regulation skills everyday include:

1. **Give the child choices:** Invite the child to express their opinion about what they'd like to do or how they'd like to do it. Offer them alternatives and respect their choices. This gives them a greater sense of autonomy as well as validation of the importance of their input.

2. **Value their opinion:** Listen to the child's ideas and be responsive to their suggestions. Acknowledge their outlook even if you disagree. Explain your ideas and opinions in simple and honest terms.

3. **Explain your reasoning:** Calmly and matter-of-factly, give them reasons for doing things in certain ways or at certain times. Don't feel 'mean' if you have to remind them of a rule; state it as an objective fact. By doing this, they'll be more willing and able to adopt the behavior.

4. **Use inclusive language:** Use of "we" and the notion of sharing thoughts, ideas and strategies can boost a child's sense that self-regulation is important for everyone. They'll have a greater sense of intrinsic motivation and won't feel singled out.

5. **Praise and give feedback.** Praise the child for using self-regulation and explain why it's important. Don't feel that you have to give them a reward although it can help to get things going. Remember, tangible rewards can actually undermine their generalization of knowledge and learning[295]. Our goal is to help the child to use self-regulation skills for their own sake and not to get a prize.

6. **Give hints and encouragement**: By giving the child with hints and encouragement, you prompt them to think for themselves and figure out what might work. When you tell them what to do, they don't have an opportunity to reflect and use their problem solving skills. After teaching the child a skill or strategy, begin asking them "What do you need to do?" or "What could you do to help yourself?" This reinforces their learning, extension and generalization of skills and strategies as well as their sense of autonomy.

PHOTO CREDITS

Page 2 - Photo by Orkun Azap on Unsplash

ABOUT THE AUTHOR

Heather MacKenzie, Ph.D., is a speech-language pathologist and educator who has spent a large part of her career developing and implementing new approaches for enhancing learning in children with special needs. She has a special interest in understanding autism spectrum conditions (ASC) and in translating current research into sound clinical practices. A major focus of her work with children has been on understanding them and how they approach learning. She has used this knowledge to develop models for optimizing their development.

Heather developed the **Learning Preferences and Strengths** model which is designed to determine each child is learning preferences and strengths and then 'harness' the preferences and strength to improve the child's learning and development. In her current book, *The Autistic Child's Guide*, she presents the **spark*** model which is an extension of her child-centered, mediational approach to teaching and learning.

Heather has provided workshops and presentations all over North America, the Middle East, Africa, in the U.K., and in Asia.

Heather's areas of expertise include autism spectrum conditions, language and communication disorders, Learning Preferences and Strengths, personality/psychological type and multiple intelligences in children with special needs.

Visit the Self-Regulation Central website (www.selfregcentral.com) for more information.

END NOTES AND REFERENCES

1 I would like to thank Simon Baron-Cohen who I believe coined the term Autism Spectrum Condition. Substituting the term "condition" for "disorder" is much more in keeping with my philosophy.

2 Sacks, O. (1996). *An Anthropologist on Mars: Seven Paradoxical Tales*. New York: Vintage.

3 Doidge, N. (2007). *The Brain that Changes Itself*. New York: Penguin Group.

4 The word 'appropriate' (as in 'socially appropriate' or 'situationally appropriate') will be used throughout this book in relation to behavior to mean actions that don't draw undue attention to the child, marginalize them or set them apart in a manner that he and/or their family don't intend or want.

5 Tangney, J. P., Baumeister, R. F., & Boone, A. L. (2004). High self-control predicts good adjustment, less pathology, better grades, and interpersonal success. *J. of personality, 72*(2), p. 271–324.

6 Levesque, C, Zuehlke, A., Stanek, L. & Ryan, R. (2004). Autonomy and competence in German and American university students: A comparative study based on Self-Determination Theory. *J. of Ed. Psych.*, 96, p. 68-84.

7 Ryan, R., Connell, J. & Plant, R. (1990). Emotions in non-directed text learning. *Learning & Individual Differences*, 2, p. 1-17.

8 Black, A. E., & Deci, E. L. (2000). The effects of instructors' autonomy support and students' autonomous motivation on learning organic chemistry: A self-determination theory perspective. *Science Ed*, 84, p. 740-756.

9 Baumeister, R., Dewall, C., Ciarocco, N. & Twenge, J. (2005). Social Exclusion Impairs Self-Regulation. *J. of Personality & Social Psych.*, 88, p. 589-604.

10 Deci, E. L., Koestner, R., & Ryan, R. M. (1999). A meta-analytic review of experiments examining the effects of extrinsic rewards on intrinsic motivation. *Psych. Bulletin, 125*, p. 627–68.

11 Deci, E. & Ryan, R. (1985). *Intrinsic motivation and self-determination in human behavior*. New York: Plenum.

12 Reeve, J., Jang, H., Harde, P. & Omura, M. (2002). Providing a rationale in an autonomy-supportive way as a strategy to motivate others during an uninteresting activity. *Motivation & Emotion*, 26, p. 183-207.

13 Reeve, J., Deci, E. & Ryan, R. (2004). Self-determination theory: A dialectical framework for understanding socio-cultural influences on student motivation. In D. McInerney & S. Van Etten (Eds.), *Big theories revisited*. Greenwich, CT: Information Age Press.

14 Assor, A., Kaplan, H., Kanat-Maymon, Y. & Roth, G. (2002). Directly controlling teacher behaviors as predictors of poor motivation and engagement in girls and boys: The role of anger and anxiety. *Learning & Instruction, 15*, p. 397-413.

15 Amabile, T. M. (1983). *The Social Psychology of Creativity*. New York: Springer-Verlag.

16 Patrick, B., Skinner, E. & Connell, J. (1993). What motivates children's behavior and emotion? Joint effects of perceived control and autonomy in the academic domain. *J. of Personality & Social Psych.*, 65, p. 781-791.

17 Reeve, J., Jang, H., Harde, P. & Omura, M. (2002). Providing a rationale in an autonomy-supportive way as a strategy to motivate others during an uninteresting activity. *Motivation & Emotion*, 26, p. 183-207.

18 Ryan, R. & Connell, J. (1989). Perceived locus of causality and internalization: Examining reasons for acting in two domains. *J. of Personality & Social Psych.*, 57, p. 749–61.

19 Hardre, P. & Reeve, J. (2003). A motivational model of rural students' intentions to persist in, versus drop out of, high school. *J. of Ed. Psych.*, 95, p. 347-356.

20 Noels, K., Pelletier, L. G., & Vallerand, R. J. (2000). Why are you learning a second language? motivational orientations and self-determination theory. *Language Learning*, 53, p. 33-64.

21 Pelletier, L., Fortier, M., Vallerand, R. & Brière, N. (2001). Associations among perceived autonomy support, forms of self-regulation, and persistence: A prospective study. *Motivation & Emotion*, 25, p. 279-306.

22 Senecal, C., Julien, E., & Guay, F. (2003). Role conflict and academic procrastination: A self-determination perspective. *European J. of Social Psych.*, 33, p. 135-145.

23 Boggiano, A., Flink, C., Shields, A., Seelback, A. & Barrett, M. (1993). Use of techniques promoting students' self-determination: Effects of students' analytic problem-solving skills. *Motivation & Emotion*, 17, p. 319-336.

24 Vansteenkiste, M., Zhou, M., Lens, W. & Soenens, B. (2005). Experiences of autonomy and control among Chinese learners: Vitalizing or immobilizing? *J. of Ed. Psych.*, 96, p. 755-764.

25 Duncan, G., Dowsett, C., Claessens, A., Magnuson, K., Huston, A., Klebanov, P., Pagani, L., Feinstein, L., Engel, M., Brooks-Gunn, J., Sexton, H., Duckworth, K. & Japel, C. (2007) School readiness and later achievement. *Dev. Psych.*, 43, p. 1428–1446.

26 McClelland, M., Morrison, F. & Holmes, D. (2000). Children at risk for early academic problems: The role of learning-related social skills. *Early Childhood Res. Quarterly*, 15, p. 307–329.

27 Perry, N. (1998). Young children's self-regulated learning and contexts that support it. *J. of Ed. Psych.*, 90, p. 715–729.

28 Fantuzzo, J., Bulotsky-Shearer, R., McDermott, P., McWayne, C., & Frye, D. (2007). Investigation of Dimensions of Social-Emotional Classroom Behavior and School Readiness for Low-Income Urban Preschool Children. *School Psych. Review*, 36, p. 44–62.

29 Zimmerman, B. J. (1989). A Social Cognitive View of Self-Regulated Academic Learning. *J. of Ed. Psych.*, 81, p. 329–339.

30 Zimmerman, B. J. (1990). Self-Regulated Learning and Academic Achievement. *Ed. Psych.*, 25, p. 3–17.

31 Mischel, W., & Ayduk, O. (2002). Self-regulation in a cognitive-affective personality system: Attentional control in the service of the self. *Self & Identity, 1*, p. 113-120.

32 Moffitt, T. E., Arseneault, L., Belsky, D., Dickson, N., Hancox, R. J., Harrington, H., Houts, R., et al. (2011). A gradient of childhood self-control predicts health, wealth, and public safety. *Proceedings of the National Academy of Sciences of the United States of America, 108*(7), p. 2693–2698.

33 Moffitt, T. E., Arseneault, L., Belsky, D., Dickson, N., Hancox, R. J., Harrington, H., Houts, R., et al. (2011). A gradient of childhood self-control predicts health, wealth, and public safety. Proceedings of the National Academy of Sciences of the United States of America, 108, p. 2697.

34 Brown, T. E. (2006), *Attention Deficit Disorder: The Unfocused Mind in Children and Adults.* New Haven, CT: Yale University Press. p. 36

35 Rimmele, U. *Neuromyths.* Center for Ed. Res. and Innovation. Retrieved from http://www.oecd.org/edu/ceri/neuromyths.htm

36 Immordino-Yang, M. H., & Fischer, K. W. (2009). Neuroscience bases of learning. In V. G. Aukrust (Ed.), *International Encyclopedia of Education*, 3rd Edition, Section on Learning and Cognition. Oxford, England: Elsevier. p. 3.

37 Elliott, R. (2003). Executive functions and their disorders. *British Medical Bulletin, 65*(1), p. 49–59.

38 Goel, V. & Grafman, J. (2000). Role of the Right Prefrontal Cortex in Ill-Structured Planning. *Cognitive Neuropsych., 17*, p. 415-436.

39 O'Hearn, K., Asato, M., Ordaz, S. & Luna, B. (2008). Neurodevelopment and executive function in autism. *Development & Psychopathology, 20*, p. 1103-1132.

40 Kana, R., Keller, T, Minshew, N. & Just, M. (2007). Inhibitory control in high-functioning autism: decreased activation and underconnectivity in inhibition networks. *Biological Psychiatry, 62*, p. 198-206.

41 Klingberg, T., Fernell, E., Olesen, P., Johnson, M., Gustafsson, P., Dahlstrom, K., Gillberg, C., Forssberg, H., & Westerberg, H. (2005). Computerized Training of Working Memory in Children With ADHD – A Randomized, Controlled Trial. *J. of the American Academy of Child & Adolescent Psychiatry, 44*, p. 177-186.

42 Rothbart, M. & Bates, J. E. (1998). Temperament.pdf. In N. Damon, W. & Eisenberg (Ed.), *Social, emotion, and personality development.* New York, NY: Wiley.

43 Gehring, W. J., & Knight, R. T. (2000). Prefrontal-cingulate interactions in action monitoring. *Nature Neuroscience, 3*, p. 516-520.

44 Holroyd, C. B., Nieuwenhuis, S. Yeung, N., Nystrom, L. E., Mars, R. B., Coles, M. G. & Cohen, J. D. (2004). Dorsal anterior cingulate cortex shows fMRI response to internal and external error signals. *Nature Neuroscience, 7*, p. 497-498.

45 Garon, N., Bryson, S. E., & Smith, I. M. (2008). Executive function in preschoolers: a review using an integrative framework. *Psych. bulletin, 134*, p. 31–60.

46 Leber, A. B., Turk-Browne, N. B., & Chun, M. M. (2008). Neural predictors of moment-to-moment fluctuations in cognitive flexibility. *Proceedings of the National Academy of Sciences, 105*, p. 13592-13597.

47 O'Hearn, K., Asato, M., Ordaz, S., & Luna, B. (2008). Neurodevelopment and executive function in autism. *Development & psychopathology, 20*, p. 1103–32.

48 Rothbart, M. K., & Posner, M. I. (2001). Mechanism and variation in the development of attentional networks. In C. A. Nelson & M. Luciana, (Eds.), *Handbook of developmental cognitive neuroscience*. Cambridge, MA: MIT Press.

49 Diamond, A. (1990). Rate of maturation of the hippocampus and the developmental progression of children's performance on the delayed non-matching to sample and visual paired comparison tasks. *Annals of the New York Academy of Sciences, 608*, p. 394-426.

50 Diamond, A. (1985). The development of the ability to use recall to guide action, as indicated by infants' performance on A-not-B. *Child Development, 56*, p. 868-883.

51 Diamond, A. & Doar, B. (1989). The performance of human infants on a measure of frontal cortex function, the delayed response task. *Dev. Psychobiology, 22*, p. 271-294.

52 Kochanska, G., Murray, K. T., & Harlan, E. T. (2000). Effortful control in early childhood: Continuity and change, antecedents, and implications for social development. *Dev. Psych., 36*, p. 220–232.

53 McCarty, M., Clifton, R. & Collard, R. (1999). Problem Solving in Infancy: The Emergence of an Action Plan. *Dev. Psych., 35*, p. 1091-1101.

54 Kopp, C. (1989). Regulation of distress and negative emotions: A developmental view. *Dev. Psych., 25*, p. 343-354.

55 Garon, N., Bryson, S. & Smith, I. (2008). A review of executive function in the preschool period using an integrative framework. *Psychological Bulletin, 134*, p. 31-60.

56 Rothbart, M. (1989). Temperament and development. In G. Kohnstamm, J. Bates, & M. Rothbart (Eds.), *Temperament in childhood*. New York: Wiley.

57 Smidts, D. (2003). Development of executive processes in early childhood. Unpublished doctoral dissertation. University of Melbourne, Australia.

58 Zelazo, P., Frye, D. & Rapus, T. (1996). An age-related dissociation between knowing rules and using them. *Cognitive Development, 11*, p. 37-63.

59 Espy, K. (1997). The Shape School: Assessing executive function in preschool children. *Dev. Neuropsych., 13*, p. 495-499.

60 Smidts, D. (2003). Development of executive processes in early childhood. Unpublished doctoral dissertation. University of Melbourne, Australia.

61 Welsh, M., Pennington, B., & Groisser, D. (1991). A normative-developmental study of executive function: A window on prefrontal function in children. *Dev. Neuropsych., 7*, p. 131-149.

62 Gerardi-Caulton, G. (2000). Sensitivity to spatial conflict and the development of self-regulation in children 24–36 months of age. *Dev. Science, 3*, p. 397–404

63 Mischel, W., Shoda, Y. & Rodriguez, M. (1989) Delay of gratification in children. *Science, 244*, p. 933–938.

64 Carlson, S., Mandell, D., & Williams, L. (2004). Executive function and theory of mind: Stability and prediction from ages 2 to 3. *Dev. Psych., 40*, p. 1105–1122.

65 Berk, L. (1992). Children's private speech: An overview of theory and the status of research. In Diaz & Berk (Eds.). *Private Speech: From Social Interaction to Self-Regulation*. Hillsdale, NJ: Lawrence Erlbaum Associates Publishers.

66 Barkley, R.A. (1997). *ADHD and the nature of self-control*. New York: The Guilford Press.

67 Kopp, C. (1989). Regulation of distress and negative emotions: A developmental view. *Dev. Psych.*, 25, p. 343-354.

68 Huizinga, M., Dolan, C., & van der Molen, M. (2006). Age-related change in executive function: Developmental trends and a latent variable analysis. *Neuropsychologia, 44*, p. 2017–2036.

69 Chelune, G., Baer, R. (1986). Developmental norms for the Wisconsin Card Sorting test. *J. of Clinical & Experimental Neuropsych.*, 8, p. 219–228.

70 Levin, H., Eisenberg, H. & Benton, A. (1991). *Frontal lobe function and dysfunction*. New York: Oxford University Press.

71 Huizinga, M., Dolan, C., & van der Molen, M. (2006). Age-related change in executive function: Developmental trends and a latent variable analysis. *Neuropsychologia, 44*, p. 2017–2036.

72 Krikorian, R., & Bartok, J. (1998). Developmental data for the Porteus Maze Test. *Clinical Neuropsych.*, 12, p. 305-310.

73 Smidts, D. (2003). Development of executive processes in early childhood. Unpublished doctoral dissertation. University of Melbourne, Australia.

74 American Psychiatric Association. (2013). *Diagnostic and statistical manual of mental disorders* (5th ed.). Arlington, VA: Author.

75 Stone, W. L., Hoffman, E. L., Lewis, S. E. & Ousley, O. Y. (1994). Early recognition of autism: parental reports vs. clinical observation. *Archives of Pediatric & Adolescent Medicine, 148*, p. 174–179.

76 Hill, E. (2004a). Executive dysfunction in autism. *TRENDS in Cognitive Sciences, 8*, p. 26-32.

77 Ozonoff, S., Goodlin-Jones, B. & Solomon, M. (2005). Evidence-based assessment of autism spectrum disorders in children and adolescents. *J. of Clinical Child & Adolescent Psychiatry, 34*, p. 532.

78 Goldstein, S. & Naglieri, J. (2009). *Autism Spectrum Rating Scales*. Toronto, CA: Multi-Health Systems.

79 Howlin, P., Goode, S., Hutton, J., & Rutter, M. (2004). Adult outcome for children with autism. *J. of Child Psych. & Psychiatry, 45*, p. 212-229.

80 Billstedt, E., Gillberg, C. & Gillberg, C. (2005). Autism after Adolescence: Population-based 13- to 22-year Follow-up Study of 120 Individuals with Autism Diagnosed in Childhood. *J. of Autism & Dev. Disorders, 35*, p. 351-360.

81 Hofvander, B., Delorme, R., Chaste, P., Nydén, A., Wentz, E., Ståhlberg, O., Herbrecht, E., Stopin, A., Anckarsäter, H., Gillberg, C., Råstam, M. & Leboyer, M. (2009). Psychiatric and psychosocial problems in adults with normal-intelligence autism spectrum disorders. *BMC Psychiatry*. Accessed December 2009 from http://www.biomedcentral.com/content/pdf/1471-244X-9-35.pdf

82 Barnard, J., Harvey, V., Potter, D., & Prior, A. (2001). *Ignored or ineligible? The reality for adults with autism spectrum disorders*. London: National Autism Society.

83 Howlin, P., & Moss, P. (2012). Adults With Autism Spectrum Disorders. *Canadian J. of Psychiatry, 57*, p. 275–283.

84 United Nations Education Science and Cultural Organization International Bureau of Education (www.ibe.unesco.org/en/access-by-country.html) reported that, in 2008, 59% of people in the United Kingdom, 75% in Sweden and 55% in France completed university or college studies.

85 The Central Intelligence Agency (www.cia.gov) reported rates of unemployment for 2008 to be 5.6% in the U.K., 6.1% in Sweden and 7.4% in France.

86 United Nations World Marriage Data 2008 (www.un.org) reported a rate of 95.5% of people in the United Kingdom and France and 95.0% of people in Sweden are married.

87 Marriage, S., Wolverton, A. & Marriage, K. (2009). Autism Spectrum Disorder Grown Up: A Chart Review of Adult Functioning. *J. of the Canadian Academy of Child & Adolescent Psychiatry, 18*, p. 324-328.

88 Marriage, S., Wolverton, A. & Marriage, K. (2009). Autism Spectrum Disorder Grown Up: A Chart Review of Adult Functioning. *J. of the Canadian Academy of Child & Adolescent Psychiatry, 18*, p. 324-328.

89 Berger, H., Aerts, F., van Spaendonck, K., Cools, A. & Teunisse, J. (2003). Central Coherence and Cognitive Shifting in Relation to Social Improvement in High-Functioning Young Adults with Autism. *J. of Clinical & Experimental Neuropsych., 25*, p. 502 – 511.

90 Szatmari, P., Bartolucci, G., Bremner, R., Bond, S., & Rich, S.(1989). A follow-up study of high-functioning autistic children. *J. of Autism & Dev. Disorders, 19*, p. 213–225.

91 Mackinlay, R., Charman, T., & Karmiloff-Smith, A. (2006). High functioning children with autism spectrum disorder: A novel test of multitasking. *Brain & Cognition, 61*, p. 14-24.

92 Kenworthy, L. E., Black, D. O., & Gregory, L. (2010). Developmental Neuropsychology Disorganization : The Forgotten Executive Dysfunction in High-Functioning Autism (HFA) Spectrum Disorders, *Dev. neuropsych., 28*, p. 809–827.

93 Chan, A., Cheung, M., Han, Y., Sze, S., Leung, W., Man, H. & To, C. (2009). Executive function deficits and neural discordance in children with Autism Spectrum Disorders. *Clinical Neurophysiology, 120*, p. 1107-1116.

94 Chan, A., Cheung, M., Han, Y., Sze, S., Leung, W., Man, H. & To, C. (2009). Executive function deficits and neural discordance in children with Autism Spectrum Disorders. *Clinical Neurophysiology, 120*, p. 1113.

95 Greene, C., Braet, W., Johnson, K., & Bellgrove, M., (2008). Imaging the genetic of executive function. *Biological Psych., 79*, p. 30-42.

96 Geurts, H., Begeer, S., & Stockmann, L. (2009). Brief Report: Inhibitory Control of Socially Relevant Stimuli in children with High Functioning Autism. *J. of Autism & Dev. Disorders, 39*, p. 1603-1607.

97 Geurts, H., Begeer, S., & Stockmann, L. (2009). Brief Report: Inhibitory Control of Socially Relevant Stimuli in children with High Functioning Autism. *J. of Autism & Dev. Disorders, 39*, p. 1603-1607.

98 South, M., Ozonoff, S., & McMahon, W. (2007). The relationship between executive functioning, central coherence, and repetitive behaviors in the high-functioning autism spectrum. *Autism,* 11, p. 441-455.

99 Shafritz, K., Dichter, G., Baranek, G. & Belger, A. (2008). The Neural Circuitry Mediating Shifts in Behavioral Response and Cognitive Set in Autism. *Biological Psychiatry,* 63, p. 974-980.

100 O'Hearn, K., Asato, M., Ordaz, S. & Luna, B. (2008). Neurodevelopment and executive function in autism. *Development & Psychopathology,* 20, p. 1103-1132.

101 Chan, A., Cheung, M., Han, Y., Sze, S., Leung, W., Man, H. & To, C. (2009). Executive function deficits and neural discordance in children with Autism Spectrum Disorders. *Clinical Neurophysiology,* 120, p. 1107-1116.

102 Sinzig, J., Morsch, D., Bruning, N., Schmidt, M., & Lehmkuhl, G. (2008). Inhibition, flexibility, working memory and planning in autism spectrum disorders with and without comorbid ADHD-symptoms. Accessed February, 2010 from http://www.capmh.com/content/2/1/4

103 Bishop, D. & Norbury, C. (2005). Executive functions in children with communication impairments, in relation to autistic symptomatology I: Generativity. *Autism,* 9, p. 7-27.

104 Kana, R., Keller, T, Minshew, N. & Just, M. (2007). Inhibitory control in high-functioning autism: decreased activation and underconnectivity in inhibition networks. *Biological Psychiatry,* 62, p. 198-206.

105 Goldstein, S. & Schwebach, A. (2004). The comorbidity of Pervasive Developmental Disorder and Attention Deficit Hyperactivity Disorder: results of a retrospective chart review. *J. of Autism & Dev. Disorders,* 34, p. 329-339.

106 Chan, A., Cheung, M., Han, Y., Sze, S., Leung, W., Man, H. & To, C. (2009). Executive function deficits and neural discordance in children with Autism Spectrum Disorders. *Clinical Neurophysiology,* 120, p. 1112.

107 Pennington, B. F., Rogers, S. J., Bennetto, L., Griffith, E. M., Reed, D. T., & Shyu, V. (1997). Validity tests of the executive dysfunction hypothesis of autism. In J. Russell (Ed.), Autism as an executive disorder. Oxford, England: Oxford University Press.

108 Kenworthy, L. E., Black, D. O., & Gregory, L. (2010). Developmental Neuropsychology Disorganization : The Forgotten Executive Dysfunction in High-Functioning Autism (HFA) Spectrum Disorders, *Dev. neuropsych.,* 28, p. 809–827.

109 Russo, N., Flanagan, T., Iarocci, G., Berringer, D., Zelazo, P., & Burack, J. (2007). Deconstructing executive deficits among persons with autism: Implications for cognitive neuroscience. *Brain & Cognition,* 65, p. 77-86.

110 O'Hearn, K., Asato, M., Ordaz, S. & Luna, B. (2008). Neurodevelopment and executive function in autism. *Development & Psychopathology,* 20, p. 1103-1132.

111 Ozonoff, S., & Strayer, D. L. (2001). Further evidence of intact working memory in autism. *J. of Autism & Dev. Disorders,* 31, p. 257–263.

112 Geurts, H. M., Verte´, S., Oosterlaan, J., Roeyers, H., & Sergeant, J. A. (2004). How specific are executive functioning deficits in Attention Deficit Hyperactivity Disorder and autism? *J. of Child Psych. & Psychiatry & Allied Disciplines,* 45, p. 836–854.

113 Poirier, M. & Martin, J. (2008). Working Memory and Immediate Memory in Autism Spectrum Disorders. In J. Boucher & D. Bowler(Eds). *Memory in Autism*. Cambridge: Cambridge University Press.

114 Hill, E. (2004a). Executive dysfunction in autism. *TRENDS in Cognitive Sciences*, 8, p. 26-32

115 Klin, A., Jones, W. Schulz, R., & Volkmar, F. (2003). The enactive mind, or from actions to cognition: lessons from autism. *Philosophical Transactions of the Royal Society London*, 358, p. 345-360.

116 Geurts, H. M., Verte´, S., Oosterlaan, J., Roeyers, H., & Sergeant, J. A. (2004). How specific are executive functioning deficits in Attention Deficit Hyperactivity Disorder and autism? *J. of Child Psych. & Psychiatry & Allied Disciplines*, 45, p. 836–854.

117 Hill, E. (2004b). Evaluating the theory of executive dysfunction in autism. *Dev. Review*, 24, p. 189-233.

118 Hill, E. (2004b). Evaluating the theory of executive dysfunction in autism. *Dev. Review*, 24, p. 189-233.

119 Kenworthy, L. E., Black, D. O., & Gregory, L. (2010). Developmental Neuropsychology Disorganization : The Forgotten Executive Dysfunction in High-Functioning Autism (HFA) Spectrum Disorders, *Dev. Neuropsych.*, 28, p. 809–827.

120 Shafritz, K., Dichter, G., Baranek, G. & Belger, A. (2008). The Neural Circuitry Mediating Shifts in Behavioral Response and Cognitive Set in Autism. *Biological Psychiatry*, 63, p. 974-980.

121 Bishop, D. & Norbury, C. (2005). Executive functions in children with communication impairments, in relation to autistic symptomatology I: Generativity. *Autism*, 9, p. 7-27.

122 Lee, L.-C., Harrington, R. a, Louie, B. B., & Newschaffer, C. J. (2008). Children with autism: quality of life and parental concerns. *J.of autism & Dev. disorders*, 38, p. 1147–1160.

123 Anderson, C., Law, J. K., Daniels, A., Rice, C., Mandell, D. S., Hagopian, L., & Law, P. A. (2012). Occurrence and family impact of elopement in children with autism spectrum disorders. *Pediatrics*, 130, p. 870–877.

124 MacDuff, G. S., Krantz, P. J., & McClannahan, L. E. (1993). Teaching children with autism to use photographic activity schedules: Maintenance and generalization of complex response chains. *J. of Applied Behavior Analysis*, 26, p. 89–97.

125 Hume, K., Loftin, R., Lantz, J., Loftin, Æ. R., & Lantz, Æ. J. (2009). Increasing independence in autism spectrum disorders: a review of three focused interventions. *J. of Autism & Dev. Disorders*, 39, p. 1329–38.

126 Stahmer, A. C., & Schreibman, L. (1992). Teaching children with autism appropriate play in unsupervised environments using a self-management treatment package. *J. of Applied Behavior Analysis*, 25, p. 447-459.

127 Dunlap, G. & Johnson, J. (1985). Increasing the independent responding of autistic children with unpredictable supervision. *J. of Applied Behavior Analysis, 18*, p. 227-236

128 Russo, N., Flanagan, T., Iarocci, G., Berringer, D., Zelazo, P., & Burack, J. (2007). Deconstructing executive deficits among persons with autism: Implications for cognitive neuroscience. *Brain & Cognition*, 65, p. 77-86.

129 Teuber, H.L. (1964). The riddle of frontal lobe function in man. *In* J.M. Warren & K. Akert (Eds). *The Frontal Granular Cortex and Behavior*, New York: McGraw-Hill, p. 333.

130 Patten, E., & Watson, L. R. (2011). Interventions targeting attention in young children with autism. *American J. of speech-language pathology*, 20, p. 60–69.

131 Werner, E., Dawson, G., Osterling, J., & Dinno, N. (2000). Brief Report: Recognition of autism spectrum disorders before one year of age: A retrospective study based on home video tapes. *J. of Autism & Dev. Disorders*, 30, p. 157–162.

132 Renner, P., Grofer Klinger, L., & Klinger, M. (2006). Exogenous and endogenous attention orienting in Autism Spectrum Disorders. *Child Neuropsych.*, 12, p. 361-382.

133 Zwaigenbaum, L., Bryson, S., Rogers, T., Roberts, W., Brian, J., & Szatmari, P. (2005). Behavioral manifestations of autism in the first year of life. *International J. of Dev. neuroscience*, 23, p. 143–152.

134 Landry, R., & Bryson, S. E. (2004). Impaired disengagement of attention in young children with autism. *J. of Child Psych. & Psychiatry*, 45, p. 1115–1122.

135 Sasson, N. J., Elison, J. T., Turner-Brown, L. M., Dichter, G. S., & Bodfish, J. W. (2011). Brief report: Circumscribed attention in young children with autism. *J. of Autism & Dev. Disorders*, 4, p. 242–247.

136 Baron-Cohen, S. (1995). *Mindblindness: An essay on autism and theory of mind*. Boston: MIT Press/Bradford Books.

137 Baron-Cohen, S., Wheelwright, S., Hill, J., Raste, Y. & Plumb, I. (2001). The "Reading the Mind in the Eyes" Test revised version: A study with normal adults, and adults with Asperger syndrome or high-functioning autism. *J.of Child Psych. & Psychiatry*. 42, p. 241-251.

138 Losh, M., Adolphs, R., Poe, M., Couture, S., Penn, D., Baranek, G. & Pivan, J. (2009). The Neuropsychological Profile of Autism and The Broad Autism Phenotype. *Arc.of Genetic Psychiatry*. 66, p. 518–526.

139 Hill, E. (2004b). Evaluating the theory of executive dysfunction in autism. *Dev. Review*, 24, p. 189-233.

140 Dawson, G., Toth, K., Abbott, R., Osterling, J., Munson, J., Estes, A., & Liaw, J. (2004). Early Social Attention Impairments in Autism: Social Orienting, Joint Attention, and Attention to Distress. *Dev. Psych.*, 40, p. 271-283.

141 Klin, A., Jones, W. Schulz, R., & Volkmar, F. (2003). The enactive mind, or from actions to cognition: lessons from autism. *Philosophical Transactions of the Royal Society London*, 358, p. 345-360.

142 Golan, O., Ashwin, E., Granafer, Y., McClintock, S., Day, K., Leggett, V., & Baron-Cohen, S. (2010). Enhancing Emotion Recognition in Children with Autism Spectrum Conditions: An Intervention Using Animated Vehicles with Real Emotional Faces. *J. of Autism & Dev. Disorders*, 40, p. 269-279.

143 Klin, A., Jones, W. Schulz, R., & Volkmar, F. (2003). The enactive mind, or from actions to cognition: lessons from autism. *Philosophical Transactions of the Royal Society London*, 358, p. 345-360.

144 Dalton, K., Nacewicz, B., Johnstone, T., Schaefer, H., Gernsacher, M., Goldsmith, H., Alexander, A. & Davidson, R. (2005). Gaze fixation and the neural circuitry of face processing in autism. *Nature Reviews Neurosciences*, 8, p. 519-526.

145 Dominick, K., Davis, N., Lainhart, J., Tager-Flusberg, H., & Folstein, S. (2007). Atypical behaviors in children with autism and children with a history of language impairment. *Res. in Dev. Disabilities*, 28, p. 145-162.

146 Field D, Garland M, Williams K. (2003). Correlates of specific childhood feeding problems. *J. of Paediatric Child Health*. 39, p. 299–304.

147 Dominick, K., Davis, N., Lainhart, J., Tager-Flusberg, H., & Folstein, S. (2007). Atypical behaviors in children with autism and children with a history of language impairment. *Res. in Dev. Disabilities*, 28, p. 145-162.

148 Williams, P. G., Sears, L. L., & Allard, A. (2004). Sleep problems in children with autism. *J. of Sleep Res.*, 13, p. 265–268.

149 Sivertsen, B., Posserud, M.-B., Gillberg, C., Lundervold, A. J., & Hysing, M. (2012). Sleep problems in children with autism spectrum problems: a longitudinal population-based study. *Autism*, 16, p. 139–50.

150 Dominick, K., Davis, N., Lainhart, J., Tager-Flusberg, H., & Folstein, S. (2007). Atypical behaviors in children with autism and children with a history of language impairment. *Res. in Dev. Disabilities*, 28, p. 145-162.

151 Dominick, K., Davis, N., Lainhart, J., Tager-Flusberg, H., & Folstein, S. (2007). Atypical behaviors in children with autism and children with a history of language impairment. *Res. in Dev. Disabilities*, 28, p. 145-162.

152 Jahromi, L., Bryce, C., & Swanson, J. (2013). The importance of self-regulation for the school and peer engagement of children with high-functioning autism. *Res. in Autism Spectrum Disorders*, 7, p. 235–246.

153 Fredricks, J. A, Blumenfeld, P. C., & Paris, a. H. (2004). School Engagement: Potential of the Concept, State of the Evidence. *Review of Ed. Res.*, 74, p. 59–109.

154 Ladd, G. W., & Dinella, L. M. (2009). Continuity and Change in Early School Engagement: Predictive of Children's Achievement Trajectories from First to Eighth Grade? *J. of Ed. Psych.*, 101, p.190–206.

155 Black, A. E., & Deci, E. L. (2000). The effects of instructors' autonomy support and students' autonomous motivation on learning organic chemistry: A self-determination theory perspective. *Science Ed.*, 84, p. 740-756.

156 Martin, J., Mithaug, D., Cox, P., Peterson, L., Van Dycke, J. & Cash, M.(2003). Increasing self-determination: Teaching students to plan, work, evaluate, and adjust. *Exceptional Children*, 69, p. 431-447.

157 Gilberts, G., Agran, M., Hughes, C., & Wehmeyer, M. (2001). The effects of peer delivered self-monitoring strategies on the participation of students with severe 85 disabilities in general education classrooms. *J. of the Association for Persons with Severe Handicaps*, 26, p. 25-36.

158 Kloo, D., & Perner, J. (2008). Training Theory of Mind and Executive Control : A Tool for Improving School Achievement ? *Mind, Brain & Ed.*. 2, p. 124.

159 Sowers, J., & Powers, L. (1995). Enhancing the participation and independence of students with severe physical and multiple disabilities in performing community activities. *Mental Retardation*, 33, p. 209-220.

160 Wehmeyer, M., Palmer, S., Argan, M., Mithaug, D. & Martin, J. (2000). Promoting causal agency: The self-determination model of instruction. *Exceptional Children, 66*, p. 439-453.

161 Eisenman, L., Chamberlin, M. & McGahee-Kovac, M. (2005). A teacher inquiry group on student-led IEPs: Starting small to make a difference. *Teacher Ed. & Special Ed., 28*, p. 195-206.

162 Test, D. W., Fowler, C. H., Brewer, D. M., & Wood, W. M. (2005). A content and methodological review of Self-advocacy intervention studies. *Exceptional Children, 72*, p. 101-125.

163 Wehmeyer, M. L. & Palmer, S. B. (2003). Adult outcomes for students with cognitive disabilities three years after high school: The impact of self-determination. *Ed. & Training in Dev. Disabilities, 30*, p. 121-146.

164 Field, S., Sarver, M. & Shaw, S. (2003). Self-Determination: A Key to Success in Postsecondary Education for Students with Learning Disabilities. *Remedial & Special Ed., 24*, p. 339–349.

165 Klingberg, T., Fernell, E., Olesen, P., Johnson, M., Gustafsson, P., Dahlstrom, K., Gillberg, C., Forssberg, H., & Westerberg, H. (2005). Computerized Training of Working Memory in Children With ADHD – A Randomized, Controlled Trial. *J. of the American Academy of Child & Adolescent Psychiatry, 44*, p. 177-186.

166 Thorell, L., Lindqvist, S., Bergman, S. Bohlin, G. & Klingberg, T. (2008). Training and transfer effects of executive functions in preschool children. *Dev. Science, 11*, p. 969-976.

167 Olesen, P., Westerberg, H., & Klingberg, T. (2004), Increased prefrontal and parietal brain activity after training of working memory. *Nature Neuroscience, 7*, p. 75–79.

168 Klingberg, T., Fernell, E., Olesen, P., Johnson, M., Gustafsson, P., Dahlstrom, K., Gillberg, C., Forssberg, H., & Westerberg, H. (2005). Computerized Training of Working Memory in Children With ADHD – A Randomized, Controlled Trial. *J. of the American Academy of Child & Adolescent Psychiatry, 44*, p. 177-186.

169 Olesen, P., Westerberg, H., & Klingberg, T. (2004), Increased prefrontal and parietal brain activity after training of working memory. *Nature Neuroscience, 7*, p. 75–79.

170 A meta-analysis combines the results from multiple studies in an effort to increase statistical power, improve estimates of the size of the effect and/or to resolve uncertainty when reports disagree.

171 Melby-Lervåg, M., & Hulme, C. (2013). Is working memory training effective? A meta-analytic review. *Developmental Psychology, 49*, 270–291.

172 Thorell, L., Lindqvist, S., Bergman, S. Bohlin, G. & Klingberg, T. (2008). Training and transfer effects of executive functions in preschool children. *Dev. Science, 11*, p. 969-976.

173 Brace, J., Morton, J. & Munakata, Y. (2006). When Actions Speak Louder Than Words. *Psych. Science, 17*, p. 665-669.

174 de Vries, M., Prins, J., Schmand, B. A., & Geurts, H. M. (2014, May). *Braingame Brian: A randomized controlled trial for an executive functioning training for children with ASD.* Poster presented at the International Meeting for Autism Research, Atlanta, GA.

175 The term 'high functioning' autism is defined in research as a person with a measured IQ of 70 or greater.

176 Owen, A. M., Hampshire, A., Grahn, J. A., Stenton, R., Dajani, S., Burns, A. S., Howard, R., & Ballard, C. G. (2010). Putting brain training to the test. *Nature*, 465(7299), 775–778.

177 Enriquez-Geppert, S., Huster, R. J., & Herrmann, C. S. (2013). Boosting brain functions: Improving executive functions with behavioral training, neurostimulation, and neurofeedback. *International Journal of Psychophysiology*, 88(1), 1–16.

178 Kouijzer, M., de Moor, J., Gerrits, B., Buitelaar, J., & van Schie, H. (2009). Long-term effects of neurofeedback treatment in autism. *Res. in Autism Spectrum Disorders*, 3, p. 496–501.

179 Kouijzer, M., de Moor, J., Berrie, J., Gerrits, B., Congedo, M. & van Schie, H. (2009). Neurofeedback improves executive functioning in children with autism spectrum disorders. *Res. in Autism Spectrum Disorders*, 3, p. 145-162.

180 Begemann, M., Florisse, E., van Lutterveld, R., Kooyman, M., & Sommer, I. (2016). Efficacy of EEG neurofeedback in psychiatry: A comprehensive overview and meta-analysis. *Translational Brain Rhythmicity*, 1(1), 19–29. https://doi.org/10.15761/TBR.1000105

181 Kubesch, S., Walk, L., Spitzer, M., Kammer, T., Laniburg, A., Heim, R. & Hille, K. (2009). A 30-Minute Physical Education Program Improves Students' Executive Attention. *Mind, Brain, & Education*. 3, p. 235-242.

182 Ellemberg, D., & St-Louis-Deschenes, M. (2010). The effect of acute physical exercise on cognitive function during development. *The Psych. of Sport & Exercise*, 11, p. 122–126.

183 Hillman, C.H., Pontifex, M.B., Raine, L.B., Castelli, D.M., Hall, E.E., & Kramer, A.F. (2009). The effect of acute treadmill walking in cognitive control and academic achievement in preadolescent children. *Neuroscience*, 159, p. 1044–1054.

184 Tine, M. T., & Butler, A. G. (2012). Acute aerobic exercise impacts selective attention : an exceptional boost in lower-income children. *Ed. Psych.*, 32, p. 821-834.

185 Kubesch, S., Walk, L., Spitzer, M., Kammer, T., Laniburg, A., Heim, R. & Hille, K. (2009). A 30-Minute Physical Education Program Improves Students' Executive Attention. *Mind, Brain, & Education*. 3, p. 235-242.

186 Ellemberg, D., & St-Louis-Deschenes, M. (2010). The effect of acute physical exercise on cognitive function during development. *The Psych. of Sport & Exercise*, 11, p. 122–126.

187 Kubesch, S., Walk, L., Spitzer, M., Kammer, T., Laniburg, A., Heim, R. & Hille, K. (2009). A 30-Minute Physical Education Program Improves Students' Executive Attention. *Mind, Brain, & Education*. 3, p. 235-242.

188 Ellemberg, D., & St-Louis-Deschenes, M. (2010). The effect of acute physical exercise on cognitive function during development. *The Psych. of Sport & Exercise*, 11, p. 122–126.

189 Lang, R., Koegel, L., Ashbaugh, K., Regester, A., Ence, W., & Smith, W. (2010). Physical exercise and individuals with autism spectrum disorders: A systematic review. *Research in Autism Spectrum Disorders*, 4(4), 565–576.

190 Lakes, K., & Hoyt, W. (2004). Promoting self-regulation through school-based martial arts training. *J. of Applied Dev. Psych.*, 25, p. 283–302.

191 Chan, A., Sze, S. L., Siu, N. Y., Lau, E. M., & Cheung, M. C. (2013). A Chinese mind-body exercise improves self-control of children with autism: A randomized controlled trial. *PLoS ONE*, 8(7), e68184.

192 Radhakrishna, S. (2010). Application of integrated yoga therapy to increase imitation skills in children with autism spectrum disorder. *International J. of yoga*, 3, p. 26–30.

193 Manjunath, N. K., & Telles, S. (2001). Improved performance in the Tower of London test following yoga. *Indian J. of Physiology & Pharmacology*, 45, p. 351–354.

194 Gothe, N., Pontifex, M. B., Hillman, C., & McAuley, E. (2013). The acute effects of yoga on executive function. *J. of physical activity & health*, 10(4), p. 488–95.

195 Teper, R., & Inzlicht, M. (2013). Meditation, mindfulness and executive control: the importance of emotional acceptance and brain-based performance monitoring. *Social Cognitive and Affective Neuroscience*, 8(1), 85–92. https://doi.org/10.1093/scan/nss045

196 Heeren, A., Van Broeck, N., & Philippot, P. (2009). The effects of mindfulness on executive processes and autobiographical memory specificity. *Behavior Research and Therapy*, 47(5), 403–409.

197 Tang, Y., Ma, Y., Wang, J., Fan, Y., Feng, S., Lu, Q., Yu, Q., Sui, D., Rothbart, M. K., Fan, M., & Posner, M. I. (2007). Short-term meditation training improves attention and self-regulation. *Proceedings of the National Academy of Sciences of the United States of America*, 104, 17152–17156.

198 Chambers, R., Lo, C., & Allen, N. B. (2008). The impact of intensive mindfulness training on executive cognition, cognitive style, and affect. *Cognitive Therapy and Research*, 32, 303–322.

199 Flook, L., Smalley, S. L., Kitil, M. J., Galla, B. M., Kaiser-Greenland, S., Locke, J., Ishijima, E., et al. (2010). Effects of Mindful Awareness Practices on Executive Functions in Elementary School Children. *J. of Applied School Psych.*, 26, p. 70–95.

200 Oberle, E., Schonert-Reichl, K. a., Lawlor, M. S., & Thomson, K. C. (2011). Mindfulness and Inhibitory Control in Early Adolescence. *The J. of Early Adolescence*, 32, p. 565–588.

201 Oberle, E., Schonert-Reichl, K. a., Lawlor, M. S., & Thomson, K. C. (2011). Mindfulness and Inhibitory Control in Early Adolescence. *The J. of Early Adolescence*, 32, p. 565–588.

202 Flook, L., Smalley, S. L., Kitil, M. J., Galla, B. M., Kaiser-Greenland, S., Locke, J., Ishijima, E., et al. (2010). Effects of Mindful Awareness Practices on Executive Functions in Elementary School Children. *J. of Applied School Psych.*, 26, p. 70–95.

203 Flook, L., Smalley, S. L., Kitil, M. J., Galla, B. M., Kaiser-Greenland, S., Locke, J., Ishijima, E., et al. (2010). Effects of Mindful Awareness Practices on Executive Functions in Elementary School Children. *J. of Applied School Psych.*, 26, p. 70–95.

204 Gallant, S. (2016). Mindfulness meditation practice and executive functioning: Breaking down the benefit. *Consciousness & Cognition*, 40, 116–130.

205 Singh, N. N., Lancioni, G. E., Manikam, R., Winton, A., Singh, A. & Singh, J. (2011). Adolescents with Asperger syndrome can use a mindfulness-based strategy to control their aggressive behavior. *Res. in Autism Spectrum Disorders, 5*, p. 1103–1109.

206 Singh, N., Lancioni, G., Manikam, R., Winton, A., Singh, A. & Singh, J. (2011). Adolescents with Asperger syndrome can use a mindfulness-based strategy to control their aggressive behavior. *Res. in Autism Spectrum Disorders, 5*, p. 1103–1109.

207 Spek, A., van Ham, N. C., & Nyklíček, I. (2012). Mindfulness-based therapy in adults with an autism spectrum disorder: A randomized controlled trial. *Research in Developmental Disabilities, 34(1)*, 246–253.

208 Kiep, M., Spek, A., & Hoeben, L. (2015). Mindfulness-based therapy in adults with an autism spectrum disorder: Do treatment effects last? *Mindfulness, 6(3)*, 637–644.

209 Sande, A., Gagnon, D., & Montgomery, J. (2017, May). *Mindfulness training with children on the autism spectrum: A pilot study evaluating the impact of mindfulness on social and cognitive outcomes.* International Society for Autism Research, San Francisco

210 Williams, M. & Shellenberger, S. (1996). *How Does Your Engine Run?: A Leader's Guide to the Alert Program for Self-regulation.* Pasadena, TX: Therapy Works Inc.

211 Barkley, R. (2012). *Executive functions: What they are, how they work, and why they evolved.* New York: The Guilford Press.

212 Barnes, K. J., Vogel, K. A., Beck, A. J., Schoenfeld, H. B., & Owen, S. V. (2008). Self-regulation strategies of children with emotional disturbance. *Physical & Occupational Therapy in Pediatrics, 28*, p. 369-387.

213 Fitch, M., & Baker-Ericzen, M. (2017, May). *Command & control cognitive training: Executive functioning intervention for teems and young adults with ASD pilot study.* International Society for Autism Research, San Francisco

214 Moyer, S. & Smith-Myles, B. (2009). *The Eclipse Model: Teaching Self-Regulation, Executive Function, Attribution, and Sensory Awareness to Students with Asperger Syndrome.* Kansas: Autism Asperger Pub. Co.

215 Moyer, S. (2008). *The ECLIPSE Model - building global skills that improve social and behavioral functioning.* Downloaded December 2012 from http://www.autism.org.uk/~/media/nas/documents/news-and-events/nas-conferences/international-conference-2008/short-seminar-presentations/sherry%20moyer%20-%20the%20eclipse%20model%20-%20building%20global%20skills%20that%20improve%20social%20and%20behavioral%20functioning.ashx

216 Bodrova, E. & Leong, D. (2007). *Tools of the Mind.* Upper Saddle River, NJ: Pearson Education Inc.

217 Diamond, A., Barnett, W., Thomas, J. & Munro, S. (2007). Preschool Program Improves Cognitive Control. *Science, 318*, p. 1387-1388.

218 Barnett, W. S., Jung, K., Yarosz, D. J., Thomas, J., Hornbeck, A., Stechuk, R., & Burns, S. (2008). Educational effects of the tools of the mind curriculum: A randomized trial. *Early Childhood Research Quarterly, 23(3)*, 299–313.

219 Cannon, L., Kenworthy, L., Alexander, L., Werner, M., & Anthony, L. (2011). *Unstuck and On Target!: An Executive Function Curriculum to Improve Flexibility for Children with Autism Spectrum Disorders,* Research Edition Baltimore, MD: Brookes Publishing.

220 Anthony, L., Cannon, L., Alexander, K., Werner, M., Wills, L., Sokoloff, J., Sharber, A., Wintrol, J., & Kenworthy, L. (2011, May). *Unstuck and On Target: An Executive Functioning Intervention for Children with High-Functioning Autism Spectrum Disorders.* Poster presented at the International Meeting for Autism Res., San Diego, CA.

221 Anthony, L., Cannon, L., Alexander, K., Werner, M., Wills, M., Sokoloff, J., Powell, K., Sharber, A., Strang, J., Rosenthal, M., Ball, E., Luong-Tran, C., Fallucca, E., Youmatz, A., & Kenworthy, L. (2012, May). *A Pilot Evaluation of Unstuck and On Target: An Executive Functioning Intervention for Children with ASD.* Poster presented at the International Meeting for Autism Res., Toronto, ON.

222 Anthony, L., Cannon, L., Strang, J., Wills, M., Luong-Tran, C., Sokoloff, J., Ball, E., Werner, E., Alexander, K., Powell, K., Sharber, A., Rosenthal, M., Wallace, G., & Kenworthy, L. (2013, May). *A Comparative Effectiveness Trial of a School- and Home-Based Executive Functioning Intervention Versus a Social Skills Intervention; Part One: Contextual Effects.* Poster presented at the International Meeting for Autism Res., San Sebastian, Spain.

223 Kenworthy, L., Werner, M., Alexander, K., Strang, J., Wills, M., Luong-Tran, M., Sokoloff, J., Bal, E., Cannon, L., Sharber, A., Rosenthal, M., Wallace, G., & Anthony, L. (2013, May). *Comparative Effectiveness Trial of School and Home-Based Executive Functioning Versus Social Skills Intervention for Children with ASD; Part 2: Performance Based Effects.* Poster presented at the International Meeting for Autism Res., San Sebastian, Spain.

224 Kenworthy, L., Luong Tran, C., Dudley, K., Werner, M., Strang, J., Armour, A., Wallace, G., & Anthony, L. (2014, May). *Longitudinal outcomes of unstuck and on target executive function intervention trial in children with ASD.* Poster presented at the International Meeting for Autism Research, Atlanta, GA.

225 Strang, J., Anthony, L., Pugliese, C., Cannon, L., Werner, M., Seese, S., Skapek, M., & Kenworthy, L. (2018, May). Improving the executive functioning of adolescents with ASD through school-based intervention: The on target for life curriculum. International Society for Autism Research, Rotterdam.

226 Kuypers, L. (2011). *The zones of regulation.* Santa Clara, CA: Think Social Publishing

227 Valkanos, C., Bettler, M., McGuire, M., Frederico, A., Kernan, B., & Mohr, A. (2016, April). *Impact of modified 'Zones of Regulation' curriculum for preschool students.* The American Occupational Therapy Association, Chicago.

228 Dignath, C., Buettner, G., & Langfeldt, H.-P. (2008). How can primary school students learn self-regulated learning strategies most effectively? *Ed. Res. Review, 3,* p. 101–129.

229 Diamond, A., & Ling, D. S. (2016). Conclusions about Interventions, Programs, and Approaches for Improving Executive Functions that appear Justified and those that, despite much hype, do not. *Developmental Cognitive Neuroscience, 18,* 34–48. https://doi.org/10.1016/j.dcn.2015.11.005

230 Self-regulated learning emphasizes teaching cognitive and motivational skills and strategies that will enhance children's academic performance.

231 Jahromi, L. B., Bryce, C. I., & Swanson, J. (2013). The importance of self-regulation for the school and peer engagement of children with high-functioning autism. *Res. in Autism Spectrum Disorders*, 7, p. 235–246.

232 Bransford, J. D., A. L. Brown, & Cocking, R.R., eds. (2000). *How People Learn*. Washington, D.C.: National Academy Press.

233 Sodian, B., & Frith, U. (2008). Metacognition, Theory of Mind, and Self-Control: The Relevance of High-Level Cognitive Processes in Development, Neuroscience, and Education. *Mind, Brain, & Education*, 2, p. 111–113.

234 Levine, M. (2007). The Essential Cognitive Backpack. *Ed. Leadership*, 64. P. 16-22.

235 These components blend well with the three main reasons for the failure of adults with ASC to achieve higher levels of education, employment and independence discussed in Chapter 1.

236 van Steensel F., Bögels S., & Perrin S. (2011). Anxiety disorders in children and adolescents with autistic spectrum disorders. *Clinical Child & Family Psych. Review*, 14, p. 302-317.

237 White, S. W., Ollendick, T., Scahill, L., Oswald, D., & Albano, A. M. (2009). Preliminary Efficacy of a Cognitive-Behavioral Treatment Program for Anxious Youth with Autism Spectrum Disorders. *J. of Autism & Dev. Disorders*, 39, p. 1652–1662.

238 Ghaziuddin, M. (2002). Asperger Syndrome: Associated Psychiatric and Medical Conditions. *Focus on Autism Other Dev. Disabilities*, 17, p. 138-144.

239 van Steensel F., Bögels S., & Perrin S. (2011). Anxiety disorders in children and adolescents with autistic spectrum disorders. *Clinical Child & Family Psych. Review*, 14, p. 302-317

240 MacNeil, B. M., Lopes, V., & Minnes, P. M. (2009). Anxiety in children and adolescents with Autism Spectrum Disorders. *Res. in Autism Spectrum Disorders*, 3, p. 1–21.

241 Canitano R. (2006). Self-injurious behavior in autism: clinical aspects and treatment with risperidone. *J. of Neural Trans.*, 113, p. 425-431.

242 Eysenck, M. W., Derakshan, N., Santos, R., & Calvo, M. G. (2007). Anxiety and cognitive performance: attentional control theory. *Emotion*, 7, p. 336–53.

243 Diamond, A., & Ling, D. S. (2016). Conclusions about Interventions, Programs, and Approaches for Improving Executive Functions that appear Justified and those that, despite much hype, do not. *Developmental Cognitive Neuroscience*, 18, 34–48. https://doi.org/10.1016/j.dcn.2015.11.005

244 Dowell. L., Mahone, E., Mostofsky, S.(2009). Associations of postural knowledge and basic motor skill with dyspraxia in autism: Implication for abnormalities in distributed connectivity and motor learning. *NeuroPsych.*, 23, p. 563–570.

245 Jansiewicz, E. M., Goldberg, M. C., Newschaffer, C. J., Denckla, M. B., Landa, R., & Mostofsky, S. H. (2006). Motor signs distinguish children with high functioning autism and Asperger's syndrome from controls. *J. of Autism & Dev. Disorders*, 36, p. 613–621.

246 Mandelbaum, D. E., Stevens, M., Rosenberg, E., et al. (2006). Sensorimotor performance in school-age children with autism, developmental language disorder, or low IQ. *Dev. Med.& Child Neurology*, 48, p. 33–39.

247 Fuentes, C. T., Mostofsky, S. H., Bastian, A. J., & Fuentes, C. T. (2010). Perceptual reasoning predicts handwriting impairments in adolescents with autism. *Neurology, 75,* 1825–1829.

248 Ashear, V., & Snortum. J. R. (1971). Eye contact in children as a function of age, sex, social and intellective variables. *Developmental Psychology: 4.* 479.

249 Ming, X., Brimacombe, M., & Wagner, G. C. (2007). Prevalence of motor impairment in autism spectrum disorders. *Brain & development, 29*(9), 565–70.

250 Ming, X., Brimacombe, M., & Wagner, G. (2007). Prevalence of motor impairment in autism spectrum disorders. *Brain & Dev., 29*(9), 565–70.

251 Whitebread, D., Bingham, S., Garu, V., Pasternak, D. & Sangster, C. (2007). Development of metacognition and self-regulated learning in young children: Role of collaborative and peer-assisted learning. *J. of Cognitive Ed. & Psych.,* 6, p. 433-455.

252 Nagel, M. (2009). Mind the Mind: Understanding the Links Between Stress, Emotional Well-Being and Learning in Educational Contexts. *The International J. of Learning,* 16, p. 34

253 Nagel, M. (2009). Mind the Mind: Understanding the Links Between Stress, Emotional Well-Being and Learning in Educational Contexts. *The International J. of Learning,* 16, p. 33-42.

254 Dominick, K., Davis, N., Lainhart, J., Tager-Flusberg, H., & Folstein, S. (2007). Atypical behaviors in children with autism and children with a history of language impairment. *Res. in Dev. Disabilities,* 28, p. 145-162.

255 Sikora, D. M., Johnson, K., Clemons, T., & Katz, T. (2012). The relationship between sleep problems and daytime behavior in children of different ages with autism spectrum disorders. Pediatrics, 130, Suppl. 2, p. 83–90.

256 Government of Canada (2007). *Canada's Food Guide.* http://www.hc-sc.gc.ca/fn-an/food-guide-aliment/basics-base/quantit-eng.php

257 Schreck K., Williams, K., & Smith, A. (2004). A comparison of eating behaviors between children with and without Autism. *J. of Autism & Dev. Disabilities,* 34, p. 433-438.

258 Lukens, C. (2005). Development and validation of an inventory to assess eating and mealtime behavior problems in children with autism. Doctoral dissertation, Ohio State University.

259 Dominick, K., Davis, N., Lainhart, J., Tager-Flusberg, H., & Folstein, S. (2007). Atypical behaviors in children with autism and children with a history of language impairment. *Res. in Dev. Disabilities,* 28, p. 145-162.

260 Dominick, K., Davis, N., Lainhart, J., Tager-Flusberg, H., & Folstein, S. (2007). Atypical behaviors in children with autism and children with a history of language impairment. *Res. in Dev. Disabilities,* 28, p. 145-162.

261 Reeve, J. & Jang, H. (2006). What Teachers Say and Do to Support Students' Autonomy During a Learning Activity. *J. of Ed. Psych.,* 98, p. 209-218.

262 Bandura, A. (1982). Self-Efficacy Mechanism in Human Agency. *American Psych.,* 37, p. 122–147.

263 Schunk, D. H. (1989). Self-efficacy and achievement behaviors. *Ed. Psych. Review,* 1, p. 173-208.

264 Fox, N. & Calkins, S. (2003). The Development of Self-Control of Emotion: Intrinsic and Extrinsic Influences. *Motivation & Emotion,* 27, p. 7-26.

265 White, R. E., & Carlson, S. M. (2016). What would Batman do? Self-distancing improves executive function in young children. *Developmental Science*, *19*(3), 419–426. https://doi.org/10.1111/desc.12314

266 Baron-Cohen, S. (2001). Theory of Mind in Normal Development and Autism. *Prisme*, *34*, 174–183. Retrieved from http://www.autism-community.com/wp-content/uploads/2010/11/TOM-in-TD-and-ASD.pdf

267 Deci, E. L., Koestner, R., & Ryan, R. M. (1999). A meta-analytic review of experiments examining the effects of extrinsic rewards on intrinsic motivation. *Psych. Bulletin*, *125*, p. 627–668.

268 Giangreco, M. F., & Broer, S. M. (2005). Questionable Utilization of Paraprofessionals in Inclusive Schools: Are We Addressing Symptoms or Causes? Focus Autism Other Dev Disablilities, 20, 10–26.

269 Bierman, K., Torres, M. & Scholfield, H. (2010). Developmental Factors Related to the Assessment of Social Skills. In D. Nangle, D. Hansen, C. Erdley. & P. Norton (Eds.). *Practitioner's Guide to Empirically Based Measures of Social Skills*. New York: Springer Science+Business Media.

270 Izard, C., Fine, S., Schultz, D., Mostow, A., Ackerman, B., & Youngstrom, E. (2001). Emotion knowledge as a predictor of social behavior and academic competence in children at risk. *Psych. Sci.*, *12*, p. 18–23.

271 Eisenberg, N., & Fabes, R. A. (1992). Emotion, regulation, and the development of social competence. In M. Clark (Ed.), *Review of personality and social Psych.: Emotion and social behavior*. Newbury Park, CT: Sage

272 Raver, C., Blackburn, E., Bancroft, M., & Torp, N. (1999). Relations between effective emotional self-regulation, attentional control, and low-income preschoolers' social competence with peers. *Early ed. & dev.*, *10*, p. 333–350.

273 Eisenberg, N., & Fabes, R. A. (1992). Emotion, regulation, and the development of social competence. In M. Clark (Ed.), *Review of personality and social Psych.: Emotion and social behavior*. Newbury Park, CT: Sage

274 Bierman, K., Torres, M. & Scholfield, H. (2010). Developmental Factors Related to the Assessment of Social Skills. In D. Nangle, D. Hansen, C. Erdley. & P. Norton (Eds.). *Practitioner's Guide to Empirically Based Measures of Social Skills*. New York: Springer Science+Business Media.

275 Bierman, K., Torres, M. & Scholfield, H. (2010). Developmental Factors Related to the Assessment of Social Skills. In D. Nangle, D. Hansen, C. Erdley. & P. Norton (Eds.). *Practitioner's Guide to Empirically Based Measures of Social Skills*. New York: Springer Science+Business Media.

276 Klin, A., Jones, W., Schultz, R., Volkmar, F., & Cohen, D. (2002). Visual fixation patterns during viewing of naturalistic social situations as predictors of social competence in individuals with autism. *Archives of general psychiatry*, *59*, p. 809–816.

277 Klin, A., Sparrow, S. S., de Bildt, A., Cicchetti, D. V., Cohen, D. J., & Volkmar, F. R. (1999). A normed study of face recognition in autism and related disorders. *J. of Autism & Dev. Disorders*, *29*, p. 499–508.

278 Silverman, L. B., Bennetto, L., Campana, E., & Tanenhaus, M. (2010). Speech-and-gesture integration in high functioning autism. *Cognition*, *115*, p. 380–93.

279 Attwood, A., Frith, U., & Hermelin, B. (1988). The understanding and use of interpersonal gestures by autistic and down's syndrome children. *J. of Autism & Dev. Disorders*, *18*, p. 241–257.

280 Baron-Cohen, S., Leslie, A. M., & Frith, U. (1985). Does the autistic child have a 'theory of mind'? *Cognition*, 21, p. 37–46.

281 Uljarevic, M., & Hamilton, A. (2012). Recognition of Emotions in Autism: A Formal Meta-Analysis. *J. of Autism & Dev. Disorders*, *43*, p.1517–1526.

282 Sucksmith, E., Allison, C., Baron-Cohen, S., Chakrabarti, B., & Hoekstra, R. (2013). Empathy and emotion recognition in people with autism, first-degree relatives, and controls. *Neuropsychologia*, *51*, p. 98–105.

283 Ekman, P. (1995). Emotional and Conversational Nonverbal Signals. D. Touretzky, M. Mozer & Hasselmo, M. (Eds.) *Advances in Neural Information Processing Systems*. Cambridge, MA: The MIT Press.

284 Ekman, P. (1995). Emotional and Conversational Nonverbal Signals. D. Touretzky, M. Mozer & Hasselmo, M. (Eds.) *Advances in Neural Information Processing Systems*. Cambridge, MA: The MIT Press.

285 Greif, E. & Gleason, J. (1980). Hi, thanks, and goodbye: More routine information. *Language in Society*, 9, p. 159-166.

286 Kylliainen, A, Hietanen JK (2004). Attention orienting by another's gaze direction in children with autism. *Journal of Child Psychology and Psychiatry*, 45, 435–444.

287 Bogdashina, O. (2003). Sensory Perceptual Issues in Autism and Asperger Syndrome. London: Jessica Kingsley Publishers

288 Marriage, S., Wolverton, A. & Marriage, K. (2009). Autism Spectrum Disorder Grown Up: A Chart Review of Adult Functioning. *J. of the Canadian Academy of Child & Adolescent Psychiatry*, 18, p. 324-328.

289 Montgomery, J. M., MacKenzie, H., & Stoesz, B. M. (2012, May). *spark*: Improving Self-Regulation, Executive Functions, and Social Competence in Children with Autism*. Poster presented at the International Meeting for Autism Res., Toronto, ON.

290 Stoesz, B. M., Montgomery, J. M., & MacKenzie, H. (2013, May). *Evaluation of executive function and autism characteristics in children with ASD participating in spark**. Poster presented at the International Meeting for Autism Res., San Sebastian, Spain.

291 Sierens, E., Vansteenkiste, M., Goossens, L., Soenens, B., & Dochy, F. (2009). The synergistic relationship of perceived autonomy support and structure in the prediction of self-regulated learning. *British J. of Ed. Psych.*. 79, p. 57-68.

292 Ryan, R. & Deci, E. (2006). Self-regulation and the Problem of Human Autonomy: Does Psych. Need Choice, Self-Determination, and Will? *J. of Personality*, 74, p. 1157-1585.

293 Katz, I., & Assor, A. (2007). When choice motivates and when it doesn't. *Ed. Psych. Review*, 19, p. 429-442.

294 Connell, J. P., & Wellborn, J. G. (1991). Competence, autonomy, and relatedness: A motivational analysis of self-system processes. In M. R. Gunnar & L. A. Sroufe (Eds.), *Minnesota Symposium on Child Psych.*, *Vol. 23*. Hillsdale, NJ: Erlbaum.

295 Deci, E. & Ryan, R. (1985). *Intrinsic motivation and self-determination in human behavior*. New York: Plenum.

www.ingramcontent.com/pod-product-compliance
Lightning Source LLC
Chambersburg PA
CBHW080643270326
41928CB00017B/3170